How to Keep From Losing Your Mind

HOW TO KEEP FROM LOSING YOUR MIND

Educating Yourself Classically to
Resist Cultural Indoctrination

Deal W. Hudson

TAN Books
Charlotte, North Carolina

Cover design by Caroline K. Green

Cover image: Fragment of colossal head sculpture by Freeda / Shutterstock.

Author headshot © Renata Grzan / RenataPhotography.com

ISBN: 978-1-5051-3077-5

Published in the United States by
TAN Books
P.O. Box 410487
Charlotte, NC 28241
www.TANBooks.com

Printed in India

To the Memory of Dr. Mortimer J. Adler

For the sole true end of education is simply this: to teach men how to learn for themselves; and whatever instruction fails to do this is effort spent in vain.

—Dorothy Sayers, "The Lost Tools of Learning," 1947

The further backwards you look, the further forward you can see.

—Winston Churchill

When I used to read fairy tales, I fancied that kind of thing never happened, and now here I am in the middle of one!

—Lewis Carroll, *Alice In Wonderland*, 1865

Praise for *How to Keep From Losing Your Mind*

Reclaiming the search for Truth, Goodness, and Beauty in our present culture is a pressing task, one required to bring about healing in a society broken by polarization and imprisoned by increasing emotional isolation. By sketching and exploring a wide variety of art, history, literature, and film, Deal Hudson points to the power of the three Transcendental Desires to express the human person beyond mere facts and to understand the world beyond mere assertions. For in the pursuit of these Transcendentals the human soul is communicable and intelligible in a way that political debates, college lectures, or public profiles cannot imitate. By renewing ourselves in the classic works of our common ancestry we can be prepared anew, not just to hear, but also to listen and understand in a more profound way.

—Bishop Thomas J. Olmsted , Diocese of Phoenix

Deal Hudson loves the Canon, the Classics, the Great Books. Yet he wants this Canon expanded. But if he loves it why change it? What criterion will he use? Will he displace the dead, white Bard of Avon to make room for some unknown Guatemalan peasant woman of color? What happens if he ignores the politically correct tropes of inclusion, diversity and multiculturalism and, instead, judges a work by its capacity to instill and elicit wonder? What if he expands the

Canon to include great film and classical music? And what if he teaches us how to detach ourselves from the thin but relentless world of digitized polemics and to use the power of our attention to rediscover the world of the good, the true and the beautiful? Then I would say that, with St. Paul, he knows that we become what we behold. "We all, beholding the glory of the Lord, are being changed into his likeness." What gets our attention gets us. The culture of postmodernism wants you, your sanity, and your freedom. Hudson wants you to escape the mind-numbing magnetism of modern media and enter into that great tradition of human creativity that challenges us to expose falsehoods, confront evil and suffering, live free, and cultivate the many shades of responsible love. Let Deal Hudson's expanded Canon show you How To Keep From Losing Your Mind.

—Al Kresta, President/CEO, Ave Maria Communications
and Host of Kresta in the Afternoon, EWTN radio

What we crave is right in front of us, no matter our age or station in life. Deal Hudson's book is an invitation to feed the heart, mind and soul. How could we forget to do so? To put off what is most satisfying in life? Yet that is exactly what we humans tend to do. Deal Hudson's book is an invitation to live fully, to fall in love with what is true and beautiful, to prevent our own spiritual, physical and emotional starvation. A secondary benefit is the best must read, hear and watch list imaginable.

—Marjorie Dannenfelser, President, Susan B. Anthony List

CONTENTS

Acknowledgments   xi

Introduction   xiii

Part I: Beauty: The Irresistible Canon

  1 You Must Change Your Life   3

  2 There *Are* Great Books   10

  3 Expanding the Canon 1: Music   24

  4 Expanding the Canon 2: Film   44

  5 Books, Poetry, Music, and Film Talk   60

  6 Wonder   77

Part 2: Truth: Bad Ideas in Motion

  7 Engaging: From Detachment to Attention   97

  8 Remembering: Knowing Requires Background   114

  9 Finding the Lever Point: The Battle Over Human Nature 129

 10 Exposing Untruth: Multiculturalism and the Therapeutic 151

 11 Unmasking the Gurus: Despots and Dictators   163

 12 Assigning Blame: Barbarians and Straw Dogs   184

Part 3: Goodness: Love Is the Crux

 13 Parental Love   205

 14 Friendship   229

 15 Eros   256

 16 Agape   280

 17 The Human   309

Bibliography   335

Acknowledgments

I want to thank my chief editor Steven Phelan for his expert and timely help. My assistant Claire Smith and former student Lisa Gaye Waddell were kind enough to read the entire manuscript and suggest important edits.

My friends Robert R. Reilly, Jens F. Laurson, Francis O'Gorman, John Kinsella, Frank Buckley, Jeffrey D. Wallin, and Dana Gioia gave me invaluable advice during my research and writing.

The years of support from Steve Clarke, my radio producer, has made the broad scope of this book possible. And it's been a pleasure to work with John Moorehouse from TAN Books.

I also want to thank Alan Carson, chair of the Morley Publishing Group, and his wife Alyssa, who have assisted and encouraged my work for over two decades. Marjorie Murphy Campbell and Bill Campbell, also longtime supporters, made it possible for me to find the time needed to write this book.

My wife, Theresa C. Hudson, who helped with the final preparation of the manuscript, patiently allowed me to work for months with quiet and little interruption. My son, Cyprian Hudson, graciously kept me supplied with iced tea and corrected several points of history. My daughter,

Hannah Hudson, though miles away, reminded me repeatedly of her love and support.

Finally, I want to express my gratitude to Frank Hanna III and David Hanna for their loyalty and generosity to my family and me.

Introduction

At the age of seventeen, I was fortunate to have met a teacher who transformed my mind and, as a consequence, my entire life. He was the janitor at my high school in Fort Worth, Texas. I was in the senior play *The Diary of Anne Frank*, and each night after play practice, he would help us clear the stage for the following day.

We would talk casually about what I was studying, what I liked, and why. One day he asked me if I knew anything about Socrates and Plato. I told him I knew the names, of course, but that was all. The next day he brought me the most beautiful book I had ever seen—*The Complete Dialogues of Plato*—in a box with a silk thread hanging outside the pages. Just like the Bible!

The janitor, whose face has remained with me even though I have regrettably forgotten his name, suggested I read the *Apology* and the *Crito* so we could talk about them the next evening. Holding such a magnificent book, I could hardly refuse. That night I read both dialogues and prepared to meet him after rehearsal the next evening.

As we sat down on some stage props, he surprised me. He didn't ask me about the dialogues but posed the question, "What comes first, existence or essence?" I was instantly intrigued and a bit afraid to give the wrong answer (I didn't know yet that philosophers have debated the question for millennia). After asking him to explain the question further, I concluded, "It must be existence!" He smiled, insisting I keep the precious book. I looked for him in the days following the performances, but I never saw him again.

It was only years later that I realized he had induced me to reflect on the mysteries of existence. What is existence? Why do things exist at all? Is existence good? How is my human existence different from that of other existing things—animal, plants, minerals, air, and water? Does God exist as I had been taught to believe? What about angels? My teacher's simple question had shaken me, and it seemed the back of my mind had opened up, letting in a flood of new questions. It was indeed life-changing.

My goal in this book is to pass on this experience.

Classic works such as Plato's dialogues are agents of wonder—they ignite the mind and the emotions. Classics turn the mind in a new direction, whether the great work in question is a book, a film, or the climactic final movement of Beethoven's Ninth Symphony.

What I call losing your mind is not about those moments when you throw up your hands in disgust; it's about losing your mind to a lie. When you buy into a false worldview, such as one that guarantees your happiness, you have made yourself captive and you have lost your freedom. All the big lies of the twentieth century—those of Hitler, Lenin, and Mao—promise a state that will meet all human needs. Once you hand that responsibility over to the state, you've enabled tyranny.

"Wisdom begins in wonder," Socrates said. The intense desire to understand an incredible sunset or an excruciatingly beautiful passage of music—it is a natural response to something inexplicable, something good, true, or beautiful.

I am one of those who believe, however, that digital technology has diminished our capacity for wonder. Too many of us stay tethered to our electronic devices, through which we have almost unfettered access to the "World Wide Web" and all the information, intrigue, and deception therein. The ease of finding almost anything spoils us. What used to be distant and hard to find is now close at hand. It is not all bad; indeed, it has many obvious benefits: vast libraries and beautiful performances are accessible on our multiple devices. The world, or at least a particular impression of it, is only a click away. Our children may never know the patience required to find just the right books, magazines, and newspapers for a research project or the jubilation of finding the rare, the out-of-print, the long-lost work.

Since three-step plans are all the rage these days, let me offer my own—this one, as the book's title suggests, for the sake of keeping our sanity and freedom. First, let us put technology to good use, to return to the classics. Many classics are now available online free or at a nominal cost. Second, let us set some time aside for leisure and contemplation. Let's adjust our habits of attention so we can read, listen, and watch without distractions. The use of social media and ubiquitous entertainment has shrunk attention spans. Third, let us engage ideas that created our civilization before they are entirely forced out of existence by the iconoclasts and book burners of today. Several generations of students have been taught lies about our civilization and have not read the classics for themselves.

This journey will be its own reward. We can pursue self-education because we live in a free society, at least for now. No one is burning books yet, though many of the classics have been eliminated from university curricula by "progressive" university professors. Thus, I don't rule out the possibility of book-burning, or its equivalent, in my lifetime. Fires are unnecessary when robust social media and search engines can prioritize information online and virtually erase those with whom they disagree.

Please don't feel badgered when I mention classic texts, films, or music you may not know. What I highlight is intended for your delight and discovery. We will begin by discussing what the Canon of Great Works consists of and why such collections became the subject of so much effort and discussion in the last century. I will argue that the widely-accepted lists of Great Books would benefit from including now-classic films and musical works in their ongoing conversation, as I believe such dialogue will open up possibilities for new audiences and discoveries. Next, I will revisit the movements in the twentieth century that together became an all-out assault on the classics, and indeed on the civilizational memory of the West. Finally, I will offer a series of dialogues between great works within the framework of the "Four Loves," as determined in antiquity and famously discussed by the great classicist, apologist, and novelist C. S. Lewis.

Along the way, we will clear away the jargon, prejudices, and specific postmodern ideas that contemporary culture has forced on all of us.

The goal is not only enjoyment of the works themselves but to recover the first mark of an educated person, his freedom in thinking. I'm not interested in helping you to check classics off a list or better prepare you to "name drop." I'm not handing you a list of "must-reads," one of the most annoying phrases of the modern social media-dominated landscape. An educational journey should not feel like a grind or an assignment handed down from above. Classics are classics because they've brought joy and understanding to generations over centuries. They are self-recommending and don't need to be pressed into your hands. It is a privilege that we live in a society where we are not forbidden access to these treasures. Even thirty years after the fall of the Berlin Wall, there remain countries that censor what is read or seen by their citizens. I grant you that a healthy society would feature "some" censorship, but the kinds of things such a society should censor—I suspect you know what I am referring to here—are heartily consumed in our own.

We have a virtually limitless amount of information at our fingertips. In researching this book, I was astounded at the resources I found on the Internet. A century ago, no one except perhaps Jules Verne and H. G. Wells could have dreamt that the contents of vast libraries would be made available in a person's hand. Centuries earlier most could only dream of having books in their home: books belonged to the privileged few, the clergy, and royalty. Every change in communication technology has resulted in more people having access to information and knowledge. What they did with that access is another topic altogether.

The Internet has exploded so much that Kevin Carey, in his 2015 book *The End of College*, predicted a "University of Everywhere" will eventually emerge on the Internet with courses, majors, and degrees offered at a fraction of today's cost.[1] We are not quite there yet, but the resources already exist for anyone with Internet access and sufficient motivation to continue his or her education in any area of learning. After all, as Carey adds, "If you take its meaning at all seriously, liberal education is the work of a lifetime."[2]

This project may well be addictive. Let us hope so if the opiate is beauty and edification. Once you start, the buzz kicks in, and you won't want to stop. Somewhere along the way, you will realize that being immersed in thought provides a deep and lasting pleasure that has few rivals in human experience. You will read, for example, *The Scarlet Letter* or go to a Shakespeare play and say to yourself, "Why haven't I done this in such a long time?" Along the way, you will learn to discriminate. Just as scholars do not rely on everything that lands on their desk, you will learn to begin to recognize the difference between the trivial, the enjoyable, the necessary, and the uplifting.

Age should not concern you—the mind is immaterial and, illness notwithstanding, remains available for growth by the student of any age. The body and the brain do age, of course, so there may be cobwebs to clear, but constant mental exercise can help retard the aging process. Bad mental

---

[1]   Kevin Carey, *The End of College: Creating the Future of Learning and the University of Everywhere* (New York: Riverhead Books, 2015), 11.

[2]   Ibid., 254.

habits accumulated over many years can be recognized and slowly corrected. Any habit, whether physical or mental, requires time to change. Habits can be changed by a few weeks of focused effort. But it is more important to consider this project, as Kevin Carey stated, the effort of a lifetime. Your habits will change, but what will hook you is your delight in reengaging the classics.

Some habits of thought are inculcated in us by culture czars who insist we see the world from their point of view. These views are often laden with assumptions, usually wrong, about life's purpose and what is most needed. In some settings, failure to "drink the Kool-Aid" can put you on the firing line. You will not merely be found wrong; you will be judged a bigot for refusing to accept their worldview, however absurd. A climate of intimidation pervades most public debate found in many of our nation's colleges and universities. Sadly, ideological indoctrination has made its way into K–12 education as well.

Remember that *culture is the school we go to every day.* I use the word advisedly: "culture," in its original definition, which had to do with veneration in a religious context, is not what we have today. Nor do we have the understanding of culture that shares its root with "cultivate," the act of toiling to grow something, such as crops. No, here I use the term in its reduced modern understanding, in which it refers to the massive collection of norms, behaviors, habits, assumptions, arts, entertainment, institutions, and interests that define a place and time. This "culture," we do have, and there is little to be proud of. We would do well to recover the word's original meaning.

If we want to change the culture, we need to remain aware of all the factors that create and sustain it. The most influential factor in shaping society is education, followed closely by media in all its various platforms. Unfortunately, traditional religion plays a relatively small and diminishing role. Thus, the messages, attitudes, and values of those controlling the schools, media, and entertainment industries are the primary sources of modern culture. Culture is also expressed by our manners, how we dress, and how we communicate, but even these are subject to regulation and manipulation. Strong religious faith and a distinctive family culture are the best antidotes to avoid being another product of cultural expectations. Attention to the classics can help to transform your culture at home.

The curiosity spurred by my encounter with Plato and Socrates began a journey that became my career. Along the way, I met one of my intellectual heroes, Mortimer J. Adler, whose example has served as a lodestar. We became friends, and I was privileged to be the Adler Fellow at the Aspen Institute for three summers in the early 1990s. As a reader, I had learned from him about how deeply the "great ideas" were rooted in the history of our civilization. I saw that it was his prodigious learning, lightly carried, which enabled him to write simply about these ideas like truth, goodness, beauty, liberty, equality, and justice.[3] Dr. Adler recoiled when anyone called them "simplified"! Anyone who has read Dr. Adler's books knows that he did not trade truthfulness for clarity. This book grows out of what I learned from Dr. Adler and the conversations we shared.

---

[3]   Mortimer J. Adler, *Six Great Ideas* (New York: Touchstone, 1997).

This book is divided into three parts: Beauty, Truth, and Goodness, three transcendental aspects of being. Each of these represents a different way, or modality, of apprehending everything that exists. Truth is being as the mind knows it. Goodness is that which we rightly desire by the will. Beauty is the splendor of all the transcendentals united, a magnet for the senses and the heart. Wherever you find one of the transcendentals, you find the others as well.

Part 1 is called "Beauty: The Irresistible Canon" because the classics have stood the test of time—they have been irresistible because we learn more from them about ourselves, the lives we lead as human persons. Classics raise questions about how to live well or whether seeking a good life is an obligation we all share. I also respectfully present the benefits of expanding the canon to include both film and classical music: filmmakers and composers have created their own masterpieces of expression and exploration about human experience.

Part 2, "Truth: About Bad Ideas," begins with reminding the reader of the habits of attention and detachment needed to engage with classics. Classics are demanding. They require detachment from the name-calling and political quarrels of the day's headlines. Contemplation, not polemics, is needed. I try to unravel postmodern ideas now dominating the academy, education, public discourse, and the media. I argue these ideas have poisoned the culture by rejecting truth, objective knowledge, and the idea of a shared human nature. With the rejection of objective knowledge, postmodernist arguments rely on power rather than reason or facts.

Part 3, "Goodness: Love Is the Crux," begins by revisiting the classic book by C. S. Lewis *The Four Loves*. Love, in all its forms, is the ground of our moral life. In each of the four chapters, I juxtapose books, film, and music, comparing how each love is expressed and portrayed. Human freedom is crucial to authentic love. A mother naturally loves her child, but she can freely abandon it. Friendships are made freely, and though Eros may feel like being possessed, it requires choice not to be swept along by it. Agape, most of all, requires the freedom of God to give and man to receive.

Let's begin, shall we? I wrote this book with a mounting sense of joy as I revisited classics I had not encountered for many years and some I was considering deeply for the first time. If this book prompts you to start on your own exploration, I will have been successful.

PART I

Beauty: The Irresistible Canon

CHAPTER I

You Must Change Your Life

D o you recall the first time you visited a great museum, such as Uffizi Gallery in Florence, or a magnificent Gothic church, like St. Patrick's Cathedral in New York City? You probably saw something that made you stop and stand still. You gazed. You became conscious of yourself staring, and perhaps you looked around to see if anyone noticed you. But you looked back, not caring what anyone else thought. You let yourself gaze until your newly-awakened thirst was quenched, at least for a moment.

Think about how that moment made you feel and what thoughts you had. Did you feel not only delighted but also challenged? It's hard to explain, but I've felt that challenge many times. A philosophy teacher at the University of Texas played the opening "Kyrie" of J. S. Bach's Mass in B Minor, and I was stunned by its beauty. Suddenly I wanted to have my teacher's ears, as it were, and his knowledge of classical music. I wanted to discover all the beauty in music. It was like my first reading of the *Apology* at the urging of the school janitor: a door was opened to treasures that have enriched my life ever since.

I've been fortunate to have teachers, friends, and family members who introduced me to what Matthew Arnold called "the best that has been thought or said." I did not "get it" on the first try. Strangely enough, it took me a while to warm up to Beethoven, not the symphonies, but the piano sonatas and the string quartets. Later I realized that my ear had needed more education, the kind that comes with many hours of listening to classical repertoire. Asking a teenager to listen to a late Beethoven string quartet is like handing them the first volume of Marcel Proust's novel *In Search of Lost Time*. But once the connection to Beethoven is felt, a sense of awe overcomes you making you wonder how anyone could feel that deeply and express it in music. That awe in itself is a challenge; namely, to plumb the depth of the human condition as profoundly as the composer. The challenge comes in the form of a question: can you follow? Yes, I answered, not because of any unique ability on my part, but because I had been happily captured, a kind of love at first sight.

Archaic Torso of Apollo

Rainer Maria Rilke (1875–1926), considered by some the greatest poet of the twentieth century, lived as a young man in Paris for several years while working as the secretary to the famous sculptor Auguste Rodin. Rilke made regular visits to the Louvre and the other museums in Paris, but one day a particular sculpture from ancient Greece caught his eye, inspiring him to write a poem:

Archaic Torso of Apollo (1908)

Although we never knew his lyric head
from which the eyes looked out so piercing clear,
his torso glows still like a chandelier
in which his gaze, only turned down, not dead,

persists and burns. If not, how could the surge
of the breast blind you, or in the gentle turning
of the thighs a smile keep passing and returning
towards that centre where seeds converge?

If not, this stone would stand all uncompact
beneath the shoulders' shining cataract,
and would not glisten with that wild beast grace,

and would not burst from every rift as rife
as sky with stars: for here there is no place
that does not see you. You must change your life.[1]

Rilke's last line comes as a surprise. Like breaking the fourth
wall in the theatre, the poet confronts the reader with a
demand: "You must change your life." It's the sculpture's
missing "lyric head," specifically its eyes "which looked out
so piercing clear" that measure us while we gaze back. Rilke
describes a moment when the roles are reversed: the artwork
is sizing up the viewer, "for here is no place that does not see
you."

The surprise of the poet's admonition wasn't in what
he said but in that he said it. It's as if Rilke chose to make

---

[1]   Rainer Maria Rilke, *Requiem and Other Poems*, trans. J. B.
Leischman (London: Hogarth Press, 1949), 115.

explicit what has been implicit in our encounters with the great work of an artist or a writer. He makes explicit what I would call the *aspiration* that's awakened. What is aspiration if not the urge to "change your life?" The root of the word is the same as that of "spirit," which is the Latin *aspirare*, meaning "to breathe." How appropriate is it, therefore, to call the beauty of art "breathtaking."

There are various ways to explain such an encounter, but the one that makes more sense than the others is the consideration that human beings are each a unity of body and spirit. St. Thomas Aquinas expresses this connection in his definition of beauty: "that which upon seeing pleases."[2] "Seeing" here stands for the power of all the senses when they encounter a pleasurable object. These objects immediately become objects of the will's desire. From the will's perspective, anything desired is a "good" because in possessing it we experience satisfaction and fulfillment. There are many things we desire, which we believe, rightly or wrongly, are connected to *the* Good.

For example, understanding is a good: the moment we understand something better, say, what we learn about prejudice from Shakespeare's *The Merchant of Venice* or the nature of romantic love from *Romeo and Juliet*, we feel satisfaction and hope. We are satisfied that we know and hopeful that the world can be understood and that we can see further into the heart of man. No one wants to walk in darkness day

---

[2]   *Summa Theologica* I.39.8. St. Thomas Aquinas, *Suuma Theologica*, trans. Fathers of the English Dominican Province, 3 vols. (New York: Benziger Brothers, Inc, 1947). All subsequent quotations are taken from this translation.

after day. This is why we are naturally drawn to happy endings, where the human struggle leads to resolution: At the end of Gustav Mahler's Second Symphony, for example, we are elevated to hear something heavenly. At the conclusion of Dickens's *Oliver Twist*, we revel in a boy being returned to his family. And in John Ford's *The Searchers*, we are relieved when a man's murderous rage towards his niece is overcome.

These moments, of course, are not consigned to endings. Think of the tragedies that leave us wiser but less satisfied—like Sophocles's *Oedipus Rex*, Shakespeare's *Macbeth*, Flaubert's *Madame Bovary*, and Kafka's *Metamorphosis*. The insight and recognition the reader experiences in tragedy, the *catharsis* of fear and pity, is itself a good that triggers aspiration for more and more lasting goods.[3] Along with the ancients, I believe this drive is rooted in the natural human desire for total fulfillment, the Good itself, which the Greeks referred to as *eudaimonia*, and which used to be translated as "happiness" but has recently more often been rendered as "well-being."

The same inner desire that delights in Keats, Mozart, or Spielberg will only be encouraged to look for a permanent, lasting satisfaction, happiness. Thus, an archaic torso of a man, lacking a head and extremities, through the power of its form can beckon you to "change your life."

---

3   Aristotle, *Aristotle's Poetics: A Translation and Commentary for Students of Literature,* trans. Leon Golden (Prentice-Hall Inc., 1968), 11.

A Confession

As a young man, I went to the Great Books looking for the Good, my eyes fixed on finding identity and definition. I was drawn to ideals for life because I lacked direction. Many of the modern works being called 'classics' put me off; their darkness troubled me. I decided they portrayed an overly pessimistic view of the world. I was looking for ideas and images to guide me. At the time, I couldn't tolerate much ambiguity and uncertainty.

For example, the shattering realism of films like *Taxi Driver* and *Apocalypse Now* went places I could not follow. I did not complain of them being depressing, as many did, but of being unintelligible—their nihilism did not make sense to me. This was also true of the celebrated artistic anti-heroes and -heroines of the '60s, such as Dennis Hopper, Andy Warhol, Jack Kerouac, Allen Ginsburg, Bob Dylan, Herbert Marcuse, Gloria Steinem, Jean-Paul Sartre, and Simone de Beauvoir. There was something there I could not see, that I was unable to understand or appreciate. Nabokov's *Lolita*, for example, which is now considered a masterpiece, I avoided reading on religious grounds until later in life only to find it was a profound moral tale. The same goes for Marquez's *One Hundred Years of Solitude*—his virtual compost of human failings initially left me cold. As much as I am annoyed by people who call serious films "depressing," I was acting in the same way without knowing it.

Time passed, and I embraced only those works that fit within my field of recognition. But years later something changed: *Taxi Driver* and *Apocalypse Now* became favorite films. The whole genre I would have called "the dark side" became recognizable to me. What had happened? Life happened. I spent twenty-three years in the academy as a student or a professor. When I started making a living outside a university, I realized my life had been cloistered. The rough-and-tumble of running a business and becoming involved in national politics introduced me to the other side of life, a wider world, where envy, wrath, and betrayal are common—in other words, the world of Homer, Virgil, Dante, and Shakespeare.

CHAPTER 2

There *Are* Great Books

Those classics that are called the Great Books are most closely associated with Mortimer J. Adler and Robert Hutchins.[1] When Hutchins became president of the University of Chicago in 1929, he hired Adler to teach philosophy in the law school and the psychology department. Upon arriving, Adler, rather brashly he admits, recommended to Hutchins a program of study for undergraduates using classic texts. Adler had taught in the General Honors program at Columbia University begun in 1921 by professor John Erskine. Hutchins asked him for a list of books to be read in such a program. When Hutchins saw the list, he told Adler that he had *not* encountered most of them during his student years at Oberlin College and Yale University. Hutchins later

---

[1] There were precursors to Adler and Hutchins's Great Books. For example, in 1886, Sir John Lubbock published his list of "The Best Hundred Books, by the Best Judges" in the *Pall Mall Gazette*. See W. B. Carnochan, "Where Did Great Books Come From Anyway?" *Stanford Humanities Review*, vol. 6, 1995, https://web.stanford.edu/group/SHR/6-1/html/carnochan.html. Sir John's list can be found here: Alex Johnson, "The Book List: Meet Sir John Lubbock, Godfather of the must-read list," *Independent*, April 24, 2018, https://www.independent.co.uk/arts-entertainment/books/features/sir-john-lubbock-the-book-list-literature-reading-godfather-mustread-listicle-a8320811.html.

10

wrote that unless Adler "did something drastic he [Hutchins here referred to himself, ed.] would close his educational career a wholly uneducated man."[2] Hutchins remained president for sixteen years before serving as Chancellor until 1951, and the following year, they did something drastic.

In 1952, Adler and Hutchins published the *Great Books of the Western World* in fifty-four volumes.[3] Adler and Hutchins included the 714 authors they considered most important to the development of Western Civilization.[4] The influence of their Great Books movement on American culture for several decades was considerable and continues to this day.

Their selection of books from over a half-century ago have held up rather well. For example, I compared them to the 2007 list published by journalist and cultural critic J. Peder Zane. Zane asked 125 leading writers to list their favorite works of fiction.[5] Zane found that the twenty most common titles listed by the writers were:

- *Anna Karenina*, Leo Tolstoy, 1877.
- *Madame Bovary*, Gustav Flaubert, 1856.
- *War and Peace*, Leo Tolstoy, 1869.

---

[2]   Mortimer J. Alder, *Philosopher At Large: An Intellectual Biography* (New York: Macmillan Publishing Co., Inc., 1977), 129.

[3]   Mortimer J. Adler and Robert Hutchins, *Great Books of the Western World*, 54 vols. (Chicago: Encyclopædia Britannica, Inc., 1952). A complete list of books can be found at "Adler's Great Book List," http://classicalcommonplace.com/knowledge-base/adler-great-books-list/.

[4]   I had the privilege of knowing and working with Dr. Adler later in his life, and I contributed several essays to his series of volumes, *The Great Ideas Today*. See bibliography.

[5]   J. Peder Zane, *The Top Ten: Writers Pick Their Favorite Books* (Boston: W.W. Norton & Company, 2007).

- *Lolita*, Vladimir Nabokov, 1955.
- *The Adventures of Huckleberry Finn*, Mark Twain, 1884.
- *Hamlet*, William Shakespeare, 1600.
- *The Great Gatsby*, F. Scott Fitzgerald, 1925.
- *In Search of Lost Time*, Marcel Proust, 1913–27.
- *Stories of Anton Chekhov*, 1860–1904.
- *Middlemarch*, George Eliot, 1871–72.
- *Don Quixote*, Miguel de Cervantes, 1602, 1615.
- *Moby Dick*, Herman Melville, 1851.
- *Great Expectations*, Charles Dickens 1860–61.
- *Ulysses*, James Joyce, 1922.
- *The Odyssey*, Homer, ninth century BC.
- *Dubliners*, James Joyce, 1916.
- *Crime and Punishment*, Fyodor Dostoevsky, 1866.
- *King Lear*, William Shakespeare, 1605.
- *Emma*, Jane Austen, 1816.
- *One Hundred Years of Solitude*, Gabriel Garcia Marquez, 1967.

Adler and Hutchins included all these books except for the two by Nabokov and Marquez. In spite of their absence, modernity is well-represented in the Great Books by Bertolt Brecht, Samuel Beckett, and William Faulkner, among others.

Zane's survey refutes the claim that lists of "greats" reflect only the opinions of middle-aged white men. The one hundred twenty writers interviewed by Zane would satisfy any diversity requirement. If someone asked the same number of philosophers, historians, or scientists about their favorite books, I predict the results would have been much the same: the new list would contain a majority of acknowledged classics with the addition of some more recent and specialist books.

Poetry

Classic poetry is well-represented in the Great Books—Homer, Virgil, Shakespeare, Dante, Milton, and Eliot are there, plus others. But poetry read in the context of the Great Books can be approached as a source of ideas or as another link in the history of ideas. This is a mistake. Poetic language is a linguistic fusion of form and content, a creation that resists being plucked for concepts to fill in the philosopher's timeline.

Someone might object to the continued relevance of poetry because no one reads poetry anymore except when assigned in a classroom. However, poet and critic Dana Gioia reports that poetry has undergone a culture revival outside of the academy, where poets have often found a steady paycheck. Gioia calls it "a tale of two cities"; a new generation of poets is finding their voice in the real world:

> They work as baristas, brewers, and bookstore clerks; they also work in business, medicine, and the law. Technology has made it possible to publish books without institutional or commercial support. Social media connects people more effectively than any faculty lounge. An online journal requires nothing but time. Any person with an iPhone and a laptop can

produce a professional poetry video. Any bookstore, library, cafe, or gallery can host a poetry reading.[6]

A 2017 study by the National Endowment of the Arts shows that 11.2 percent of American adults, 28 million people in the US, still read poetry.[7] But young adults, in particular, ages eighteen to twenty-four, are leading the return, with 17.5 percent reporting regular poetry reading, a doubling of interest since the last such study in 2012 (8.2 percent). Regardless of how many poetry books you have on your shelves, or how many you see at your local bookstore, poetry thrives. Human beings need to sing, to express themselves beyond the limits of discursive reasoning. Like music, poetic language engages the reader at an emotional level that goes untouched by philosophical reasoning. Before the philosophers, it was Homer who instructed the Greeks about gods and heroes. But his epics were sung, not read. The *Iliad* and *Odyssey* were sung by bards who held them in memory for a thousand years before they were written down.

Wilfred Owen

If someone tasked me with the job of introducing poetry to neophytes, one of the first books I would assign my students is the poetry of Wilfred Owen (1893–1918). His life was short because he went to war, dying exactly one week before the end of WWI. After college, Owen went to Paris

---

[6]   Dana Gioia, "Introduction," *Best American Poetry 2018*, guest editor, Dana Gioia (New York: Scribner, 2018).

[7]   Sunil Iyengar, "Taking Note: Poetry Reading Is Up—Federal Survey Result," June 7, 2018, https://www.arts.gov/art-works/2018/taking-note-poetry-reading-—federal-survey-results.

where he taught both English and French. He witnessed the beginning of the war and two years later returned to England where he was commissioned as a second lieutenant. His experience in battle is recorded in the poetry which was inspired, in part, by time spent in a hospital with the already-established poet Siegfried Sassoon. Owen could have stayed home but returned to the trenches where he died four months later. I'm amazed at what Owen wrote before turning twenty-six. In "Disabled," he writes about a soldier returned home without his legs, in a wheelchair, watching football from the sidelines:

> About this time Town used to swing so gay
> When glow-lamps budded in the light blue trees,
> And girls glanced lovelier as the air grew dim,—
> In the old times, before he threw away his knees.
> Now he will never feel again how slim
> Girls' waists are, or how warm their subtle hands;
> All of them touch him like some queer disease.[8]

In "Strange Meeting," Owen imagines a soldier jumping into a crater in no man's land and finding the corpse of an enemy soldier staring at him: "By his dead smile I knew we stood in Hell." The live soldier addresses the dead one: "Strange friend," I said, "here is no cause to mourn." But the corpse interrupts:

> "None," said that other, "save the undone years,
> The hopelessness. Whatever hope is yours,

---

8   Wilfred Owen, *The Collected Poems of Wilfred Owen* (New York: New Directions Publishing Company, 1993), 67.

> Was my life also; I went hunting wild
> After the wildest beauty in the world[9]

The glory of war as told by Homer, Virgil, Herodotus, Thucydides, and Caesar Augustus was read in school by soldiers on both sides of the trenches. What this soldier found instead was "the pity of war, the pity war distilled." With his thoughts of glory extinguished by death, he imagines himself back in battle:

> Then, when much blood had clogged their chariot-wheels,
> I would go up and wash them from sweet wells,
> Even with truths that lie too deep for taint.
> I would have poured my spirit without stint
> But not through wounds; not on the cess of war.
> Foreheads of men have bled where no wounds were.
> I am the enemy you killed, my friend.
> I knew you in this dark: for so you frowned
> Yesterday through me as you jabbed and killed.
> I parried; but my hands were loath and cold.
> Let us sleep now. . . ."

A spiritual sense pervades these lines: "I would have poured my spirit without stint." The bloody "chariot-wheels," a reference to Homer's *Iliad*, are cleansed "from sweet wells," like Jacob's Well (Jn 4:5–6), a pilgrim site in the ancient city of Nablus for centuries. The dead soldier tells the one living, "I am the enemy you killed, my friend," and then offers him his forgiveness with the words, "Let us sleep now." At the end of this ghastly encounter, Owen concludes on a note

---

[9]   *The Collected Poems of Wilfred Owen*, 35.

of nobility and common cause. Reading Owen answers our questions about what men experience in battle, how they are able to face death, and how they cope with the experience of battle. The best literature takes us to places and circumstances we can only vaguely imagine and gives us access into the interior lives of people we would otherwise never know.

Making Lists

An indispensable guide to classics is *The Western Canon: The Books and School of the Ages* by literary scholar Harold Bloom.[10] He organizes his book around twenty-six select authors, including the poets Shakespeare, Dante, Chaucer, Milton, Goethe, Whitman, Dickinson, Neruda, and Pessoa. His appendices, however, include lists of other books he considers canonical catalogs by era—Theocratic, Aristocratic, Democratic, and Chaotic—and by country. Bloom's book is one of the best sources I have found to help one become familiar with the names and works of important writers around the world, and he has published a remarkably helpful set of lists for the reader.[11]

Although classic texts are included in some high school and college curricula, it's the rare student who can deeply appreciate *King Lear* or *Macbeth* as a teenager or young adult. The worldly profundity of Flaubert's *Madame Bovary* or Edith Wharton's *Age of Innocence*, for example, is lost on

---

[10]   Harold Bloom, *The Western Canon: The Books and School of the Ages* (New York: Riverhead Books, 1994).

[11]   "Harold Bloom Creates a Massive List of Works in The 'Western Canon': Read Many of the Books Free Online." http://www.openculture.com/2014/01/harold-bloom-creates-a-massive-list-of-works-in-the-western-canon.html.

all but a few teenagers, as it was lost on me. Books like *Moby Dick*, *The Scarlet Letter*, and *The Great Gatsby* pose the same challenge. We want to introduce young readers to the classics, but, frankly, these, like many other classics, are books for grown-ups.

Philosophy and theology are central to any version of the Great Books—they address discursively those questions that have arisen in the lives of every person since Adam and Eve—meaning, morality, truth, justice, love, death, and eternity. Some philosophers and theologians, however, are more easily approached than others. There are always technical terms to master; for example, in Greek philosophy the concept of *Logos* ("word," "reason," or "order") which also plays a central role in Christianity: John 1:1 "In the beginning was the Word" (λόγος, Logos).[12] Every philosopher and theologian wrote in a historical tradition. Readers who pick up, for example, St. Thomas Aquinas will quickly see that he quotes from Scripture, Greek philosophers, Patristic Fathers, Roman writers, and Arab theologians. However, with some patience and access to online reference works, readers can acquire enough background knowledge to read Aquinas intelligently. Later philosophers, such as Kant, Hegel, and Heidegger, are more difficult and test the patience of the non-specialist. With the reader in mind, I will discuss mainly the ancients and medievals. These works are foundational for understanding Western civilization, and their

---

[12] Oxford University Press provides a free online PDF of key philosophical terms, "Glossary of Philosophical Terms," http://global.oup.com/us/companion.websites/9780199812998/studentresources/pdf/perry_glossary.pdf.

influence is seen throughout the philosophy and theology that followed.

Greats and Classics

Greatness is measured in many ways, and any list of greats should be subject to criticism. I remember asking my then college dean at a dinner party to name his top ten novels, and he answered that "top ten" lists were "nonsense." A bit surprised, I replied, "But they are such great conversation starters!" He reluctantly agreed, but I had made a more important point than I realized at the time. Reliable lists are the answer to, "Where do I go next?" Let's imagine a situation that I am sure has happened over and over: You're listening to the car radio, flipping through channels; you hear a snatch of music that makes you stop, and you listen enthralled to the end. (This has happened to me more than a few times.) You wait to hear the announcer name the piece and the composer. You hear, "That was the *Violin Concerto* of Samuel Barber."[13] "Who is Samuel Barber?" you ask yourself. What else did he write? Does anyone else write music that sounds like that? The Internet has made the answers very easy to find. You can read about Samuel Barber (1910–1981), see a list of his works and the best available recordings. Search further and you can find other composers who, like Barber, wrote music in a "late-Romantic" style. Good lists are invaluable to tell me what I don't know.

---

[13]   The *Violin Concerto* (1939) of Samuel Barber is a treasure. You can hear violinist Gil Shaham play it with the conductor David Robertson and BBC Symphony Orchestra: https://www.youtube.com/watch?v=NVcwiXHk5FI.

Barber's *Violin Concerto* inspires me to declare my description, not definition, of greatness. A book, a film, or a musical composition is great when you think to yourself, "I want to listen to all the music (or read the books and watch the movies) by this composer right away." You may consider this too subjective, but I know I'm not alone in having that thought after reading Tolstoy, Shakespeare, Dostoevsky, Proust, Homer, Dickens, or Jane Austen; listening to Brahms, Dvorak, or Stravinsky; or watching the films of Kurosawa, Welles, or Eisenstein. As the renowned literature professor Harold Bloom puts it, "I think that the self, in its quest to be free and solitary, ultimately reads with one aim only: to confront greatness."[14]

Let me clarify one thing: I am using the words *great* and *classic* as though they were interchangeable. There's a distinction. Take, for example, *All Quiet on the Western Front* by Erich Maria Remarque. It's a well-known classic novel about the First World War. Remarque portrayed the absurdity of the war for the soldiers on both sides who were expected to "go over the top" day after day. Remarque's novel, published in German in 1928, had the good fortune of being translated into English the following year. Then the novel was made into an Oscar-winning 1930 film, *All Quiet on the Western Front*, directed by Lewis Milestone.[15] Remarque's book is still very readable, a classic novel about war and the First World War in particular.

---

[14]   Harold Bloom, *The Western Canon: The Books and School of the Ages* (New York: Riverhead Books, 1994), 485.

[15]   Hilton Tims, *Erich Maria Remarque: The Last Romantic* (New York: Carroll & Graf Publishers, 2003), 55–60, 69–72.

However, when you compare Remarque's novel to *Magic Mountain* (1924)[16] by Thomas Mann, the limitations of Remarque's novel are evident. Whereas Remarque explores the experience of life in the trenches of WWI, Mann's scope is more universal, possessing layers of meaning about the shattering of European civilization as the *result* of the First World War. *Magic Mountain* depicts a turning point in Western culture through the fate of one man, Hans Castorp, who lives in a sanitorium for seven years trying to recover his health.

The most important criteria to use in determining greatness is the opinion of experts. Everyone has their personal favorites—arguing about why, say, one film is better than another is part of the delight of film-going. Experts, however, are qualified to make the hard call: to answer the question, where does this film or that book rank in comparison to the others? When I want to buy a new car, I ask the opinion of the mechanic who has been working on my cars for twenty years. Anyone who knows what is required to be an expert at anything will recognize the depth of knowledge needed to measure a book, a movie, a musical composition against all that has come before.

But it should be said, experts are not always right. Consider the list of Nobel Prize winners for literature.[17] The

---

[16]   *Der Zauberberg* by Thomas Mann was published in German in 1924. It was translated into English in 1927 by H. T. Lowe-Porter with an afterword by the author, *The Magic Mountain* (London: Secker and Warburg, 1927). A highly-acclaimed new English version was published in 1995: *The Magic Mountain*, trans. John E. Woods (New York: Alfred A. Knopf, 1995).

[17]   "All Nobel Prizes in Literature," https://www.nobelprize.org/

first literature prize, given in 1901, went to the French poet René François Armand (Sully) Prudhomme (1839–1907) "in special recognition of his poetic composition, which gives evidence of lofty idealism, artistic perfection and a rare combination of the qualities of both heart and intellect." Prudhomme was a strange choice given the competition. In the previous decade, Dostoevsky had published *Brothers Karamazov* (1880). The next year, Henry James published *A Portrait of a Lady* followed by *The Bostonians* in 1896. Twain's *Huckleberry Finn* was published in 1854, Robert Louis Stevenson's *Dr. Jekyll and Mr. Hyde* in 1886, along with Thomas Hardy's *Tess of the d'Ubervilles*. In addition, Tolstoy published his "Kreutzer Sonata" in 1890. Searching for Prudhomme, I found only one of his books in English translation, the 1875 *Les vaines tendresses*.[18]

Imagine being Sully Prudhomme when he received a letter from the Nobel committee and realizing he had beat out Dostoevsky, Tolstoy, Twain, Stevenson, Hardy, and Henry James. He may have also thought of other writers active at the time: Guy de Maupassant, Emile Zola, Rudyard Kipling, W. B. Yeats, Paul Verlaine, Arthur Rimbaud, August Strindberg, Henrik Ibsen, and George Bernard Shaw. In the work of these 'also-rans' we find inexhaustible stories of the human condition, universal in scope, all told with faultless command of language. All lists measuring greatness are subject

---

[18]   prizes/lists/all-nobel-prizes-in-literature/.
Sully Prudhomme, *The Vain Tenderness* (Dead Dodo Vintage, 2012): https://www.amazon.com/Vain-Tenderness-Annotated-Sully-Prudhomme-ebook/dp/B0083V6B8I/ref=sr_1_3?keywords=Sully+Prudomme&qid=1551387306&s=gateway&sr=8-3-spell.

to reconsideration—the truly great remain on the list with the passing of centuries.

CHAPTER 3

Expanding the Canon 1: Music

We all have music we love, music that never fails to move us, particularly when it's associated with special people and significant moments in our lives. My list of favorites, however, veers towards the classical. During college, pop music completely lost its hold on me when I heard Debussy's *Afternoon of a Faun*.[1] As a result, I'd much rather *Rhosymedre*[2] by Ralph Vaughan Williams be played at my funeral than "Blowin in the Wind"[3] or, God forbid, "On Eagles Wings." If someone brings a guitar, I hope my friends will grab the casket and run.

Before there were books, there was music. The earliest known visual art depicts man making music. Archaeologists have unearthed a variety of musical instruments in Egypt, Sumer, Babylon, and present-day Europe that were used for

---

[1]   Here is the story of my 'conversion' to classical music in college: Deal W. Hudson, "How the Beatles, My Great Aunt, and Debussy Changed My Life," http://www.thechristianreview.com/how-the-beatles-my-great-aunt-and-debussy-changed-my-life/.

[2]   Listen to an orchestral version of *Rhosymedre*, based upon a hymn tune from the late nineteenth century here: https://www.youtube.com/watch?v=kymJPJTUftY.

[3]   A video of Bob Dylan singing "Blowing in the Wind" live on TV, March 1963, can be seen here: https://www.youtube.com/watch?v=vWwgrjjIMXA.

both religious and social purposes.[4] We read about music in Homer's epic poems (800–700 BC). Within the epics, singing choruses play a crucial, ritual role in funeral rites. After a body was laid out and prepared for burial, the funeral procession would start with women wailing their grief while musicians played a funeral dirge. In this passage from *The Iliad*, Andromache laments the death of her husband, Hector, at the hands of Achilles:

> And white-armed Andromache led their songs of sorrow,
> cradling the head of Hector, man-killing Hector
> gently in her arms: "O, my husband
> cut off from life so young! You leave me a widow.
> lost in royal halls—and the boy only a baby,
> the son we bore together, you and I so doomed."[5]

The Greeks were also the first to treat music theoretically, trying to understand its power to attract and to please the human ear. Music critic and historian Robert R. Reilly describes how Pythagoras took a single string, plucked it, noted the tone, and then began plucking strings half the length, progressively hearing higher tones matching the previous ones—he had discovered the octave. As Pythagoras[6] kept plucking his string in various lengths, he discovered all

---

4   The European Music Archaeology Project is amassing all the information and artifacts beginning at 40,000 BC, the Upper Paleolithic period. Read about the project at http://www.emaproject.eu.

5   Homer, *The Iliad*, trans. Robert Fagles, introduction and notes by Bernard Knox (New York, Penguin Books, 1990), 25:850–55.

6   The original texts of Pythagoras with translations can be found in G. S. Kirk and J. E. Raven, *The Presocratic Philosophers: A Critical History With a Selection of Texts* (Cambridge: Cambridge

the ratios, such as 3:2 and 4:3, that pleased the ear due to their consonance.[7] This consonance of sounds, or notes, is called "tonality." Pythagoras's theorem was based upon two facts: first, that sounds remained consonant with each other played at measurable ratios, and, second, that the human ear naturally recognized those sounds as pleasant, satisfying, and beautiful.

When Pythagoras concluded that "harmonic music is expressed in exact numerical ratios of whole numbers, he concluded that music was the ordering principle of the world."[8] As Reilly explains, this insight became a key ingredient of Greek cosmology, metaphysics, and ethics. What Pythagoras called "the harmony of the spheres" represented a universal ordering principle that should also govern persons. This cosmology is what lies behind Lorenzo's claim in Act 5, Scene 1 of Shakespeare's *The Merchant of Venice*:[9]

> The man that hath no music in himself,
> Nor is moved with concord of sweet sounds,
> Is fit for treasons, stratagems and spoils;
> The motions of his are dull as night

University Press, 1957), 217–231.

[7] Robert R. Reilly and Jens F. Laurson, *Surprised by Beauty: A Listener's guide to the Recovery of Modern Music* (San Francisco: Ignatius Press, 2016), 17.

[8] Ibid., 17–18.

[9] Ralph Vaughan Williams set Shakespeare's words to music. His *Serenade to Music* composed in 1938 is written for orchestra and sixteen soloists. An outstanding recording can be heard here: https://www.youtube.com/watch?v=QDYi4JgQA2I.

And his affections dark as Erebus:

Let no such man be trusted.[10]

If you are not "moved by concord of sweet sounds," you're out of harmony with the universe, at least, according to Shakespeare. In 1987, Allan Bloom, a respected classics professor, applied this view of music, also subscribed to by Plato,[11] to popular music. Bloom argued in *The Closing of the American Mind* that the lives of his students were being diminished by the music they consumed. The response from academia and media was pure fury. How can a white male *classics* professor make moral judgments about the popular music of teenagers?

I taught *The Closing of the American Mind* in my introduction to philosophy courses, and I recall a student throwing her book against the wall. Perhaps what infuriated both students and the elites was his description of a thirteen-year-old boy listening to rock music through headphones or watching (then very-influential music video channel) MTV: "In short, life is made into a nonstop, commercially prepacked masturbational fantasy."[12] Sadly, Bloom's book became prophetic rather than medicinal. Popular music has only gotten worse

---

[10]   Shakespeare, *The Merchant of Venice*, 5.1.83–89, *The Complete Works of Shakespeare*, ed. Hardin Craig (Atlanta: Scott, Foresman and Company, 1961), 528.

[11]   Plato, *Republic*, III.398-403, trans. G. M. A. Grubbe (Indianapolis: Hackett Publishing Company, 1974), 68–74.

[12]   Alan Bloom, *The Closing of the American Mind: How Higher Education Has Failed Democracy and Impoverished the Souls of Today's Students*, foreword by Saul Bellow (New York: Simon and Schuster, 1988), 75.

with politics and ideology added to the classic "sex, drugs, and rock & roll," making the result even more disgusting.

Beginning With Organum

What we call "classical music" began with the chant melodies of the early and medieval Church which themselves were iterations of music in Jewish worship. The Hebrew Scriptures are abundant with songs of praise. For centuries, chants differed from region to region and were sung without musical notation. In the fifth century, a Schola Cantorum was established in Rome to study and perform the chants. Pope Gregory (540–604) reorganized the Schola and began codifying chant: for that reason chant is often called "Gregorian."[13] Very little is known about Western popular music until the early twelfth century when the Troubadour poets roamed from court to court singing songs of love.[14] During the same period, sacred music composers began to be known by name. One of the first composers we know is the Benedictine abbess Hildegard of Bingen (1098–1179). Much of her music has been preserved, including the liturgical drama *Ordo Virtutum* about a soul's struggle to resist temptation.[15] In the next century, composers Léonin and

---

[13]   Derrick Henry, *A Listener's Guide to Medieval & Renaissance Music* (New York: Facts On File, Inc. 1983), 8–10.

[14]   Bernard de Ventadorn (1130–1190) is one of the best known Troubadours. Here his "Can Vei la Lauzeta Mover" ("When I See a Lark") is performed by the Clemenic Consort, https://www.youtube.com/watch?v=e0JNIukJv1k.

[15]   Paul Senz, "*Catholic Composers: Hildegard von Bingen*," *Catholic World Report*, September 17, 2018, https://www.catholicworldreport.com/2018/09/17/catholic-composers-hildegard-von-bingen/.

Pérotin at the Cathedral of Notre Dame in Paris introduced into music a second melodic line, giving the choral sound a sense of depth.[16] Two distinct melodies sung together was called "organum" and gave to music what could be called perspective, analogous with what emerged in the painting of Cimabue (1251–1302) at the beginning of the Italian Renaissance.

Music has always played an integral part in important rituals of passage—birth, death, marriage, worship, any step taken from one stage of life to another. Music is also part of our *play* when we enjoy and celebrate our living for its own sake. Play, in this sense, is a kind of gratitude, a recognition that life is a gift and not to be treated as the only means of obtaining material ends. In play, we celebrate the moment and music is its most vivid expression. Play is a human need, not to be spoken of as an extravagance, "when I get the time."

Music, like the written word and visual art, is communicative. Music says something that the ear hears and translates through mind and emotion into human meaning. Music has a unique power in this respect. In studying music, writes music historian Paul Henry Lang, "We are seeking the human being in the plenitude of his always new and yet typically related creations, because we find that every tune from the past raises an echo in us today."[17]

The neurologist and scientist Dr. Oliver Sacks explores music's power beginning with the way it can unexpectedly

---

[16]   Listen to an example of organum by Leonin: https://www.youtube.com/watch?v=ngCRm7uLirA.

[17]   Paul Henry Lang, *Music In Western Civilization* (New York: W.W. Norton & Company, Inc. 1941), xxii.

and immediately transport us to a place of heightened awareness or deep pleasure. In his *Musicophilia*, Dr. Sacks describes
an experience which many of us immediately recognize:

> On my morning bike ride to Battery Park, I heard
> music as I approached the tip of Manhattan, and then
> saw and joined a silent crowd who sat gazing out to sea
> and listening to a young man playing Bach's *Chaconne
> in D* on his violin. When the music ended and the
> crowd quietly dispersed, it was clear that the music had
> brought them some profound consolation, in a way
> that no words could ever have done. Music, uniquely
> among the arts, is both completely abstract and pro-
> foundly emotional. It has no power to represent any-
> thing particular or external, but it has a unique power
> to express inner states or feelings. Music can pierce the
> heart directly; it needs no mediation.[18]

Sacks specifically explores how this power translates into
therapeutic benefit for those with mental afflictions—
autism, Parkinson's, dementia, and Williams syndrome. He
attributes this power to music's "Proustian mnemonic, eliciting emotions and associations that had been long forgotten,
giving the patient access once again to mood and memories,
thoughts and worlds that had seemingly been completely
lost."[19]

Far from apologizing for including music in our curriculum, I consider it a treat, like inviting a friend to sit down to

---

[18]   Oliver Sacks, *Musicophilia: Tales of Music and the Brain* (New
York: Vintage, 2008), 329.
[19]   Ibid., 380.

eat an exquisitely prepared meal. If you are unfamiliar with classical music, I predict you will find in it the kind of joy that arises from the reading of a great literary work. Great music is also medicinal. At the age of ten, Pablo Casals, the great cellist, started each day playing Bach's *Preludes and Fugues* on the piano after a morning walk.[20] When asked by a reporter at the age of eighty-five whether his daily habit grew boring, he replied, "No," playing each day "was a new experience, an act of discovery."[21] That sounds to me like a prescription for sanity.

Classical music puts us closer to history; it can reveal the sensibility and aspirations of the era in which it was created. Cultural historians normally associate plainsong—a single melody—with the Christian piety and Catholic institutions of the Middle Ages. The history of chant in the Roman Church's liturgy is well-documented, and different forms of chant remained the primary form of liturgical music in the churches that split from Rome in the twelfth century. Renaissance polyphony—multiple voices singing equivalent lines in harmony—represents the quantum leap in scientific learning and accelerating social developments during that period. The Baroque era began in the late seventeenth century with the works of Bach and Handel. They transformed polyphony into homophony: Counterpoint was shaped into a single dominant voice supported by one or more additional voices. The Baroque period coincided with the

---

[20]   Luis Claret, "Pablo Casals: Artist and Humanitarian," *cellobello. org*, https://www.cellobello.org/legacy-cellists/pablo-casals-artist-and-teacher/.

[21]   *Musicophilia*, 237, n. 13.

beginning of the Enlightenment which was the first significant step towards the modern age in philosophy, literature,
and politics. The Classical Age of Mozart and Haydn per-
fected the use of homophony through the development of
sonata form—exhibition, development, and recapitulation.
The second half of the eighteenth century marked the high
point of the Enlightenment in works such as Mozart's opera
The Magic Flute (1791) and Haydn's *The Creation* oratorio
(1797). With the arrival of the Romantic era, composers like
Beethoven and Schubert turned towards greater emotional
expression and musical experimentation. Romanticism's
dual preoccupations of exploring the self and celebrating
human freedom are expressed in the music, literature, and
philosophy of the age.

The modern age, with its protest against tradition and
increasing social fragmentation, started before the cata-
strophic First World War. The riot at the 1913 Paris premiere
of composer Igor Stravinsky's *The Rite of Spring* was prophetic of what was to come.[22] Artists, writers, philosophers,
scientists, and political radicals aimed at all the established
ideas and institutions: kingship, tonality in music, linear
narrative in literature, Scripture (and faith itself), as well as
assumptions about truth, morality, and the canon of beauty.

Music historian Paul Henry Lang considered it ridic-
ulous to omit music in historical writing: "It's difficult to
understand why some of the most eminent historians of our
modern era, unlike their predecessors, do not restrict their
attention to wars, treaties, and royal dynasties, but consider

---

[22]   Modris Ekstein, *Rites of Spring: The Great War and the Birth of the
Modern Age* (Boston: Marriner Books, 2000), 10–16.

the history of arts and letters, politics and religion, economics and science, an integral, and perhaps the most important, part of history writing, are still completely uninformed about the role of music in the history of civilization."[23]

Lang goes on to criticize an admired historian of the Renaissance who "deems a scant page or so sufficient to deal with an art which graced the daily life of people, adorned the festivities of the princely courts, and ennobled the mystic ritual of the ancient church and sturdy liturgy of the new." To emphasize his point, Lang adds a playful bit to remind the historian about a famous organist of the Italian Renaissance, "When Merulo played, the church had to be closed to prevent people from crushing each other in their eagerness for admission." To leave such facts out of a history of the Italian Renaissance is indefensible.

O Magnum Mysterium

Just as music has its place in history, it has long been integral to religious practice. Composers set the sacred texts into a work of such beauty that they become rooted in memory. Music infuses religious rituals and liturgies around the world. But the gift of music to people of faith is not limited to the classics such as J. S. Bach's *Mass in B Minor*, Handel's *Messiah*, and Mozart's *Requiem*.

There has been an abundance of sacred music written in the twentieth and twenty-first centuries. The *O Magnum Mysterium,* composed in 1994 by Morten Lauridsen (b. 1943), has become one of the most-performed pieces

---

23   *Music In Western Civilization,* 249.

of choral music in the world.[24] Its reverent, ecstatic beauty stands side-by-side with the most admired sacred music of the old world.

The beauty of Lauridsen's *O Magnum Mysterium* is quite a contrast to much of the classical music written since the revolt against tonality. This perversity began in 1908 with composer Arnold Schoenberg's (1874–1951) Second String Quartet, Op. 10.[25] After atonality, Schoenberg created 12-tone, where each note has the same musical value as another—the result was an inhumane cacophony.[26] Without a doubt, the assault on beauty following the devastation of Europe by the First World War caused disillusion among artists and writers. Some lost their religious faith and their faith in Western civilization. Composers expressed their estrangement from tradition with a deliberate rejection of tonality.

The tonal scale is an arrangement of seven notes built upon a tonic key used by composers since ancient Greece and, presumably, before. It's tonality that the human ear instinctively recognizes as pleasing. In his critique of musical modernism, John Bortslap writes, "The phenomenon of

---

[24]   A live performance of Lauridsen's *O Magnum Mysterium* by the Westminster Cathedral Choir can be seen and heard here: https://www.youtube.com/watch?v=9y9yM53TowA&t=37s.

[25]   Schoenberg's String Quartet No. 2 with soprano is written in his earlier late romantic style, but the composer's turn to atonality begin in the last movement. It can be heard here performed by New Vienna String Quartet and soprano Evelyn Lear: https://www.youtube.com/watch?v=eB5I5iU0OoE.

[26]   Arnold Schoenberg's "Suite for Piano, Op. 25, (1921-1923) was one of his first 12-tone pieces: It can be "heard" here: https://www.youtube.com/watch?v=bQHR_Z8XVvI.'

tonality is a condition *sine qua non* for the creation of music and for giving music its expressive qualities."[27] Composer Leonard Bernstein made the defense of tonality the focus of his 1976 Charles Norton Eliot Lectures at Harvard University, *The Unanswered Question.*[28] In his lectures which were made into videotapes, Bernstein explained why tonality is the key to the meaning of music.[29] Both Bortslap and Bernstein regard the break with the tonal tradition as more than an aesthetic matter—it was a manifestation of a spiritual crisis in the West. Tonality is the musical equivalent of intelligibility in philosophy, of narrative structure in literature, and the grammar of filmmaking. In theology, it's equivalent to the death of God.

Surprised by Beauty

Robert Reilly and Jens F. Laurson devoted a book to composers who, like Morten Lauridsen, have served the cause of beauty over the past century, choosing to reject both atonality and the 12-tone music that became fashionable after Schoenberg in the mid-twentieth century.[30] In *Surprised by Beauty*, Reilly and Laurson rewrite the history of modern music, doing the world of music an excellent service by expanding, and correcting, the canon of great twentieth-century music.

---

[27]   John Bortslap, *The Classical Revolution: Thoughts On New Music In the 21st Century* (New York: Dover Publications, 2017), 21.

[28]   Leonard Bernstein, *The Unanswered Question: Six Talks at Harvard* (Boston: Harvard University Press, 1976).

[29]   Composer and conductor Leonard Bernstein explains tonality in five minutes while sitting at a piano: https://www.youtube.com/watch?v=Gt2zubHcER4&t=277s.

[30]   *Surprised by Beauty*.

The composers featured in *Surprised by Beauty* includes John Adams, Malcolm Arnold, Samuel Barber, Maurice Duruflé, Frank Martin, Roy Harris, George Rochberg, John Kinsella, Edmund Rubbra, Gerald Finzi, Erich Korngold, and Ralph Vaughan Williams. These are composers whose devotion to tonality led to their being denied the accolades that went to fashionable composers writing unlistenable music. Both atonality and 12-tone music were an intellectualist fantasy which substituted musical theory for musical beauty

The inclusion in *Surprised by Beauty* of Erich Korngold, Bernard Herrmann, and Nino Rota, each well-known film composers, is a reminder of the role film composers played in keeping tonal music before audiences between the 1930s and the 1980s. I hope that film music will make its way into more concert halls in the future, such as the music of Ennio Morricone, John Barry, Henry Mancini, Elmer Bernstein, John Williams, Miklos Rózsa, Franz Waxman, Max Steiner, along with Herrmann, Korngold, and Rota. As Reilly and Laurson show, there was plenty of tonal music written during those fifty years, but orchestras programmed only a small portion of it.

The canon of music in the twentieth century is far from settled, but regarding the music that came before, experts agree. In his recent book *The Indispensable Composers: A Personal Guide*, New York Times critic Anthony Tommasini chooses Monteverdi, Bach, Handel, Haydn, Mozart, Beethoven, Schubert, Chopin, Schumann, Verdi, Wagner, Debussy, Puccini, Schoenberg, Stravinsky, and Bartok.[31]

---

[31]   Anthony Tommasini, *The Indispensable Composers: A Personal Guide* (New York: Penguin Press, 2018).

Tommasini could have easily included composers such as Brahms, Berlioz, Tchaikovsky, Liszt, Strauss, Rachmaninov, Ravel, Mahler, Bruckner, and Dvorak, among others. After my discovery of classical music, my first indispensables were Debussy and Ravel. But I didn't have any friends who knew enough to suggest more composers until I went to graduate school. I followed my ears at the time but was much helped by *The Lives of the Great Composers* by Harold C. Schonberg first published in 1970.[32] This book remains my favorite to put in the hands of the novice music lover, though it should be supplemented by *Surprised by Beauty*.[33]

There's no accepted list of greatest classical compositions, and for good reason: it would be hopelessly random. How do you choose, say, from Domenico Scarlatti's 555 keyboard sonatas, Haydn's 106 symphonies, Bach's 216 cantatas, Beethoven's 16 string quartets and 9 symphonies, or Mozart's operatic masterpieces? Would Chopin's *Preludes Op. 28* count as one piece or twenty-four? You see the problem. It's not that some geek couldn't come up with a plausible list of, say, the 500 best. But trying to put them in order would be foolishness. How do you judge the ranking of an opera versus a piano sonata, an oratorio versus a piano trio? Music lovers, however, are not shy about making lists of the best recordings of all time.[34]

---

32   Harold C. Schonberg, *The Lives of the Great Composers,* 3rd Edition (W. W. Norton & Company, 1997).

33   Another reliable guide is David Dubal, *The Essential Canon of Classical Music* (North Point Press, 2003).

34   "The 50 greatest recordings of all time, The must-have classical performances on disc," August 23, 2018, http://www.classical-music.com/article/50-greatest-recordings-all-time.

No Training Required

Anyone can hear the greatness in music; a musical background or education isn't needed. The Vienna-born musicologist Victor Zuckerkandl described music as "a mystical aspect of human existence" that crosses all cultures. In *The Sense of Music*, he wrote:

> One cannot insist too strongly on the truth of the assertion that the experience of great music does not presuppose a special gift or special learning. This is precisely the unique thing about music: it *speaks a language that is understood without learning*, understood by everyone, not just the so-called musical people. If this were not so, folk music would not be the universal phenomenon it is. Fundamentally, Bach and Beethoven speak no other language than the folk song. . . . Many a person has felt the full impact of a great work of the tonal art and been moved by it from the bottom to top at the first meeting. If there had not been some understanding, some communication, he would not have felt the impact, he would not have been so moved.[35]

I found this to be the case in 1980 when I taught one of my first college-level courses—music history—at the Federal Prison in Atlanta. My twenty students were tough men, from the inner-cities, mostly in on various drug charges. I had little doubt the great works would affect them. As a self-taught lover of classical music, I followed the trail of beauty

---

[35]   Victor Zuckerkandl, *The Sense of Music* (Princeton: Princeton University Press. 1959), 4, emphasis added.

from the early twentieth-century composers back to the beginning, chant, then forward again through all the ages of music history. Along the way, I made mental notes of the music that meant the most to me, the music that possessed the greatest immediacy. It was this music I chose to share with my students, several of whom wept when I played one of the *Penitential Psalms* of Orlando de Lassus, and it got very weepy when I played Ravel's *Pavane for Dead Princess*.[36] There wasn't a period or style of music, except for the atonal, which failed to connect with these men. It was easily one of my most memorable teaching experiences because the music erased the social and cultural differences between us. As Zuckerkandl said, music "speaks a language that is understood without learning."

British neurologist and music theorist Oliver Sachs offers an example of how classical music connects with the average listener. "Dido's Lament" is a famous aria from the 1688 opera *Dido and Aeneas* by the English composer Henry Purcell (1659–1695).

> One does not need to know anything about Dido and Aeneas to be moved by her lament for him; anyone who has ever lost someone knows what Dido is expressing.[37] And there is, finally, a deep and

---

[36] Here is Ravel's own orchestration of the piano version of *Pavane pour une infante défunte* (1899) played by the London Symphony Orchestra conducted by Andre Previn: https://www.youtube.com/watch?v=ke7kwQ4CGCw.

[37] "Dido's Lament" is performed here by Elin Manahan Thomas, the Orchestra Of The Age Of Enlightenment, and conducted by Harry Christophers It follow the brief aria, "Ah, Belinda." https://www.youtube.com/watch?v=uGQq3HcOB0Y.

mysterious paradox here, for while such music makes one experience pain and grief more intensely, it brings solace and consolation at the same time.[38]

There's no mistaking the mourning expressed by the vocal line of swirling, descending notes, communicating linguistically incommunicable exhaustion and sadness. Dido's attempts to rise above herself and overcome her grief falls back to the earth, under which she will soon be buried. Death comes at her own hand.

Mass in B Minor

The only way to make a living as a composer in the eighteenth century was to be employed by the church or the court. We regard Johann Sebastian Bach as a giant among composers, but during his lifetime, he was seen as a highly-coveted organist, choral director, and composer, nothing more. Bach worked hard throughout his life serving at courts in Weimar and Köthen before signing a contract to serve as music director (*Kapellmeister*) at the St. Thomas Church in Leipzig in 1723. He was thirty-eight years old. When he died in 1750 at age sixty-five, he left behind a corpus of work second to none in the history of music.

There is one composition, however, that stands out—the elements of the *Mass in B Minor* were composed as early as 1733, but it was not completed until 1747. We don't know if Bach ever heard his masterpiece performed. Its uniqueness lies in this: the *Mass in B Minor* is a Catholic work. Bach was a devout Lutheran, a Lutheran composer who all his life had

---

[38]   *Musicophilia*, 329–30.

served in the Lutheran churches in Northern Germany. But his *Mass in B Minor* sets the entire Roman Catholic Mass, something no other Lutheran composer had done before. As conductor and Bach scholar John Eliot Gardiner wryly remarks, Bach had chosen "an unusual form for a Lutheran composer."[39]

The Lutheran liturgy contained only the first part of the Catholic Mass—the Kyrie and Gloria. In his *Formula missae* of 1523, Martin Luther created the template for all Lutheran worship that followed. The present Divine Service of the Lutheran Church includes the Kyrie and Gloria as part of the "Service of the Word."

Why did Bach take this step? Gardiner speculates that "the Ordinary of the Mass allowed him to concentrate on universal themes in a language weathered by time. At all stages in Christian history, it has provided a point of reference and the central means by which individuals can find and redeem themselves."[40]

Bach's Mass is not an entirely new composition; it's what's called a "parody Mass," meaning that the composer borrowed extensively from his previous compositions, some of which were secular works. Bach wasn't trying to cut corners; he chose music that would best express the text of the Mass, suggesting that he might have thought of this work as a summation of his life's work.[41] The *Mass in B Minor* is a substantial work lasting about two hours featuring eighteen

---

[39]   John Eliot Gardiner, *Bach: Music In the Castle of Heaven* (New York: Vintage Books, 2015), 480.

[40]   Ibid., 481.

[41]   Wilfred Mellers, *Celestial Music? Some Masterpieces of European Religious Music* (Woodbridge: The Boydell Press, 2002), 67.

choruses and nine arias—solo or duet—employing five solo-ists, chorus, and orchestra.

As I mentioned in chapter 1, when I first heard Bach's Kyrie in a college classroom, I was stunned. I had a minimal musical background, most of which consisted of listening to LPs of Broadway musicals in the basement of my family home. What was it about this music that, on first hearing, captured the mind and heart of a nineteen-year-old student at the University of Texas?

Kyrie eleison, of course, means, "Lord, have mercy." Those who hear it regularly in worship may have grown so used to it that the words register little of their meaning. Bach's musical setting of these words will make you listen as if hearing these words for the first time. The work opens with the single word *Kyrie* sung by the chorus on such dramatic chords your attention is seized: Kyrie eleison is sung like the pleading of a soul who knows his guilt and has nowhere else to turn except towards God's mercy. After less than a minute, the orchestra takes over repeating the same musical themes of the chorus but adding the complexity of inner voices.

After the orchestral interlude, a fugue starts to build beginning with the tenors, and a second fugue follows with the basses, and suddenly the sound of the Mass becomes richer, raising the voices upward. Gardiner describes this perfectly: "an ascending, aspiring delineation of prayer."[42] As I listen, the music's fugal structure feels as if layers of sound are being laid over me, totally enveloping me, until I am entirely inside the music. After another short orches-tral interlude, the basses enter, followed by the tenors, and

---

[42]   *Bach*, 488.

both women's sections—the music becomes overwhelming in its sense of purpose, prompting me to ask myself, can any human heart be this pure in its contrition? If so, how could God resist?

In the chapters that follow, we will open a dialogue between writers, composers, and filmmakers. If you want to see a great piece of sculpture, you should look at it from all directions. Like looking at a human life, no one angle of vision tells the whole story.

CHAPTER 4

Expanding the Canon 2: Film

Film as an art form is the new kid on the block. Yet, it's not as new as people assume. The average film fan is aware of silent films but probably knows little about them and has little interest in seeing them. But to understand film as an art form, some of its history is worth knowing. For example, before the "talkies" arrived in 1928 with *The Jazz Singer*, the movie business had long been a commercial success and a cultural force.

The motion picture business began in 1894 with the invention of Thomas Edison's peephole kinetoscope.[1] Four years later in 1898, filmmaker W. K. L. Dickson filmed twelve scenes with Pope Leo XIII in the Vatican[2] which was premiered at Carnegie Hall.[3] The audience, we are told,

---

[1]   Charles Musser, *The Emergence of Cinema: The American Screen to 1907* (Berkeley: University of California Press, 1994), 1.

[2]   Dickson made five films in 1898 with the titles *Pope Leo XIII Carried Through the Vatican Loggia On His Way to the Sistine Chapel* (35 mins); *Pope Leo XIII in His Carriage Passing Through the Vatican Gardens* (40 mins); *Pope Leo XIII, In His Chair* (50 mins); *Pope Leo XIII, Resting On his Way to His Summer Villa* (1 hour); *Pope Leo XIII Walking Before Kneeling Guards* (25 mins): https://anttialanenfilmdiary.blogspot.com/2018/06/1898-anno-tre-w-k-l-dickson-and.html.

[3]   *The Emergence of Cinema*, 219.

received the film with enthusiasm. One reviewer recorded that their favorite scene was when "His Holiness blessed the instrument which had recorded his movements, and through it . . . those who would see the picture afterward."[4] This was the first time a papal blessing had been delivered using visual technology. It's no surprise that Dickson's scenes with the pope were particularly welcome in cities like Boston with large Irish populations. Before the beginning of the twentieth century, films had entered the mainstream of American culture.

A Trip to the Moon

These short films were shown in theatres or storefronts until the Nickelodeon chain of film theaters arrived in 1905. The name was a combination of "nickel" (the shows cost five cents to see) and the Greek word for covered music hall, *odeion*. Film-dedicated storefront theaters started springing up around the country like mushrooms. By 1906, there were eight thousand Nickelodeons nationwide, but that number quickly doubled, and movies became big business.[5] By 1907, over two million people *each day* went to a Nickelodeon, and one-third of them were children.[6] This new market led to larger theaters, which started replacing the Nickelodeons which enabled longer feature films to be shown to the audience sitting in comfort. By 1930, more than 65 percent of the population went to the movies weekly.[7]

---

[4]   Ibid., 220.
[5]   Ibid., 449.
[6]   *A History of the Cinema*, 42.
[7]   Catarina Cowden, "The Long-Term Movie Attendance Graph

The first big hit of the film industry came in 1902's *A Trip to the Moon* by pioneer French filmmaker George Méliès. Méliès has been called "the first film director" by many critics and historians due to his ability "to weave a fabric of screen fiction."[8] *A Trip to the Moon* lasts from nine to eighteen minutes, depending on the projection speed, and is hand-colored frame by frame. Based on the fiction of novelist Jules Verne, it depicts a scientific lunar expedition, the exploration of the moon's surface, an attack by its inhabitants, and a daring escape.[9]

American filmmakers were not far behind: The next year, 1903, director Edwin Stanton Porter released *The Great Train Robbery*, which outdid Méliès's debut through its use of composite editing, frequent camera movement, and exterior locations.[10] Porter also provided the audience an image which they most likely remembered the rest of their lives: the leader of the robbers pointed his gun into the camera and emptied the barrel of all six bullets. Audiences jumped for cover.[11]

However, it was an American from the Deep South, D. W. Griffith (1875–1948), who developed the grammar, or the *how*, of filmmaking as an art form. Griffith began making films in 1908, churning out a total of forty-eight

---

Is Really, Really Depressing," https://www.cinemablend.com/new/Long-Term-Movie-Attendance-Graph-Really-Really-Depressing-68981.html.

8   *A History of Cinema*, 4.

9   *A Trip to the Moon* can be viewed here: https://www.youtube.com/watch?v=CEQQefvfnk4.

10   *The Emergence of Cinema*, 352–55.

11   *The Great Train Robbery* can be viewed here: https://www.youtube.com/watch?v=zuto7qWrplc.

"one-reelers" each lasting fifteen minutes. His output grew in subsequent years, but his first two-reeler, *Enoch Arden*, wasn't made until 1911. *Judith of Bethulia* (1914), his first four-reeler, represents "American cinema's foremost transition movie from shorts to features," according to film historian Matthew Kennedy.[12] But it was his landmark twelve-reel film, "*The Birth of a Nation*," that became, and remains, one of the most profitable films ever made.[13] With the success of this film, American movie culture took an even firmer hold with the invention of the movie palace with their Arabian Nights interiors, luxurious feel, live orchestra, and costumed attendants.

Way Down East

To explore Griffith's films, I would begin with what the director called "A Simple Story of Plain People," his 1920 drama *Way Down East*, starring two of the leading stars of silent cinema, Lillian Gish as Anna Moore and Richard Barthelmess as David Bartlett. Anna is a pretty but poor young woman from a New England village.[14] She meets Lennox, the son of a wealthy family who, wanting to get her into bed, manipulates Anna into a fake marriage. Once pregnant, Lennox leaves her, and Anna gives birth to the baby—she names him Trust Lennox. Cast back into poverty, Anna

12   Matthew Kennedy, "Making History: D. W. Griffith on DVD," https://brightlightsfilm.com/making-history-d-w-griffith-on-dvd/#.XHG10C3Mx0I.

13   Richard Schickel, *D. W. Griffith: An American Life* (New York: Limelight Editions, 1984), 281.

14   An unrestored print of *Way Down East* can be seen here: https://www.youtube.com/watch?v=MgYA4jUr4o0).

watches her baby boy die. She gets a job with Squire Bartlett whose son, David, falls in love with her. When the Squire finds out about the baby, he sends Anna away during a furious snow storm. After publicly outing Lennox as the father of her dead child, Anna ends up on an ice floe where David attempts to rescue her. The scenes on the frozen river stretch the viewer's capacity for suspense as far as it will go. The scene is as terrifying as it was for the actors themselves who worked out in the cold and on the river making little use of doubles.

Griffith's camera and lighting make Gish look translucent with a radiating innocence that makes Lennox's deception even more despicable. The scene in the bedroom after the marriage displays Gish in clinging lingerie like a lamb prepared for slaughter. *Way Down East* is a perfect example of why the "how" of movie making is more important than the "what." The "what" of this film is pure melodrama; the visual grammar of Griffith elevated the story, making it one of the finest films of the silent era.

In just over a century, film became the dominant art form in the world. At the same time movies were starting to attract millions, the president of Harvard University, Charles William Eliot, published his fifty-one-volume collection of great works, the *Harvard Classics* (1909). He told an audience of working men that a five-foot shelf full of good books could provide "a good substitute for a liberal education in youth to anyone who would read them with devotion, even if he could spare but fifteen minutes a day for reading."[15] Eliot's project suggests that a classical education

---

15   Adam Kirsch, "The Five-Foot Shelf Reconsidered," *Harvard*

was already losing its appeal and prestige. This was no doubt the case: a cultural revolution was in the making. The ideal of education through reading books and admiring "high art" was being challenged by the rise of a popular culture that loved going to the movies. Just as the change in technology made the new creative form available, the law of supply and demand kicked in. In 1909, the same year the *Harvard Classics* were published, film director D. W. Griffith made and released 140 one-reelers for public consumption.[16] The pace of change was only accelerating.

Film as Art

In 1936, German philosopher Walter Benjamin wrote that the movies were a further development of what started with the invention of photography. His concern was with how technology affected art and culture, arguing that artists' embrace of new technology to create art removed its "aura."[17] An artwork that becomes so widely available would lack the permanence, uniqueness, and authenticity that defined the high art of the previous two centuries. Without intending to, the earliest filmmakers were subverting the artistic traditions that provided the original elements of their art form. No doubt, Benjamin was onto something. But he did not recognize that filmmakers were already creating

Magazine, November-December 2001, http://harvardmagazine. com/2001/11/the-five-foot-shelf-reco.html.

[16]   Richard Schickel, *D. W. Griffith: An American Life* (New York: Limelight Editions, 1996), 618–19.

[17]   Walter Benjamin, "The Work of Art in the Age of Mechanical Reproduction" (1936), trans. Harry Zohn, https://www.marxists. org/reference/subject/philosophy/works/ge/benjamin.htm.

unique, authentic, and permanent works. When Adler[18] and Hutchins launched their Great Books project in 1952, books still reigned supreme as cultural signposts. That year the general public was being dazzled by Gene Kelly's *Singin' in the Rain* (itself containing a certain commentary on the turn from silent movies to "talkies"). It was also the year of *High Noon*, *The Quiet Man*, and *The Greatest Show on Earth*, which won the Oscar for best film. In spite of the significant artistic accomplishments that these now-classic films represent, movies, in general, were not yet taken very seriously as an art form among the elite.

Film criticism had not won much respect, even though the practice was initiated in the silent era by respected writers such as Vachel Lindsay and Carl Sandburg. Lindsay was the first in the United States to write about the aesthetics of film, *The Art of the Moving Picture*, 1914.[19] As one historian of film remarked, "The literary, it could be, were blinded by their literacy from understanding the language of the cinema; so it is not surprising that it needed a poet."[20]

Modern film studies did not begin until the 1950s; most of the major film studios had been in business since at least the 1920s—20th Century Fox (founded in 1935), RKO

---

[18]   On a personal note, when I tried to engage Dr. Adler in 1992 on the question of treating films as "Great Books," he demurred, though he was spurred to write a short book about art, *Art, the Arts and the Great Ideas*, (New York: Scribner, 1994). All classic "works of art" are treated but neither film nor movies are ever mentioned.

[19]   *American Movie Critics: An Anthology from the Silents Until Now*, ed. Phillip Lopate (New York: Literary Classics of the United States, 2006), 3–26.

[20]   *A History of the Cinema*, 32.

Pictures (1928), Paramount Pictures (1912), Warner Bros. (1923), and Metro-Goldwyn-Mayer (1924). The output of what's called the "studio system" dramatically impacted American culture. In 1930, out of a population of 120 million, 80 million Americans attended a film.[21] Until television started to arrive in large numbers of living rooms in the mid-fifties, visiting the local movie theater was an American ritual for families, especially for children. It was inevitable that with each passing decade, the importance of films in shaping the culture would increase exponentially, and not only in the United States.

The critical assessment and ranking of films began with a 1968 book by Andrew Sarris, *The American Cinema: Directors and Directions 1929–1968*.[22] The leading film critic of the time, Pauline Kael, strongly objected to Sarris treating films like a serious art form: "There is so much talk now about the art of film that we may be in danger of forgetting that most of the movies we enjoy are not works of art."[23] Kael was in favor of keeping movie-going what the audience considers it to be, a few hours of entertainment. In the controversy among critics that followed, Kael's opinion did not win out, though her writing remained influential to fellow and future critics.

21   Catarina Cowden, "The Long-Term Movie Attendance Graph Is Really, Really Depressing," https://www.cinemablend.com/new/Long-Term-Movie-Attendance-Graph-Really-Really-Depressing-68981.html.

22   Andrew Sarris, *The American Cinema: Directors and Directions 1929–1968* (New York: Dutton, 1968).

23   Pauline Kael, "Trash, Art, and the Movies," *American Movie Critics: An Anthology From the Silents Until Now* (New York: The Library of America, 2006), 339.

A Film Canon

Lists of great films have continued to appear since Sarris broke the ice either by individual critics such as Roger Ebert[24] or Jonathan Rosenbaum,[25] but the most highly-recognized list is published in the British Film Institute's magazine, *Sight and Sound*.[26] Since the first list in 1999, the results have been remarkably uniform. Going through a number of lists, I have listed the twenty most often mentioned (in no particular order):

- *Battleship Potemkin*, Serge Eisenstein, 1925.
- *The Passion of Joan of Arc*, Carl von Dreyer, 1928.
- *Sunrise: A Song of Two Humans*, F. W. Murnau 1929.
- *Man with a Movie Camera*, 1929.
- *The Rules of the Game*, Jean Renoir, 1939.
- *Citizen Kane*, Orson Wells, 1941.
- *Bicycle Thieves*, Vittorio de Sica, 1948.
- *Singin' in the Rain*, 1952.
- *Tokyo Story*, Yasujirō Ozu, 1953.
- *Seven Samurai*, Akira Kurosawa, 1954.
- *The Searchers*, John Ford, 1956.
- *Vertigo*, Alfred Hitchcock, 1958
- *8½*, Federico Fellini, 1963.
- *Andrei Rublev*, Andrei Tarkovsky, 1966.
- *Au Hasard Balthasar*, Robert Bresson, 1966.

---

24   Roger Ebert's list of great films can be found here: https://www.rogerebert.com/great-movies.

25   Jonathan Rosenbaum, *Essential Cinema: On the Necessity of Film Canons* (Baltimore: The Johns Hopkins University Press, 2004).

26   Ian Christie, "The 50 Greatest Films of All Time," July 30, 2018, https://www.bfi.org.uk/news/50-greatest-films-all-time.

- *2001: A Space Odyssey*, Stanley Kubrick, 1968.
- *The Godfather*, Francis Ford Coppola, 1972.
- *The Mirror*, Andrei Tarkovsky, 1975.
- *Apocalypse Now*, Francis Ford Coppola, 1979.

Many of us have strong feelings not only about which films we love the most, often extending that affection to what we believe is "the greatest." No doubt films like *The Searchers*, *Singin' In the Rain*, and *The Godfather* will be familiar and should encourage readers to try the rest. *Seven Samurai*, for example, is as entertaining as any John Ford western. The comparison is not accidental: its director, Akira Kurosawa, was an earnest admirer of John Ford. Carl Theodor Dreyer's *The Passion of Joan of Arc* is one of the most realistic and powerful portrayals of spirituality ever created. The least known of the films above, *The Mirror* and *Andrei Rublev*, were both directed by Andrei Tarkovsky (1932–1986). Never heard of him? Neither had I until I started seeing his name on various lists of great films. Of this rather obscure auteur, Ingmar Bergman said, "Tarkovsky for me is the greatest (director), the one who invented a new language, true to the nature of film, as it captures life as a reflection, life as a dream."[27] After watching *Andrei Rublev*, I am persuaded to believe that Bergman is right. The challenge of films like *The Mirror* is similar to reading *Don Quixote*, *Middlemarch*, or *War and Peace:* they are enjoyable but long and demanding. The

---

[27]   Peter Culshaw, "Andrei Tarkovsky – 'a mystic and a fighter,'" December 1, 2007, https://www.telegraph.co.uk/culture/film/starsandstories/3669621/Andrei-Tarkovsky-a-mystic-and-a-fighter.html.

payoff to engaging such films is exposure to astonishing storytelling and ravishing beauty.[28]

These masterpieces of filmmaking are long overdue in
joining the canon. Great art in every genre is, as we have
discussed, first and foremost, enjoyable in itself, but it is also
helpful in understanding a historical era. Some significant
artists have become commonplace as associations with a time
and place: The fourth century BC sculptor Praxiteles with
ancient Greece; Lully and Rameau with the French culture
of Louis XIV; Picasso and the Spanish Civil War; the paintings of Kaspar David Friedrich and German Romanticism;
Edvard Munch's painting *The Scream* and the modern age;
Gothic architecture and medieval culture; poets like Wilfred
Owen, Siegfried Sassoon, Edward Thomas, Issac Rosenberg,
and Rupert Brooke and the First World War.

Some films have taken root in the public imagination and
are seen as illuminating representations of historical eras or
events: D. W. Griffith's *The Birth of a Nation* (1915) and
the KKK; Charlie Chaplin's *The Dictator* and Adolph Hitler;
Metropolis (1927) by director Fritz Lang along with Stanley Kubrick's *2001: A Space Odyssey* (1984) and the impact
of modern technology; Michael Cimino's *The Deer Hunter*
(1978) and Francis Ford Coppola's *Apocalypse Now* (1979)
for the Vietnam War; Spielberg's *Saving Private Ryan* (1998)
and World War II; *A Man for All Seasons* and the Catholic
Church; William Friedkin's *The Exorcist* (1971) and demonic

---

[28]   Fiction writer and film critic David Gilmour recounts his
experience allowing his fifteen-year-old son to drop out of high
school if he agrees to watch three films with him each week. His
son, Jesse, agrees and the results are quite remarkable and moving;
see *The Film Club: A Memoir* (New York: Twelve, 2007).

possession; *The Ten Commandments* and the Jews escaping from Egypt; *It's a Wonderful Life* and the meaning of Christmas. Even without having seen these films, images and clips from them are so often used that they become familiar.[29]

The impact, both financial and demographic, of the film industry around the world is overwhelming. In 2018, 1,346,146,776 movie tickets were sold worldwide, with a total box office take of $12,074,939,346.[30] Printed book sales in the same year were 695,000,000.[31] Both film and book sales are strong for their respective medium; however, when books bought are a fraction of the number of movie tickets sold, the difference in relative impact is obvious.

Don't worry about the booksellers—their business is strong and getting stronger: studies show that in 2016, Americans still read an average of twelve books a year, and it appears the availability of e-books and audiobooks are aiding in readership.[32] The explosion in the availability and popularity of film, contrary to common belief, has hurt neither book sales nor actual reading. As it turns out, the advance of digital media has led to adaptations by the producers of both film and books: publishers have added e-books and audiobooks, and the movie business is transitioning towards the streaming platforms to win even larger audiences. But in

---

29   "All-Time Box-Office Top 100 Films," https://www.filmsite.org/boxoffice.html.

30   "Domestic Movie Theatrical Market Summary 1995 to 2019," https://www.the-numbers.com/market/.

31   "Unit sales of printed books in the United States from 2004 to 2018 (in millions)," https://www.statista.com/statistics/422595/print-book-sales-usa/.

32   Andrew Perrin, "Book Reading 2016," September 1, 2016, http://www.pewinternet.org/2016/09/01/book-reading-2016/.

producing films that go straight to online platforms such as Netflix, like the recent award-winning *Roma*,[33] the future of the movie theater is put into doubt.

Defending the Canon

Criticism of choosing a film canon has been addressed by Paul Schrader, one of America's most respected film directors and screenwriters. His twenty-four screenplays include such notable films as *Taxi Driver, American Gigolo, Raging Bull, Affliction*, and *First Reformed*. He wrote and directed *Mishima: A Life in Four Chapters* (1984), which is included in the great films list of noted film critic Roger Ebert.[34]

Schrader's writings about film are as enjoyable to read as they are insightful. In 2006, he explained why he never followed through on his promise to write the book that would be the film genre's equivalent of Harold Bloom's survey of great literary works.[35] Any such canon, he writes, would be "twentieth-century heresy." Rather than spend time defending the traditional standards for determining which works belong in the film canon, Schrader offers a "nonjudgmental" canon determined by the following criteria: beauty, strangeness, unity of form and content, tradition, repeatability, and morality.

---

[33]   Brian Tallerico, "*Roma*," November 21, 2018, https://www. rogerebert.com/reviews/roma-2018.

[34]   Roger Ebert, "Mishima: A Life in Four Chapters," December 5, . 2007, https://www.rogerebert.com/reviews/great-movie-mishima-a-life-in-four-chapters-1985.

[35]   Paul Schrader, "Canon Fodder: Paul Schrader's Canon Criteria," *Film Comment*, September/October 2006.

You will be surprised, as I was, to see *morality* among the traits relevant to determining canonical works. "Movies will always have a moral component," Schrader explains, because whenever a filmmaker tells a story about real life, a moral dimension is inevitable. He thinks any great film will have "moral resonance," but it is "better implied than spelled out," a point with which I am in full agreement. Too often "message movies" make themselves look stupid by setting up cardboard characters walking through a predictable plot to an end everyone knows is coming.

Schrader wants to "expand the parameters" of beauty as a criterion of the canonical films to include the "ability to qualitatively transform reality." He cites Picasso and Jackson Pollack as artists who did not seek to make something beautiful or pleasurable but who wanted to change the world. I can see his point in thinking about the impact a beautiful work of art can have on its viewer—such an experience can disturb a person's self-understanding, prompt reflection, and can indeed be life-changing. The *strangeness* of a film can add to its transformative power, though it can also limit its impact by limiting its audience. As an attribute of a work of art, strangeness can cause the elite and perhaps following generations to puzzle over it, to debate it, to be awed by it.

Schrader also, wisely, includes *tradition* because judgments about a film should not be limited to the film *per se* but should also consider their place in the history of filmmaking. (I would add that evaluation of any art form is impossible without reference to other notable works of art, especially those which have been regarded as reference points.) *Repeatability* has been for me the sure sign that a film is in a unique class: there are some films I watch at least once a year, and I am always surprised by their expressive power. A canonical film should be one that has layers of meaning that are inexhaustible.

The World Is a Screen

New York University professor, Mitchell Stephens argues that this transition from written works to visual media is epochal.[36] Stephens sees in the "rise of the image" an opportunity to counter the sense of despair that inflicts our age, in spite of its affluence. The image, he says, "provides us with the tools—intellectual and artistic tools—needed to construct new, more resilient ways of looking at our lives."[37] Would that all artists took this wise counsel to heart so that this common-sense moral guidance would be reflected in their work.

By looking at books, music, and films together, we can test Mitchell's thesis about the moving image and its "tools" to enrich self-reflection making it less vulnerable to currents of change. While reminding us that he is an "inveterate reader and writer," Mitchell wants to make the case that video "moves easily, ineluctably to an ironic distance and might, therefore, lead us to whatever truths lie beyond ironic distance. It has the potential to present us with new mental vistas, to take us to new philosophic places, as writing once did, as printing once did."[38] This claim about the power of

---

[36]   Mitchell Stephens, *the rise of the image and the fall of the word* (New York: Oxford University Press, 1998), xi.
[37]   Ibid.
[38]   Ibid. xii.

films is not, I think, unique to that art form. But as Mitchell explains, it's the nature of the filmed image to remain at a distance, say, as compared to reading a book, that allows a viewer to be drawn into a film without withdrawing into the safety of the familiar.

Considering films as part of a canon is going to leave out many of your favorite films. That's only to be expected because just as we don't confine our reading or listening to classics, we all have movies we enjoy seeing, as Pauline Kael wrote, just for an evening's entertainment. On the other hand, you may be surprised to find that some popular favorites are very highly regarded by the critics. For example, *Some Like It Hot* (Billy Wilder, 1959) was on everybody's list of best films. I had never thought of Tony Curtis dressing up as a woman as more than a trick to lure Marilyn Monroe into his upper bunk on the train. Yes, there's a lot here to reconsider, and that's part of the pleasure.

CHAPTER 5

Books, Poetry, Music, and Film Talk

I recently went to a concert featuring the *Symphonie Fantastique* (1830) by Hector Berlioz. Berlioz wrote it as a kind of love letter to win the heart of a famous Irish actress, Harriet Smithson.[1] He had been obsessed with Smithson for three years after seeing her in Shakespeare's *Hamlet.* His attempts to woo her by moving near her and sending her a multitude of letters had failed.

In the fourth of the symphony's five movements, Berlioz depicts the execution by beheading of an artist for the murder of his beloved. I wonder what was going on in Berlioz's mind to make him think this storyline would win Smithson over. As it turns out, the beheading worked. After Smithson heard the symphony in 1832—she missed the premiere— she agreed to marry him. The marriage lasted only a few years; they had a son, Louis, but separated soon afterward.

Such a personalized narrative piece of music draws in the average listener—it did Smithson—but it also says something about the artist and his milieu. To understand an

---

[1]   "Berlioz's *Symphonie Fantastique*," https://www.pbs.org/keeping score/berlioz-symphonie-fantastique.html.

artist like Berlioz, we should see him, as he saw himself, as a kind of Romantic hero, a leading figure in the Romantic movement that encompassed Europe in the first decades of the nineteenth century. That's precisely what the late man of letters Jacques Barzun did in his monumental two-volume work *Berlioz and the Romantic Century* (1950).[2] Barzun was my tutor in interdisciplinary studies, an approach to learning which we are putting to work in this book. When I encountered Barzun's book as a doctoral candidate in interdisciplinary studies, I was preparing to write a dissertation focusing on three key figures of the nineteenth century—Charles Baudelaire, Friedrich Nietzsche, and Soren Kierkegaard—tracing their response to the Romantic movement.[3] Each thought himself to be anti-romantic, but none of them was entirely free from the essential characteristics of romanticism—a preoccupation with the self and an impatience with tradition. By focusing on their mutual rejection of romanticism, I was able to find a starting point for comparing them.

Barzun's work on Berlioz sets the standard for interdisciplinary thinking; the way he moves between art forms, discussing their connections, is effortless. Barzun shows that understanding a composer and his music involves far more than musical and biographical analysis: "In a high civilization all social facts and forces become the matrix, and sometimes the subject, of the artist's work; and in the forms and

---

2   Jacques Barzun, *Berlioz and the Romantic Century*, 2 vols. (New York: Columbia University Press, 1969). This is a reprint of Jacques Barzun: *Berlioz and the Romantic Century*, 2 vols. (Boston: Little, Brown & Co., 1950).

3   Deal W. Hudson, *Three Reactions to Romanticism: Baudelaire, Nietzsche, and Kierkegaard*, The Graduate Institute of Liberal Arts, Emory University, 1978.

conditions of a collective art like music we find the element of a familiar history — politics, economics, and other struggles of human groups."[4]

Barzun dismisses the narrowness of music scholars who focus only on a composer's score to measure his work. An art critic, Barzun argues, can compare a realist painting to life because it contains familiar objects like tables and chairs. No one objects. But easy acceptance of this comparison risks making a false assumption that the painter in question believes life can be depicted by copying recognizable objects. Both life and art are far more complicated. In the case of music, a less representational medium, how can it speak to the listener about life? This is where Barzun illumines much: he explains how music can converse with other art forms: "To the artist, life consists of sensations, and these may be reproduced with equivalent effect by widely different physical means. A chord, a shape, or a word are such means. The meaning in the so-called representative arts thus arises from contrasts, rhythms, and evocations which exactly correspond to the contrasts, rhythms, and evocations in music."[5]

Life itself is where great books, music, and films meet. What all these have in common is the human desire and need to explore our lived experience. What starts creatively as a means of expression is received by the attentive reader/listener/viewer as a communication of insight. Such an understanding derived from a work of art opens the door to a conversation with conceptual works of philosophy, history, criticism, biography, science, and social science. Each pursues the kind of understanding appropriate to its methodology.

---

[4]   *Berlioz and the Romantic Century,* "Author's Note."
[5]   Ibid., 9.

Ultimate Concern

The goal of such a conversation is to better understand oneself, others, society, morality, politics, beauty, the world, and the Absolute. Paul Tillich, a philosopher and theologian of the mid-twentieth century, proposed that, regardless of one's religious faith, everyone has an "ultimate concern."[6] It was up to each person to determine for himself what this concern was and the degree of importance it would have in his life. Some will notice in Tillich's theory an echo of Aristotle's teleology: all humans act towards an end "which is always desirable in itself and never for the sake of something else."[7]

Every work we will consider here is a product of a creator's ultimate concern. Sometimes the artist or author is aware of this, sometimes not. The artist who claims his works have no significance beyond themselves is delusional, dishonest, or just dumb. In his description of ultimate concern, Tillich echoes St. Augustine's "restless heart"[8] and St. Thomas Aquinas's "infinite desire for God."[9] This inner urging toward an ultimate is in every person whether he is aware of it or not. Tillich puts it this way: "The human heart seeks the infinite because that is where the finite wants to rest."[10]

---

[6]   Paul Tillich, *Dynamics of Faith* (New York: Harper Colophon Books, 1957), 2–3.

[7]   Aristotle, *Nicomachean Ethics*, 1097a30-34, trans. by Martin Ostwald (Indianapolis: Bobb-Merrill, 1980), 14–15.

[8]   "Because you make us with yourself as our goal, and our heart is restless until it rests in you," St. Augustine, *Confessions*, 1.1, trans. Sarah Ruden (New York: Modern Library, 2017), 3.

[9]   *Summa contra gentiles* III.I.48, trans. Vernon J. Bourke (London: The University of Notre Dame Press, 1975), 162–67. All quotations from the *Summa contra gentiles* are from this volume.

[10]   *Dynamics of Faith*, 13.

Of course, some works are created primarily for a transitory pleasure or delight (or disgust and insult, for that matter), but for that very reason, such "art" isn't found on the list of great works. In this book, we consider pieces of a puzzle, as it were; though we do not yet know how the pieces will fit together, we know what we hope to find when it is made whole—to see, to understand, to see and affirm what really *is, what really exists.* From its centuries of reflection on human existence, the Western tradition has derived concepts of human rights, human dignity, democracy, freedom of religion, and the common good. Are these just convenient fictions used for "virtue-signaling" or other forms of manipulation?

Aristotle, Aquinas, and Tillich remind us that every person seeks to find answers to the fundamental questions. These questions cannot be shut out, despite the busyness and distraction of modern life, at least not for long. Our shared existence possesses a vulnerability, a fragmentary quality, because each of us is in the process of finding wholeness.

Answers

Poet and critic Dana Gioia describes the British poet Elizabeth Jennings (1926–2001) as "England's best Catholic poet since Gerard Manley Hopkins."[11] Jennings's faith directly informed her poetry, and she wrote voluminously: her *Collected Poems* is 1,100 pages long.[12] Jennings succeeded as a poet both among her peers and, as is not frequently the

---

[11]   Dana Gioia, "Clarify Me, Please, God of the Galaxies: In Praise of the Poetry of Elizabeth Jennings," *First Things*, May 2018.

[12]   Elizabeth Jennings, *Collected Poems*, ed. Emma Mason (Manchester: Carcanet Press, 2012).

case, in finding an audience. Fifty thousand copies of her *Selected Poems* were sold in 1979, a phenomenal amount for a poet. She did not, however, succeed much at life. As Gioia explains, at forty years old, she was impoverished and struggled with mental illness to such a degree that she could not hold a steady job.[13]

In this poem, Jennings catches one of the moments when the "big answers" inevitably confront us in a way that we can no longer hide behind the comfort of "small answers."

Answers

I kept my answers small and kept them near;
Big questions bruised me but still I let
Small answers be a bulwark to my fear.

The huge abstractions I kept from the light;
Small things I handled and caressed and loved.
I let the stars assume the whole of night.

But the big answers clamoured to be moved
Into my life. Their great audacity
Shouted to be acknowledged and believed.

Even when all small answers build up to
Protection of my spirit, still I hear
Big answers striving for their overthrow

And all the great conclusions coming near.[14]

---

13   "Clarify Me, Please, God of the Galaxies."
14   *The Oxford Book of Twentieth Century Verse*, chosen by Philip Larkin (London: Oxford University Press, 1973), 564.

There are times in life when we all experience the "great audacity," when fundamental questions about life become inescapable. Those "small answers" delay the encounter while we attend to the daily duties. But, the poet writes, "Big answers striving for their overthrow." Jennings captures the moment when our thoughts are struck by wonder, taking us out of the moment and to a place where we sense "all the conclusions coming near."

Darkness at Noon

Some events wake up an entire generation, forcing many to start looking for the big answers. In 1940, British author Arthur Koestler published his novel *Darkness at Noon,* set in Communist Russia. The topic was timely for the English, as Britain had forged an alliance with Soviet Russia against Hitler and the Nazis. This alliance served to encourage further intellectuals in Europe, England, and the United States who were enamored of Stalin's regime. In Hollywood, Communist sympathizer and screenwriter Dalton Trumbo would later boast of keeping Koestler's anti-Soviet novel from being made into a motion picture.[15] Supporters of Communism ignored reports of Stalin executing party members and anyone else who displeased him. At least 1,550,000 were arrested, a million or more died, in Stalin's "Great Purges" of 1936–1938. Stalin believed that if only 5 percent of those

---

[15]   Michael Weiss, "The McCarthyism canard," *The New Criterion,* September 7, 2010, https://www.newcriterion.com/blogs/dispatch/the-mccarthyism-canard.

arrested and killed turned out to be enemies, "that would be a good result."[16]

Koestler's book put an end to any infatuation with Stalin. He depicts the absurdity of the main character, Comrade Rubashov, who has been captured, imprisoned, interrogated, and given a "show trial."[17] Comrade Rubashov is a former party leader now accused of treason during one of Stalin's purges. Throughout the ordeal, Rubashov tries to make sense of the situation, only to fail because there's no way to understand it except as a decision of "Number 1" (Stalin). Only after Rubashov finally signs a confession and receives a death sentence does he wake up. This moment described in the last ten pages of *Darkness at Noon* is among the most powerful in modern fiction. It's in these pages that we read about Rubashov accepting the reality of the absurdity; he sees it for what it is and takes responsibility for the lie he has been living.

After his final sentencing, he is taken back to his prison cell to wait for the executioner. Rubashov is relieved that he "no longer had to howl with the wolves,"[18] the pack that hunts and kills for Number 1 without regard for humanity. He remembers a speech he memorized as a youth: the speech by the French revolutionary Danton to his tribunal after being condemned to death. "Tyranny is afoot, she had torn her veil, she carries her head high, she strides over our dead bodies." Then Koestler gives the reader a view into

---

[16]   Orlando Figes, *Revolutionary Russia:1891-1991* (New York: Metropolitan Books, 2014), 194.

[17]   Ibid., 195.

[18]   Arthur Koestler, *Darkness at Noon,* trans. Daphne Hardy (New York: Macmillan Publishing Company, Inc, 1941), 254.

Rubashov's thoughts as he contemplates his fate. Rubashov still has "certain questions to which he would have liked to find an answer before it was too late. They were rather naive questions; they concerned the meaning of suffering, or, more exactly, the difference between suffering which made sense and senseless suffering."[19]

Wondering if the vastness of the suffering inflicted by the regime made any sense, he locates the flaw in the Soviets' moral logic: they thought of mankind only in the abstract, not "the real human of bone and flesh and blood and skin."[20]

Rubashov feels an "oceanic sense" come over him, recognizing that as a Party leader he would have dismissed it, but now, "In death, the metaphysics became real." In other words, in facing the reality of death, questions about being, existence, time, and eternity cannot but arise. Notice here the corollary between Rubashov's insight and Stalin's famous but possibly apocryphal quip: "A single death is a tragedy, a million deaths is a statistic." Rubashov recalls that as a child he loved astronomy and regretted not answering the question of his interrogator, "What about the infinite?" That's the source of his guilt, "Could there be a greater?" The "oceanic sense," he realizes, is "counter-revolutionary." The Party had taken away his free will, his capacity for wonder, his urge to ask questions about good and evil.

The Party had reduced all of humanity's troubles to "economic fatality," a cause he had faithfully served for forty years. No matter how cruelly the Party acted on this assumption, people were no better off than before. Rubashov muses,

---

19   Ibid., 254–55.
20   Ibid., 255.

"Premises of unimpeachable truth had led to a result which was completely absurd." Waiting in his prison cell for the executioner to arrive, Rubashov says to himself, "No, one cannot build a Paradise with concrete."

The page-long passage in *Darkness at Noon* just before the anticipated knock of the executioner on the door reaches a near-mystical height. Rubashov realizes that the evil principle of "the end justifies the means" was the "defective compass" that set the direction of the Party, and, as a result of that realization, he imagines a new party emerging: "Perhaps the members of the new party will wear monk's cowls, and preach only purity of means can justify the ends."

From reading this, you might never guess that Koestler had himself been a member of the Communist Party. After the purge of 1936–1938, during which many friends and acquaintances disappeared, he left Russia, taking with him an insider's knowledge of Communism in there and throughout Europe. The *Boston Globe* literary critic George Scialabba remarks that Koestler's novel forever diminished the appeal of Communism with intellectuals and may have kept Communists from winning the 1946 election in France.[21] In 1973, Aleksandr Solzhenitsyn's *The Gulag Archipelago*, which revealed the grisly nature and scope of the Soviet political prison system, would finish Koestler's project, dealing a death blow to Communism's intellectual defenses in the West.

---

[21]   George Scialabba, "Review of Arthur Koestler: The Homeless Mind by David Cesarani," *Boston Globe*, January 23, 2000, http://georgescialabba.net/mtgs/2000/01/arthur-koestler-the-homeless-m.html.

It is notable that *Darkness at Noon* certainly had considerable influence on European politics and intellectual life during and after the war, but we cannot emphasize too strongly the effect of the more personal insight revealed at the story's climax: "In death, the metaphysics became real." Rubashov, like all of us, eventually faces questions about the ultimate concern. Often these require a moment of tremendous fear or resignation, such as being dealt a death sentence, to break through our resistance. Koestler demonstrates in this great work how the indirectness of fiction, like other art forms, can pack a greater wallop than merely descriptive discourse. We instinctively take a step back from the challenge of direct speech, but seeing the same thought embodied in a compelling story is more likely to reach us where change occurs, in the intersection of heart and mind.

The Impact of Movies

So, while it is true that great works of literature have at times had truly transformative effects on a society precisely by reaching people where they live, far from the classroom and lecture hall, another medium has even greater reach, especially today. Many critics and historians have argued, for example, that film is more effective at lowering our defenses than any other medium, particularly in its ability to unite other art forms in service of a single story. Film scholar Stephen Apkon explains, "But the combination of moving image, spoken word, text, and music—plus the way that combination shoots like a needle straight into the cerebral cortex—makes the movie the most powerful and compelling text we have yet created."[22]

Film, Apkon adds, is the artistic medium that comes closest to "the ideal of unmediated communication."[23] It sounds good on the surface, but one may fairly ask: Is film truly an "unmediated" experience? After all, movies contain all sorts of obviously mediated elements—speech, music, characters, plot, to name a few. For something to be unmediated, it must communicate with the viewer without any intervening thought; it must simply, in a sense, pop into one's head. (Aquinas explained angelic knowledge as immediate and intuitive, a way of knowing which Descartes tried to adopt in his *Meditations*.[24]) No, considering just the large production apparatus required to create a film and the care taken by the director to perfectly capture a scene are enough to demonstrate that film is anything but "unmediated communication."

Apkon has in mind a different notion of immediacy than that which philosophers consider. Filmmakers want to keep the construction of the film hidden from the viewer. For example, Apkon says the audience should feel but not be aware of camera movement.[25] He proposes an ideal of "Continuous editing: unmediated, direct, personal, and

---

[22]   Stephen Apkon, *The Art of the Image: Redefining Literacy In a World of Screens,* foreword by Martin Scorsese (New York: Farrar, Straus, and Giroux, 2013), 39.

[23]   Ibid.

[24]   Deal W. Hudson, "Adler from An Angel's Eye," *The Aspen Institute Quarterly,* Winter, 1995, vol. 7, no.1, 86–99.

[25]   *The Art of the Image,* 158.

immersive reality."[26] I don't see how that is different from a good novelist, poetry, or composer, all of whom want their creation to be experienced as a whole. Anything else is like wearing a suit inside out with all the seams showing.

Apkon might have held a view of film's immediacy at a far more practical level; namely, the immersive experience of watching a movie versus reading a book, listening to music, going to the theatre, or looking at paintings and sculpture. On this, I agree with him with one qualification. It's one thing to watch a film in a darkened theater with an eighty-foot wide screen and Dolby sound filling your ears from every direction, and quite another to watch the same film on your tablet at home. It's a case of total immersion without distraction versus partial immersion with inevitable distractions. The direction the film business is going, towards streaming on individual devices, will diminish the sense of immersion and near-total immediacy, which is undoubtedly already affecting the art form of film.

Apkon is more helpful in his understanding of how to "redefine literacy," by which he means "the ability to comprehend and have facility with those areas that are deemed critical to our being full participants in the world."[27] This is important for our understanding of how books, music, and art converse.

My generation, the heart of the post-WWII "baby boom," was confronted by visual media; up went the rabbit ears over the TV set with three channels, and we believed every word we heard. It wasn't until the Vietnam and Watergate era

---

[26]   Ibid., 69.
[27]   Ibid., 139.

that we began to realize how uncritically we had received the information being fed to us by the new medium. All training in visual media was gained by trial and error in an effort to look behind the image on the screen. We had been taught critical thinking about books. This new world of television was magical for a time—the immediacy of a World Series, a political convention, the landing of a man on the moon—but the magic was lost when the audience realized the manipulation of the medium.

Visual literacy can be understood by analogy to literacy in the language arts. We learn not only how to read a text—to understand its use of narrative voice, metaphor, simile, symbol, imagery, plot, character, action, spectacle, and so on—but we learn how to write, how to create a text. When it comes to visual literacy, there is very little formal education offered in the American educational system, which is hard to understand since film and now other forms of visual communication have become so dominant.

Wagner as Precursor

The medium of film, however, had an important precursor, a man who succeeded in incorporating all the arts forms of his era into one gigantic work of art, a four-part opera, *The Ring of the Nibelungen*. Thirty-nine years before the first "talkie" film, *The Jazz Singer* (1927), composer Richard Wagner's *Ring Cycle* was first performed between August 13–17, 1882. With this seventeen-hour operatic work, Wagner stretched the traditional boundaries not merely of opera but of modern art itself. Recall that musical theatre is one of the oldest art forms, appearing first in Ancient Greece where choruses were integral to the narrative. Many cultural derivations later, opera as we now know it emerged in the late sixteenth century and gradually became the dominant art form in most of Europe, its apex is seen in the works of Mozart in the eighteenth century and those of Puccini and Wagner in the nineteenth. Yet, in essays published by a young Wagner in 1840, we find the desire to create the *'Gesamtkunstwerk,'* a *complete work of art* in operatic form. The vision wasn't realized until 1876 with *The Ring of the Nibelungen*[28] when it was first performed in full (parts of it were staged, not entirely in accordance with Wagner's wishes, beginning in the 1860s).

With the full work, Wagner had composed seventeen hours of music for a huge orchestra, with elaborate sets and costumes, in an opus that would be presented over a period of four days. Those who have experienced a *Ring* perfor-mance done well, as I have, will attest to its unique power. Starting with an emotionally-charged storyline based in Norse mythology, Wagner's *Ring* melds all of the available arts with a surging late romantic score of alternating har-monic themes into an experience that can elicit a kind of awe that approaches the religious. This was Wagner's precise intent to replace traditional faith with the spiritual ecstasy of his music.

---

[28]   You can hear and see the first opera of the cycle, *Das Rheingold*, conducted by Pierre Boulez at Wagner's own opera house, Bayreuth, in 1980: https://www.youtube.com/watch?v=3ZP-yXsNV2E.

Teaching Yourself

Interdisciplinary approaches to classics and the arts sometimes face the charge that such studies limit the depths to
which one can go in a single discipline. There is some truth
to that, but only some, for it assumes that authentic scholarship is too demanding to be spread across disciplines. In my
opinion, such interdisciplinary studies can also serve more
people by looking across disciplines to gain a better understanding of an era, an idea, or a movement. And what we
aim for in this work is not scholarship per se, but rather to
begin a process of self-directed classical education, to fall in
love with the greatest works and, through that process, to
protect our intellectual freedom and develop the habits that
foster clarity of thought. I'm grateful to the biographer of
Victor Hugo,[29] and I know he wouldn't be irked by my use
of his biography in an overview of Parisian culture in the
nineteenth century. I assume that's why the biographer studied Hugo's life for so many years, to make a deeper appreciation of Hugo available to the rest of us non-specialists and
not merely to fellow scholars.

Learning, after all, never occurs in a prescribed way. It's
just not how persons naturally learn! The sequencing of
courses based on a hierarchy of knowledge works for some
students but not all. Of course, children must learn how to
read and write, just as they should learn basic mathematics as well as how to express clearly what they are thinking.
Those skills are required before any comprehensive education
can take place. Beyond these basic building blocks, older

---

[29]   The best biography is Graham Robb, *Victor Hugo: A Biography*
(New York: W. W. Norton & Company, 1998).

children and adults learn when they are ready—when they *care enough*. This is true of literature, history, government, or geography, all of which require using skills acquired earlier.

Similarly, one does not teach a student to be virtuous by merely having her memorize the virtues and other moral teachings. This fact does not make such basic education optional however; memorization and direct engagement with the most fundamental moral texts are necessary. Thinking about morality enables us to appraise our lives and others against an ethical standard, but when virtues are actually *acquired*, they direct thoughts, emotions, and actions in an orderly way, which is especially important in difficult circumstances. The classics portray heroes and criminals, spiritual victory and loss, the anguish of indecision, the boredom of indifference—in these stories we see mirrors of ourselves and the lives around us. By attending to them, we see more clearly.

CHAPTER 6

Wonder

American poet Wallace Stevens attended Harvard College, went to New York Law School, and started practicing law in 1904 at the age of twenty-five. His first book of poems, *Harmonium,* was not published until 1923 when he was forty-four.

Stevens lived in two worlds: in Hartford, where after 1916 he was an attorney for Hartford Accident and Indemnity Company, becoming vice president in 1936; and in the Florida Keys, which became the setting for the majority of his poetry, beginning in 1922.[1] On his final visit to the Keys, Stevens picked a fight with Ernest Hemingway: "So it began, with Stevens swinging at the bespectacled Hemingway, who seemed to weave like a shark, and Papa hitting him one-two and Stevens going down 'spectacularly,' as Hemingway would remember it into a puddle of fresh rainwater."[2] Stevens, by the way, won the Pulitzer Prize in 1955 for his *Collected Poems,* two years after Hemingway, who was nine years younger, and one year after Hemingway's Nobel Prize.

---

[1] Michael Schmidt, *The Lives of Poets* (New York: Alfred A. Knopf, 1999), 626–29.

[2] Paul Mariani, *The Whole Harmonium: The Life of Wallace Stevens* (New York: Simon & Schuster, 2016), 207.

Have you ever been there, standing on the beach as dusk becomes night, looking up at the cloudy sky and the horizon, dumbstruck at such beauty? We don't have the words to describe what we see, but we want to capture the moment, to remember or to communicate it. It takes a poet, I suppose. Here is how Wallace Stevens captures the wonder that such a moment inspires:

Fabliau of Florida

Barque of phosphor
On the palmy beach,

Move outward into heaven,
Into the alabasters
And night blues.

Foam and cloud are one.
Sultry moon-monsters
Are dissolving.

Fill your black hull
With white moonlight.

There will never be an end
To this droning of the surf.[3]

The only serious challenges to the reader come with the first line and the last. "Barque of phosphor"? Perhaps you remember reading Edgar Allen Poe's "To Helen," in which he describes her beauty, "Like those Nicéan barques of yore."

---

3   Wallace Stevens, *The Collected Poems of Wallace Stevens*, ed. John N. Serio and Chris Beyers (New York: Vintage Books, 2015), 25.

A barque is a ship. We know "phosphorescent," but is that the same as "phosphor"? Trusting that it is, we move to the next line and the remainder of the poem. The narrator is on a beach where ships, plural as it turns out, "Move outward into heaven," entering a matrix of bluish colors. Then all that we see is united as if we are on one of the ships as the colors merge into a blackness—"foam and cloud are one." As everything darkens, moonlight is invited to fill the boat; then the narrator strangely comments that the "droning of the surf" will never end.

What does he mean? A droning on of the surf's sound or the disappearance of the surf under a dark sky? There have been no references to sound in the poem. Here I think Stevens is looking past the senses: the "droning of the surf" can mean the simple fact of the never-ending cycle of water going out and coming in, what we all see when walking an ocean beach. The droning surf becomes an image for, "There will never be an end." The poet leaves us wondering, but not in an agnostic way; we have seen enough through his eyes of what amazes him in the darkening horizon. There seems to be some tone of regret registered there. Stevens's bold wondering raises questions, some of which have no immediate answer.

Maxims and Aphorisms

In engaging a new work of poetry, one can choose to be washed away in the rhythm and imagery, or he can delve into the work, seeking to understand. Rarely is a poem nakedly descriptive, explicit about its meaning, as one would expect from philosophy. The bridge between poets and philosophers is not as narrow as is often described. Plato wrote in the fictional form of dialogues, having characters voice different perspectives, with his protagonist Socrates usually (not always) winning the day. This is where we get the term "Socratic method" of dialogue and questioning in education, which is also the basis for our approach in this book.

We don't know what Socrates thought except through his student, Plato. Socrates was not a fan of writing, thinking that philosophy was necessarily a work of dialogue, which was to be spoken. Thankfully for us, Plato disagreed. The Greek tradition of oration was already well established when Socrates came on the scene in the fifth century BC, as its history was rendered in epic poetry such as that of Homer. Such "pre-Socratic" reflection merges description and narrative with the poetic. This effective mode of thought and communication reappears throughout history. The Danish philosopher Søren Kierkegaard (1813–1855), for example, recognized the power of "indirect communication" and couched most of his arguments, like Plato, in the form of philosophical fictions written under various names to distinguish points of view. By "indirect," he meant nothing more than speaking through characters and a narrative.[4]

Classicist and philosopher Friedrich Nietzsche (1844–1900) also experimented with non-discursive forms. He wrote a philosophical novel, *Thus Spake Zarathustra* (1883–1891), and several books of aphorisms. It's generally overlooked that

---

[4]   Søren Kierkegaard, *The Point of View for My Work as An Author: A Report to History*, trans. Walter Lowrie, ed. Benjamin Nelson (New York: Harper Torchbooks, 1962), 5–27.

Nietzsche, though German, preferred French culture. The *Maxims* (1665) of François de La Rochefoucauld (1613–1680) spurred him to adopt an aphoristic, or "wise saying," style or writing. La Rochefoucauld, unlike Nietzsche, made no pretense of being a philosopher. The *Maxims,* published anonymously, contain the insights of a worldly and wise man who observes the jockeying for power and privilege in the court society of Louis XIII and Louis XIV. One is likely to find their equal in a self-help book today.

> 20 The constancy of the wise is only the art of containing their agitation in their hearts.[5]
> 25 One needs greater virtues to hold out against good fortune than bad.[6]
> 38 We make promises according to our hopes, and we keep them according to our fears.[7]

Pensées

Blaise Pascal (1623–1662) was writing aphorisms at the same time. His *Pensées* ("Thoughts") were published in 1670, eight years after his death. The work, consisting of pages lying randomly in stacks, had to be put in order by his editors. Unlike his contemporary, he addresses his aphorisms to work on the perennial questions. A polymath and a genius, Pascal developed a mechanical calculating machine

---

[5] François de La Rochefoucauld, *Maxims; La Rochfoucault,* trans. Stuart D. Warner and Stépane Douard (South Bend: St. Augustine's Press, 2001), 7.

[6] Ibid., 8.

[7] Ibid., 10.

(later named the "Pascaline") at the age of nineteen. He had a genius's aptitude for mathematics, geometry, and both the natural and social sciences.

Despite his many and lasting contributions in mathematics and atmospheric sciences, the *Pensées* is his most remembered work. Born Catholic in Catholic France, Pascal felt drawn in his early twenties toward a sect known as the Jansenists, which emphasized the fallenness of the human race and the necessity of grace for any individual to act in a meritorious way. Five doctrines of Jansenism were condemned by Pope Innocent X in 1653. Pascal, however, was not deterred. One year later, a religious experience prompted Pascal to write about his faith in the *Pensées*. The tone here feels aggressive, impatient, even angry. He sounds like a man on an evangelical mission, his evangelism employing the tools of his immense learning. Wonder, for Pascal, is not about sunsets over the sea: Wonder teaches us about our place in the universe. In *pensée* number 199, "The Disproportion of Man,"[8] he compares man to the infinite and the universe. Pascal asks us to look first at nature, then beyond nature, allowing us to see that "the whole visible world is only an imperceptible dot in nature's ample bosom." Realizing his insignificance, a man will ask himself, "What is a man in the infinite?"

At this point, Pascal surprises us: he does not rely on the wide sky as his only metaphor. He wants to "show him a new abyss," namely, the "immensity of nature enclosed in this miniature atom." This leaves man caught between two

---

[8]   All the quotes are taken from Blaise Pascal, *Pensées*, trans. A. J. Krailsheimer (New York: Penguin Press, 1984), 88–95.

absolutes: the *nothingness* "from which he emerges" and the *infinite* "in which he is engulfed." Then Pascal reveals the complementarity that he as a scientist finds between the created order and truths of his faith. Scientific curiosity becomes wonder, making him "more disposed to contemplate them in silence than investigate them with presumption." He concludes by confessing, "The author of these wonders understands them: no one else can."

Pascal quotes Aristotle in agreement: "For it is owing to their wonder that men both now begin and at first began to philosophize."[9] Aristotle would have known the story told by Plato about how the earliest known philosopher, Thales, was mocked by a Thracian servant-girl for falling into a well while he was gazing at the stars: "He was eager to know the things in the sky, but that which was behind him and just by his feet escaped his notice."[10] Those words would be to several artists a badge of honor, but there's no record of how Thales took them. Wonder[11] is the natural human response to what the sky represents, the seeming vastness of things.

Wonder can be life-changing, as it was for Pascal. It is the metaphysical awareness that lies behind Wallace Stevens's ode to the darkening sky. Wonder is not an emotion, though it does often arrive with emotions, provoking awe, delight, or even fear. Wonder begins when the senses light up the

---

[9]   Aristotle, *Metaphysics*, 982b 11-983, *The Basic Works of Aristotle*, ed. Richard McKeon, introduction by C. D. C. Reeve (New York, Modern Library Classic, 2001), 692–93.

[10]   *The Presocratic Philosophers*, nos. 74, 78.

[11]   From θαῦμα (*thaûma*), meaning to wonder or to marvel, F. E. Peters, *Greek Philosophical Terms: A Historical Lexicon* (New York, New York University Press, 1967), 22.

intellect, eliciting poetry, music, metaphysics, and matters of the ultimate concern.

Primary Wonder

Denise Levertov moved to America from England in 1947 and became one of the best poets of the post-war generation. She published twenty books of poetry, but her first, *The Double Image* (1946), gained her national recognition in the UK when she was only twenty-one. Her 1959 collection, *With Eyes at the Back of our Heads*, established her reputation in the United States. During the fifties, Levertov had been influenced by American transcendentalists, which helped to free her to channel her innate Romanticism. During the sixties, Levertov exhausted herself in anti-war activism and feminism, and her poetry, some say, suffered. In this poem, it is Levertov the romanticist who describes how amid "a host of diversions" the mind can be unexpectedly visited by what she calls "Primary Wonder."[12]

Primary Wonder

Days pass when I forget the mystery.
Problems insoluble and problems offering
their own ignored solutions
jostle for my attention, they crowd its antechamber
along with a host of diversions, my courtiers, wearing
their colored clothes; caps and bells.
And then

---

[12]   Denise Levertov, "Primary Wonder," *Selected Poems*, ed. Paul A. Lacey (New York: New Directions, 2002), 192.

once more the quiet mystery
is present to me, the throng's clamor
recedes: the mystery
that there is anything, anything at all,
let alone cosmos, joy, memory, everything,
rather than void: and that, O Lord,
Creator, Hallowed One, You still,
hour by hour sustain it.

Events have long and often unpredictable afterlives. What once felt like a joyful moment years ago can come back and hit you like a slap across the face. For example, the memory of a child's birth will keep circling back as she grows older, eliciting more reflections about one's own life, its direction and purpose, and about what might have been. Built into that process is an aspect of self-questioning and self-examination—you can sound the depths, or you can resist by seeking distraction. Wonder is an admission both of finitude and mystery. There are persons, sadly, who live in denial of both. Wonder can sneak up on us: "the mystery / that there is anything, anything at all."

Since Aristotle observed that philosophy begins in wonder, we should not be surprised that he places the habit of contemplation at the summit of his requirements for a happy life. In book ten of his *Nicomachean Ethics,* Aristotle argues that happiness requires steady use of the best part of oneself, the intelligence, and be applied to knowledge sought for its own sake, which leads to self-sufficiency, which we might understand as a certain kind of personal freedom. Contemplation is an activity that requires free time. He recognizes that finding the time is difficult for men and women who are bound to practical activities—families, business, military, government. Those who live to seek amusement are fated to be the least contemplative of all.[13]

For those of us not living in ancient Greece, the meaning is clear: we need to find time to study and protect it—time undisturbed by the practical necessities of life. Indeed, Aristotle believed such study exercises to be our most distinctive human ability, one that is its own reward and bestows lasting pleasure: "what is by nature proper to each thing will be at once the best and the most pleasant for it. In other words, a life guided by intelligence is the best and most pleasant for man, since intelligence belongs to man alone. Consequently, this kind of life is the happiest."[14]

Thus, the hunger for higher things stirred by wonder should lead to the actual contemplation of those higher things. For Aristotle, to wonder is to seek answers, and happiness belongs to those who find them. Wonder opens the mind, and contemplation focuses the mind on possible and actual truths. It may also mean stripping ourselves of some adult pretensions.

Dies Natalis

Childlikeness is an often-forgotten aspect of wonder. Children look at the world with wide-eyed innocence, reminding adults of their own lost innocence, of wonder left far behind. But it needn't be. Poets reawaken wonder with words that viscerally evoke wonders we have known and unseen wonders just in front of us.

---

[13]   Aristotle, *Nicomachean Ethics*, 1176a30-1177b25, 287-89.
[14]   Ibid., 1178a5-9, 291.

The poet Thomas Traherne (1636–1674) belongs to the seventeenth-century metaphysical school, though not as well-known as Donne, Herbert, and Marvel. His most noted work is the mystical *Centuries of Meditation*.[15] It's an extended prose-poem of remarkable spirituality, probing and mystical.

In a section entitled "Wonder," he imagines a child entering the world, "When first among His works I did appear." The English composer Gerald Finzi (1901–1956) set this section to music, a five-movement cantata for solo voice and orchestra, *Dies Natalis*, which premiered in 1939. Like Traherne, Finzi is not as celebrated as his contemporaries, Gustav Holst and Ralph Vaughan Williams. But Finzi possessed a remarkable gift for setting words to music. Music critic and historian Robert R. Reilly describes *Dies Natalis* as a work of art in which "The unsullied joy, the sense of wonder, and the celebration of creation are conveyed with a spontaneity and rapture that is breathtaking."[16]

Finzi was by nature a contemplative and disposed toward the celebration of childhood experience. He enjoyed long walks through the English countryside, its beauty spurring his composition. He had the initial inspiration for setting Traherne's prose-poem from the *Centuries*[17] on a walking tour of East Anglia in 1927. Finzi saw a sixteenth-century

---

[15] Thomas Traherne, *Centuries Thomas Traherne 1637-1674*, The Faith Press, 1960. A free download is available here: https://archive.org/details/centuries_of_meditations_1412_librivox.

[16] Robert R. Reilly and Jens F. Laurson, *Surprised by Beauty: A Listener's Guide to the Recovery of Modern Music* (San Francisco, Ignatius Press, 2016), 107.

[17] *Centuries*, 3rd Century.

church roof with three tiers of angels with outspread wings and was reminded of Botticelli's painting *Mystic Nativity*. Afterward, Finzi read more in the *Centuries* and chose an excerpt for each of the four movements. Here is the text of the second.[18]

How like an angel came I down!
How bright are all things here!
When first among His works I did appear
O how their glory me did crown!
The world resembled His Eternity
In which my soul did walk;
And every thing that I did see
Did with me talk.
The skies in their magnificence
The lovely, lively air,
O how divine, how soft, how sweet, how fair!
The stars did entertain my sense;
And all the works of God, so bright and pure,
So rich and great, did seem,
As if they ever must endure
In my esteem.
A native health and innocence
Within my bones did grow,
And while my God did all His Glories show,
I felt a vigour in my sense
That was all Spirit. I within did flow
With seas of life, like wine;

I nothing in the world did know
　　But 'twas Divine.

The tenor line achieves an ecstatic glow at the words "With seas of life, like wine" that is unnerving for its unabashed beauty. His outright declamation of "Divine" at the end makes Traherne's intention clear, although the agnostic Finzi did not share his faith. As Robert R. Reilly comments: "In my own experience with agnostics, I have found they are often particularly close to God—intimate enough to hold a personal grudge," particularly in cases involving the suffering of children and death.[19] Finzi lost his father at the age of seven; his three older brothers and music teacher, Ernest Farrar, would die in the trenches of the First World War while he was a teenager. Perhaps his experience of death made his encounters with the beauty in nature and art, by contrast, all the more meaningful and arresting—ecstatic experiences he put into his music. Or, perhaps, the experience of birth.

3 Godfathers

Wonder requires slowing down and taking time to look around. Men running from the law through a windy desert, by contrast, are unlikely to be in such a mood. In John Ford's film *3 Godfathers* (1948), however, we meet three characters who are about to be surprised, and changed, by wonder. Starring John Wayne (Robert Hightower), Harry Carey Jr. (William Kearny), and Pedro Armendáriz (Pedro), *3 Godfathers* does not conform to Ford's signature narrative about tough guys fighting it out. Instead, Ford here tells a story

---

[19]   *Surprised by Beauty*, 106.

about the beauty and power of a newborn child to transform outcast men.

The three ride into town intent on bank robbery but stop to laugh at the sign "B. Sweet" on a fence. A man, "Buck" Sweet, played by Ward Bond stands up from behind the fence, and a friendly chat ensues. He is the local sheriff who, sensing something fishy about them, sends them off with, "I'll be seeing you boys, probably."

They see him very soon indeed while racing out of town after robbing the bank: Buck is already armed and organizing a posse. Having escaped, they stop in the desert to rest, finding a bullet hole in their water bag. Flabbergasted, they see a covered wagon standing alone in the blowing sand.

These three outlaws now resemble the three Magi finding a mother and child they had not expected to meet—they want to escape, but they have to stop. Robert tells the other two that there is a woman alone in the wagon and she is about to have a baby. He is angry that her absent husband has foolishly blown up a water supply. She's been alone for days, and the water has run out. Pedro, himself a father, goes to help with the birth. Pedro takes off his hat, walks towards the rear of the wagon, while the music sets a mood of reverence.

The camera shoots Pedro from inside the wagon, his face is framed by the wagon's cover like a Gothic window, with several dead trees on a high sandhill behind. Pedro's luminous face contrasts with Richard's, who turns from the camera, bends towards the ground, in turmoil, and covers his face.

At twilight, the baby is born. Cinematographer Winton C. Hoch's magical scene shows Robert and William from a distance staring at the wagon, lamplight warming the twilight shadows; wind whipping up the sand.

Pedro emerges, saying "She wants to see you, all of us, together," to enter the wagon.

Robert interrupts, "What does she have?"

"A big boy," Pedro answers. Robert takes off William's gun, then his own, and his hat. His demeanor grows softer. Wonder awaits.

Inside, it's the effect of both mother and child on Robert that most interests the camera. Pedro says his name is Pedro Rocca Fuerte, suggesting St. Peter. She pleads, "Please save my baby." Robert is the first to answer, "Yes, ma'am, I'll save him." Pedro and William also promise. Her speech to the baby before she dies is heartbreaking, "You'll be alone in the world when mother leaves you . . . no one to tuck you into bed at night." She cries. Turning away and back, she says, "I want you, all of you, to be my baby's godfathers."

They are surprised but accept. Robert helps her kiss her baby, and then she dies. Robert cradles the baby tightly while a lamp expires in front of the sand hill.

There is a spare burial scene. All three godfathers are transformed by their wonder at a new life, by their love for the child, and by the promises made to his dying mother. As the story progresses, Ford tests the transformation harshly: William dies of thirst, refusing to take any water from the child; Pedro kills himself after a fall with the child; Richard stumbles with baby Pedro into the town of New Jerusalem on Christmas Day, nearly dead.

Although replete with obvious Christian allusions and imagery, Ford's direction keeps the film from seeming heavy-handed. Movie critic Joseph McBride disagrees: he contrasts the powerful scenes in the desert, "a religious pilgrimage," with the scene where a disoriented Robert meets a donkey who miraculously guides him to New Jerusalem.[20] To me, the pilgrimage was so replete with religious symbolism, I would have been surprised if the sheep had *not* shown up when Hightower was lost and in despair!

In the final scene, Hightower and the sheriff are playing chess, waiting the for the train to take him to a prison where he will serve a short sentence. The sheriff jokes, "The jail will do you real good." The town sings a hymn as he boards the train. Given the extraordinary sacrifice of all the godfathers, this return to normalcy is disconcerting. But wonder is present: Buck was going to hang Robert for murder, and the town was preparing for it, now they are singing instead.

To experience wonder, mind and heart must be receptive. In Aristotle's contemplation of the Good and Finzi's "esteem" of creation, receptivity is evident. But Hightower was different; he wasn't receptive, but he was overwhelmed by love for the child despite himself. All three, however, undergo some loss of self and with that gain vulnerability, allowing the vision to take over their lives. Wonder gains awareness of the new or the newly-recognized; it's an expansion of human consciousness, an opportunity for transformation and transcendence. Receptivity is key to seeing with innocent eyes, to losing oneself in awe of a great work of

---

[20]   Joseph McBride, *Searching for John Ford: A Life* (New York: St. Martin's Press, 2001), 442.

nature or art. We shouldn't assume that some dazzling event will open our eyes.

As I was finishing this chapter, I gave a short speech on a panel discussing the culture and the arts. I asked the audience how many of them had read or seen a play of Shakespeare in the past year. I told them I was writing this book about going back to the classics. Afterward, a visibly upset woman asked me why I had asked that question about Shakespeare. I tried to explain it was an example of going back to the classics, but she wasn't listening. She seemed angry like a student being called out for not doing her homework. What struck me was her lack of piety towards Shakespeare, as if Shakespeare had nothing more to offer. She had read him, she told me, and that was that. She didn't recognize in Shakespeare's plays and poetry an inexhaustible work of art. Perhaps one day she will feel curious enough to pick up, say, *The Tempest*—if she does, I trust her wonder will be rekindled.

PART 2

Truth: Bad Ideas in Motion

Chapter 7

Engaging: From Detachment to Attention

Many years ago, in college, I read some lines from "Ash Wednesday"[1] by T. S. Eliot. The poet, addressing God, is seeking direction in what he finds to be a very challenging spiritual path. One of the blessings he requests is this:

> Teach us to care and not to care
> Teach us to sit still.

"Not to care" was a thought that grabbed my mind: It felt like freedom. Those years, the late sixties, were full of pressure to conform, which was ironic since the causes to which we were supposed to conform were freedom and non-conformity. The pressure was on to reject "the establishment." I tried half-heartedly to join in, but I knew those causes were not for me. I cared about other things, such as my Shakespeare class, my discovery of Eliot's poetry, or how to look cool throwing a frisbee in the quad. But in Eliot's poem, I met an idea that started to reorient me and has

---

[1]   T. S. Eliot, "Ash Wednesday," *The Poems of T.S. Eliot: The Annotated Text, Vol. 1, Collected and Uncollected Poems,* ed. Christopher Ricks and Jim McCue (Baltimore: Johns Hopkins Press, 2015), 97.

guided me all my life. I could choose what to value and to care about. Maybe Eliot gave me a "hippie" mindset after all!

I found out that freedom requires the habit of detachment, the ability not to be swept away by the zeitgeist. Note that "detachment" as I use it here is not indifference, what the French call *ennui,* or what the Christian moralists called *sloth.* We want to care, we should care, but about what really matter *to us.* "Teach us to care and not to care", Eliot writes, and, I might add, what to care about . . . or not.

Without detachment, a person's attention wanders to and from whatever is in the news. We speak as if scripted from the day's most recent input. It's not easy to go off-script, to go your own way, and suffer being considered odd. After playing golf with a new group of guys for four hours, one of them usually asks what I "do." When I tell them that I taught philosophy for fifteen years, they stare back at me not knowing what to say. There is one advantage, however, when a face lights up—I know I have met a potential friend.

The need for detachment is also evident when we jump to conclusions. Consider reading the daily news, which for many these days comes as a social media "feed." When you look at the headline, do you immediately form an opinion on the article based upon the source, whether CNN, FOX, *Washington Post, New York Times*? As attention spans become shorter, we don't take the time to read beyond headlines or to weigh opinions. Catching and correcting this habit is integral to *forming your opinion.* To do this, you need to consider the balance of the facts presented: recognizing the choice of quotations and words coloring the story. You may realize much of your thinking is being done for you without you realizing it.

The lack of detachment abounds: It's rare to find a public intellectual, writer, reporter, or public figure who embodies it. Compared with the sixties and seventies, what's admired in public figures has changed dramatically. The highly entertaining jousts of the late conservative intellectual William F. Buckley with his liberal guests, like his good friend John Kenneth Galbraith,[2] was replaced by the descendants of the sentimental Phil Donahue,[3] who on his show explored and exploited the feelings of his guests and studio audience. The long line of imitators has followed, culminating in the increasingly freaky 'reality show' television. The result has been entertainment based upon inciting a conflagration of emotions and stirring a deep pool of tears.

But there is more. Note that in "Ash Wednesday" Eliot asked that he be taught "to sit still." The poignancy of such a simple line challenges daily habit. Literary scholar Harold

---

[2] *Firing Line* ran for thirty-three years (1966–1999) on PBS. John Kenneth Galbraith, the leading liberal economist of his time, was frequently on *Firing Line* with host William F. Buckley. In this conversation from July 11, 1996 they discuss, "Have We Learned Anything About the Good Society," https://www.youtube.com/watch?v=vchsMpuf90g.

[3] The *Phil Donahue Show* ran for twenty-six years (1970–1996 on various networks). Looking over the episodes, he had very interesting and provocative guests from all points on the political spectrum. But his way of conversing with them and interacting with the audience very often explored emotional reactions rather than reasons. Here is a show from March 1993 on sexual abuse among Catholic clergy with Rev. Andrew Greeley, SJ, Barbara Blaine, and Jason Berry, https://www.youtube.com/watch?v=WBtUKALOvWA.

Bloom underscores the need for quiet: "Real reading is a lonely activity,"[4] and we pursue it "to enlarge solitary existence."[5] Bloom defends the difficulty of understanding a great book or artwork. He scoffs at the teachers who no longer require students to read the play *Julius Caesar* in its entirety but instead assign just a few passages and have them make shields and swords from cardboard rather than essays and arguments about the genius of Shakespeare's writing. Bloom assigns the blame to scholars, those who "encourage everyone to replace difficult pleasures by pleasures universally accessible precisely because they are easier."[6] There's a lesson here for all of us.

Walden

Solitude is difficult for most, a kind of spiritual exercise. In his *Pensées,* Pascal wrote, "All of humanity's problems stem from man's inability to sit quietly in a room alone."[7] Wise hyperbole aside, a serious education requires solitude and sustained attention. One writer who found a way to sit still was Henry David Thoreau (1817–1862).

> I went to the woods because I wished to live deliberately, to front only the essential facts of life, and see if I could not learn what it had to teach, and not, when I came to die, discover that I had not lived. I did not wish to live what was not life, living is so dear; nor

---

4   *The Western Canon,* 485.
5   Ibid, 484.
6   Ibid., 486.
7   *Pensées,* nos. 137, 67.

did I wish to practice resignation, unless it was quite
necessary.[8]

The Thoreau I met in high school was a kind of intellectual
monk/hippie who gave up the company of society, returning
to nature for two years to seek wisdom in a cabin beside a
lake. As I found out later, Thoreau didn't live a fully monas-
tic existence. He often walked the mile into Concord, New
Hampshire to visit friends or give a lecture. His mother did
his laundry. Friends and strangers visited him in the hut
that had only three chairs; sometimes it was standing room
only. In the remote cabin, he also protected runaway slaves.
Although Thoreau did not possess an iPhone, he remained
tethered to the world beyond in a way any of us might do in
similar circumstances.

For maintaining such ties, Thoreau has been criticized. In
a 2015 essay entitled "Pond Scum," Kathryn Schulz writes,
"Thoreau did not live as he described, and no ethical principle is emptier than one that does not apply to its author.
The hypocrisy is not that Thoreau aspired to solitude and
self-sufficiency but kept going home for cookies and company."[9] The hypocrisy charge stretches the point about Thoreau's laundry and his forays into Concord. But Schulz digs
further: She describes Thoreau's *Walden* as akin "in spirit
to Ayn Rand: suspicious of government, fanatical about

---

[8]   *Walden* was not written while Thoreau lived in the hut but seven
        years later in 1854. Henry David Thoreau, *Walden; Or, Life in the
        Woods* (Dover Thrift Editions, 2016), loc. 1158 of 4224, Kindle.
[9]   Kathryn Schulz, "Pond Scum: Henry David Thoreau's moral
        myopia," *The New Yorker*, October 19, 2015, https://www.
        newyorker.com/magazine/2015/10/19/pond-scum.

individualism, egotistical, élitist, convinced that other people lead pathetic lives yet categorically opposed to helping them. It is not despite but because of these qualities that Thoreau makes such a convenient national hero."

There were several spirited responses[10] to Schultz's attack on Thoreau, but none of them responded to the insinuation about the character of American readers—that we are, like the characters in Ayn Rand's novels, narcissistic.[11] It's an odd flourish for Schulz to make, and entirely unsubstantiated. She characterizes our appreciation of Thoreau as a product of elitist and self-centered readers. Knowing a bit about Ayn Rand, she would not have spent more than a few minutes in Thoreau's cabin—her taste would be offended. Why can't Schultz recognize the obvious? Thoreau was a cranky but friendly man; a writer, and thinker, who found he did his best work in isolation. There's no reason to disbelieve the author of *Walden,* whose most famous passage still stirs the spirit:

> I wanted to live deep and suck out all the marrow of life, to live so sturdily and Spartan-like as to put to rout all that was not life, to cut a broad swath and shave close, to drive life into a corner, and reduce it to

---

[10]   Donovan Hohn, "Everybody Hates Thoreau," *The New Republic,* October 21, 2015, https://newrepublic.com/article/123162/everybody-hates-henry-david-thoreau.

[11]   Since her death, Ayn Rand (1905–1982) has gained a large following who embrace the "virtue of selfishness" of both her non-fiction writings and her novels. He major novels are *The Fountainhead* (1943) and *Atlas Shrugged* (1957). I enjoyed reading both these works in high school, but my appreciation sharply dimmed as I delved further into the classics.

its lowest terms, and, if it proved to be mean, why then to get the whole and genuine meanness of it, and publish its meanness to the world; or if it were sublime, to know it by experience, and be able to give a true account of it in my next excursion.[12]

In what was intended as a compliment, literary scholar Jeremiah Purdy calls Thoreau "a genuine American weirdo" and defends his call to find time for attention to life itself rather than just daily tasks:

Most of us move, like him, between engagement and detachment, between feeling the justice and wrongs of our communities as our own and becoming insensate to them. Thoreau is no model, but he is a useful and difficult conversation partner across the centuries, a difficult friend as he was a difficult citizen. He did not solve any of our problems, but he felt their extreme poles so acutely that he still casts his broken shaft of light on them today.[13]

In addition to this, I think Thoreau is a powerful reminder of two things: to take whatever measures are necessary to think for oneself and to remember, in spite of technology, writing remains the act of putting pen to paper.

---

[12] Henry David Thoreau, *Walden; Or, Life in the Woods* (Dover Thrift Editions, 2016), loc. 1158 of 4224, Kindle.

[13] Jeremiah Purdy, "In Defense of Thoreau: He may have been a jerk, but he still matters," *The Atlantic,* October 20, 2015, https://www.theatlantic.com/science/archive/2015/10/in-defense-of-thoreau/411457/.

Open to Everything

We sometimes hear talk of "carving out" time for leisure, as if leisure was viewed as optional, less important than what it is to be "carved out" *from*. In 1952, T. S. Eliot wrote an introduction to a book by the German philosopher Josef Pieper, *Leisure: The Basis of Culture,* recommending the book for its attempt to realign philosophy with "an attitude which presupposes silence, a contemplative attention to things, in which man begins to see how worthy of veneration they really are."[14]

The "leisure" that Pieper explicates is a contemplative "form of silence" which is "open to everything."[15] Indeed, it is a precursor to wonder. Pieper is not writing for an educated elite: he addresses everyone, regardless of education or class, who have come to regard leisure time as merely restorative:

> The point and justification of leisure are not that the functionary should function faultlessly without a breakdown, but that the functionary should continue to be a man—and that means that he should not be wholly absorbed in the clear-cut milieu of his strictly limited function; the point is also that he should continue to be capable of seeing life as a whole and the world as a whole; that he should fulfill himself, and come to full possession of his faculties, face to face with being as a whole.[16]

---

[14]   Josef Pieper, *Leisure: The Basis of Culture,* intro. T. S. Eliot, trans. Alexander Dru (London: Faber and Faber LTS, 1952), 20–21.
[15]   Ibid., 53.
[16]   Ibid., 57.

Why would Pieper call leisure "the basis of culture"? Culture, as I have said, is the school we attend every day. It teaches us the dominant set of values and way of life in our society. Yes, we are taught these things even if we choose to reject them. If our culture equates leisure with time off from work, that attitude will be expressed through various means: customs, manners, lifestyle, and work. Living in a culture is like breathing the air. We do it every day but hardly notice it. Only by reflection does a culture's messaging become explicit.

But we also use the term *culture* in a normative way. We call someone "cultured" who is familiar with history, languages, and the kind of books, movies, and music we are discussing here. It's important to keep these uses distinguished. In the descriptive sense, in our present culture, leisure is equated with relaxation—play, sport, exercise, hobbies. Even those activities are regarded as taking time away from the valuable or obligatory duties of work and family. Now substitute Pieper's view of leisure for what takes away from work and family—"I'm going to spend the afternoon in the backyard reading *War and Peace*." Is that taking time away from the family or is it a necessary part of nurturing well-being, for oneself and one's family?

Many families have gotten so used to binging on TV series or taking in the next *Star Wars* episode that they don't notice how many hourly candles were burned on the altar of mindless entertainment. We don't *have to care* about it.

Thinking Freely

You can choose what to read, hear, and see, rather than bending to the pressure of what's popular. That's also part of forming your own opinion about how you spend your time and attention. The recent addiction to looking at screens is being challenged by studies of "captology" that explains how technology is designed deliberately to manipulate and capture our attention.[17] I wonder how many brains cells are dying from hours of uninterrupted screen-gazing.

There are the "cultural bosses" who determine the facts and values voiced by the media, entertainment, politicians and parties, education, and popular religion. They want us tethered to our screens. These bosses dominate the cultural markers with their headlines, tweets, movies, television shows, curricula, lectures, even sermons, and religious teaching. Once you become aware of their manipulative power, you can "just say no."

Everything you see in print, view on a screen, or hear on the radio is the product of an editor. It may be obvious to most, but many people don't realize the fact that an editor stands between you and whatever information is being presented. Failure to think critically means that editor owns your mind. The editor is also responsible for *what is not included.* Editors decide what news or opinion is worthy of being seen by their audience. They choose who gets invited to the show, the topic for conversation, and the length of

---

[17]   Corentin Dautreppe, "The mind distracted: technology's battle for our attention," March 6, 2019, https://news.yahoo.com/mind-distracted-technologys-battle-attention-034909034.html?soc_src=community&soc_trk=ma.

time for each segment. In short, editors choose what you will learn or not learn from their platform.

Become your own editor: Ask yourself questions about what you read. Do the facts and arguments support the editor's opinion? What essential information or evidence is missing? What questions have *not* been posed? Is the presentation one-sided, heavily weighted to one side or the other?

Good Readers

Remember Plato's famous allegory of the cave from Book VII of *The Republic*.[18] Prisoners sit inside the cave, in chains, seeing only shadows passing along the stone wall. They see what is in front of them and cannot turn their heads around. A fire above and behind them sends light past their heads to the wall in front. Between the fire and prisoners, there is a walkway. Socrates asks Glaucon, his interrogator, to imagine people carrying various objects along the walkway so that the light throws an image of the object on the front wall. Because they see nothing else, the inhabitants regard what they see as real.

There is a good reason why this allegory remains relevant in every age. The predominance of the screens leads directly to the basic question posed by Plato about knowledge. Our preoccupation with screens makes us voluntary prisoners. According to Nielsen, in 2016 the average American spent over ten hours of the day looking at a screen.[19] We don't

---

[18] *Republic*, VII, 514–16, 168–69.
[19] Jacqueline Howard, "Americans devote more than 10 hours a day to screen time, and growing," July 29, 2016, https://www.cnn.com/2016/06/30/health/americans-screen-time-nielsen/index.html.

need chains or anyone compelling us to watch. Accepting whatever you read on your screen makes you a prisoner. Your thinking is being done for you by someone else, an editor whom you should not necessarily trust. That problem multiplies alarmingly in a society where millions are doing the same, having their thoughts and opinions formed by another mind. Becoming your own editor not only means questioning content but also becoming aware of the medium through which content is passed, its power to persuade, create dependence, foster addiction, or even self-alienation.

For example, it is alarming to see nearly everyone holding up their cell phones to record video, their eyes moving back and forth between their video image and the event itself. It seems as if the more important the event, the more cell phones are held aloft. Being present at the event, fully experiencing it, becomes secondary to recording it. This act of distancing oneself for a self-important "I was there!" alienates a person from his or her immediate surroundings, making the recorded record of the event more important than the lived experience itself. Videos replace the need for memories, just as our increasing resort to devices to remember basic things such as numbers and dates relieves us of our ability to recognize those and countless other things. Most of us are voluntarily making ourselves prisoners, crafting for ourselves not only the chains but the wall upon which a darkened version of real life is projected.

Ask yourself what habits of mind you may have developed in a culture dominated by social media and intense cultural indoctrination. Use of social media has diminished our capacity for attention, whether reading, viewing, speaking, or listening. It is not surprising that one study has found that between the years 2000 and 2013, average attention spans dropped from twelve seconds to eight, the same as a goldfish.[20] Another study notes the average office worker checks email thirty times a day—nearly eight times each working hour.[21] Online publication *Slate Magazine* did a survey of how many of its readers read to the end of an article. Most readers get to the middle of an article, then fall away rapidly. *Slate* concluded that only about 5 percent of people who land on *Slate* pages are actually engaged in a significant way.[22]

Online reading habits such as this discourage serious reading. Indeed, the time spent reading by Americans has sharply declined. This is the case in spite of the fact that book sales remain strong. Perhaps someone should survey what percentage of purchased books remain unread. A 2014 study by the US Bureau of Labor Statistics found average Americans spend nineteen minutes per day reading, while adults between ages 25 and 34 read eight minutes per day on weekends and holidays and those aged 20 to 24 average around 10 minutes.[23] What's the fate of education in this

---

[20] Kevin McSpadden, "You Now Have a Shorter Attention Span Than a Goldfish," *TIME*, May 14, 2013, http://time.com/3858309/attention-spans-goldfish/.

[21] TJ Ray, "The brain's dwindling attention span," *The Oxford Eagle*, September 23, 2018, https://www.oxfordeagle.com/2018/09/23/the-brains-dwindiling-attention-span/.

[22] Farhad Mojoo, "You Won't Finish This Article: Why People Online Don't Read to the End," *Slate*, June 6, 2013, https://slate.com/technology/2013/06/how-people-read-online-why-you-wont-finish-this-article.html.

[23] Bijan Stephen, "You Won't Believe How Little Americans Read,"

kind of culture? It will be up to you, the reader, to swim against the current of constant distraction.

A serious return to the classics requires highly focused attention. In his recent and indispensable book *The Novel: A Biography*, literary critic and historian Michael Schmidt repeats the call from Eliot, Thoreau, Harold Bloom, and others to "sit quietly":

> To become a 'good reader' one must give oneself over to a regime of concentrated pleasure. One does not set out to read a book a day (there is no necessary pleasure in that) but may spend two or three years on a book (as I did on Thomas Mann's *The Magic Mountain*), read only portions of another, devour a third at a single sitting. Reading for school is different from reading we do for ourselves: geared to 'course-outcomes,' the former entails reading about, the novel stunned like a creature in an abattoir, while a class crawls over it, prodding, appraising, slicing.[24]

Good readers, Michael Schmidt adds, want *to prolong* the reading of great books. Only in silence and solitude will the story unfold and its meanings start to pour out. Complex or long texts demand time and attention, which most readers claim to no longer have enough of in the case of the former and often truly lack in the case of the latter. The claims are that they won't "enjoy" it, or that reading this book "feels

---

TIME, June 22, 2014, http://time.com/2909743/americans-reading/.

[24]   Michael Schmidt, *The Novel: A Biography* (Boston: The Belknap Press at Harvard, 2014), 9.

like work." "What am I going to get out of this?" If only they knew!

Spem in alium

We think that music taxes our attention less than reading, but that's most likely because the music we listen to doesn't demand anything from us: heavy rhythms from the drums, some catchy guitar chords, and a singer to deliver mostly, thankfully, inaudible lyrics. Classical composers created works that were both highly complex and immediately appealing, but it is an appeal that makes you want to listen harder. Such is the case of Thomas Tallis (1505–1585), a Catholic composer who served in the courts of Henry VIII, Edward VI, Mary I, and Elizabeth I. Elizabeth did not trust the Catholics around her, but Tallis continued to flourish under her reign. This is surprising since, as a Catholic composer, Tallis composed brilliantly in the polyphonic style which Elizabeth discouraged. Polyphony made the words, of the *Word*, unintelligible according to Protestant critics. This attitude towards sacred music pervaded Protestant Europe and became an issue debated by the Catholic bishops at the Council of Trent (1545–1563). Fully aware of his queen's attitude towards polyphony, Thomas Tallis composed a motet with forty different melodic lines, or parts. *Spem in alium* is rightly considered a polyphonic masterpiece, but whether or not Elizabeth ever heard it we do not know. We do know the composer was never sent to the Tower.

Polyphonic compositions usually made use of four to eight parts. A forty-part motet is just in your face; there's no other way to put it. The results are spectacular, as if Tallis captured in music the view from the inside of a Gothic cathedral. The music blossoms, expanding further and further out and up, while within you hear the continuous interaction, called counterpoint, of the forty parts. *Spem in alium*[25] requires fives choirs of eight voices each—every chorister singing a separate melodic line, quite a challenge to both singers and the conductor.

The text is unusual for a composer in the court of Elizabeth I. It's taken from the passage in *Judith* just before she cuts off the head of Holofernes: "I have never put my hope in any other but in Thee, God of Israel." Tallis had seen quite a few heads fall while working at the Tudor court. Tallis was twenty years old when St. Thomas More was executed. Given Elizabeth's attitude towards polyphony, it's unlikely Tallis performed it during her reign. Scholars disagree; some say it was performed in 1570, others say not until 1610, fifteen years after the composer's death.

Great music, like great poetry, makes focused attention easy, just as in worship beautiful music helps us to pray. Beauty by its very nature arrests the eye and the ear. Perhaps you have seen videos of "flash mobs" on YouTube. Singers and instrumentalists dressed like ordinary shoppers begin to sing and play. It begins with a single voice. Some of the shoppers stop and turn to listen while other keep walking but look back. Then other voices or instruments join in, and soon all the shoppers are standing still with big grins of astonishment. The effect is powerful because the beauty of

---

[25]   There are many fine recordings of *Spem in alium*, but I suggest starting with this one by The Tallis Scholars conducted by Peter Philips: https://www.youtube.com/watch?v=iT-ZAAi4UQQ.

the music comes unexpectedly and transforms an ordinary shopping trip with a flash of joy.

CHAPTER 8

Remembering: Knowing Requires Background

It wasn't until my mid-fifties that I started to study history in earnest. I came to realize there was a weakness in my education—a lack of historical knowledge. I viewed myself as classically-educated, a long-time proponent of the Great Books. My education was in philosophy and classics at the University of Texas-Austin; Christian doctrine at Princeton Theological Seminary; and theology and literature at Emory University. Outside the classroom, I read the classic novels from throughout the world, listened to and studied classical music, and, eventually, I began watching movies intent on becoming familiar with film history and all its classics.

A professor of philosophy, I knew a broad timeline of Western history, but I didn't realize my need to dig deeper, making connections that do not appear in an overview. Like many of us, I regarded history as a narrative for memorization—a series of epochs, each with a dominant culture; important leaders and events; ideas; forms of government; institutions; works of art—all encompassed in a timeline starting with its rise, continuing through its flourishing, and ending with its decline and demise.

History Lessons

One lesson I've taken away from historical study is that no kingdom, no matter how dominant, lasts forever. Remember the heyday of the Greeks, Romans, Carthaginians, Vikings, Normans, and the empires of Britain, Spain, Germany, and Portugal; the nations we call the Netherlands, Spain, France, Japan, Greece, Italy, and Russia were born in the twentieth century.

More important was the realization that history taught a side of human nature different from what I had read in the philosophers—call it, "the dark side." What I take away from my reading of history is simple—I was naive. I assumed people would generally do the "right thing." Reading the philosophy of Plato, Aristotle, St. Thomas Aquinas, and modern Thomists did not prepare me for what I learned about the human condition from my "deep dive" into history. This may be due to my philosophical propensity to focus on the ideal for man and society, what we should all aspire to be and do. But when I read, for example, about the peace conference at Versailles after the First World War and its disastrous consequences, virtue theory does not suffice.[1] What was the Treaty of Versailles other than a product of "great men" with flawed characters clashing over claims of idealism, vengeance, ownership, and guilt? Shakespeare, not Aristotle, should have prepared me to expect this.

I had read Shakespeare and Dostoevsky, but I had not taken them to heart. My only explanation is this: As I read *Brothers Karamazov*, *The Underground Man*, *Macbeth*,

---

[1]   Margaret Macmillan, *Paris 1919: Six Months That Changed the World* (New York: Random House, 2002).

Richard III, and *King Lear,* I didn't think of these characters as contemporaries, as existing in my time or community. I felt distanced from them, as if they were historical, not fictional, characters. Why did I do that? Perhaps I was distracted by the status of these books as classics, the guideposts of the Western tradition. At the same time, my mind was becoming deeply etched with the theories of morality and virtues and failed to notice the distance between the philosophers and the novelists. As a good friend of mine once said to me, "Everyone has a little larceny." He was probably charitable. It's truer to say everyone has a little larceny, but some have more than a little.

What about my Christian faith? What did it teach me about human nature that would help me put the philosophers in a broader context: The first we see of human beings is their Fall and a few chapters later God, seeing the "wickedness of men", floods the earth (Gn 6:5). Jesus Christ is abandoned by all but one of his disciples, betrayed by Judas, denied three times by the "rock" Peter. The same people who welcomed him into Jerusalem with palms choose to save Barabbas rather than him. In the history of the Church itself, which contains all the plot twists of a two-thousand-year mini-series, we see periods of decadence and corruption alternating with those graced by wise and sacrificial leadership. Is there a better example of sinful and flawed "man of God" than King David? History and human experience helped clear away my resistance to seeing human nature in the raw.

But I want to add another reason which was prompted by a comment made by the English writer John Cowper

Powys (1872–1963)[2] about Dostoevsky: "His Ideal is sanctity—not morality."[3] Dwelling too much on the theme of morality, I think, diverted me from recognizing the spirituality of characters who sin greatly. To put it another way: a character's moral condition is not the most important thing about them. And it's a mistake to equate their moral plusses and minuses with their standing before God. That would have devastating results for all of us.

Looking It Up

I'm part of a generation that was assigned history to memorize—lots of dates, names, events, and places. If those facts were associated with something significant, such as the causes of the Civil War, they were remembered. Even if my generation was alive to the significance of what we memorized, modern education no longer demands much memorization about timelines, significant dates, and prominent historical figures. Students still are required to memorize the multiplication tables, but the significance of years like 1066, 1215, 1492, 1776, 1789, 1860, 1917, and 1963 don't matter. Why? Because we have the Internet. Students and

---

[2]   John Cowper Powys is little read these days but deserves to be known by anyone who admires great writing and storytelling. His novels, often infused with Welsh mythology, are known for their marvelous writing, sensitivity to nature, and sensuously-driven characters: A good place to start would be one of these: *Wolf Solent* (1929); *A Glastonbury Romance* (1932); *Maiden Castle* (1936); *Owen Glendower* (1941); or *Porius* (1951).

[3]   John Cowper Powys, *One Hundred Best Books: With Commentary and an Essay on Books and Reading* (New York: G. Arnold Shaw, 1916), 36.

teachers no longer recognize the need for memorization in the humanities but "Google it" across the curriculum.

In her stinging critique of contemporary education, Daisy Christodoulou asserts, "We cannot rely on just looking it up."[4] She tears into the assumption that digitization has freed us from having to memorize, to create a reservoir of long term memory: "The more knowledge we have, the more problems we can solve. The reason why we need that knowledge in long-term memory and cannot rely on it being in the environment is that our working memories are limited. Working memory can only hold three to seven new pieces of information at once."[5]

Working memory, conscious reflection at work, is limited and relies on long-term memory to keep it from becoming overloaded. The long-term memory holds facts for use by the working memory. Let's say you are reading an article about rioting in Paris and the author compares the rioters to "the Terror" and the "Jacobins." Long-term memory uploads to working memory the understanding of both terms from the French Revolution. You can keep reading without having to skip the reference or look it up. When we are forced to constantly search for information on the Internet, we exhaust the resources of working memory which "means we do not have that space available to process the new information or to combine it with other information."[6]

---

[4]   Daisy Christodoulou, *Seven Myths About Education* (London: Routledge, 2013), 49.

[5]   Ibid., 61.

[6]   Ibid., 64.

How would a chess master, for example, play without the combination of long-term and working memory?

Technology puts an encyclopedia at our fingertips but does not take the place of a well-educated long-term memory. How frequently we look up information on the computer or phone should remind us of how little we have committed to memory and the necessity of knowing facts in an informed discussion. However, retrieving a single fact is like having a topographical map showing only hills and mountains but without the coordinates to connect them. Google searches cannot be supplied with broad historical background knowledge.

Thus, there's no way to get around the memorization that has become so unpopular in education. Students need to memorize more than basic mathematics. The outsourcing of our memory to internet-based-organs weakens the power of memory and undermines our ability to tell fact from fiction in online sources.

Cultural history scholar Camille Paglia argues for the return to "broad survey courses based in world history and culture, proceeding from antiquity to modernism."[7] She is right: students of any age need a historical framework if they are to understand their times. For me, a historical timeline is necessary to understanding whatever I am thinking about: say, the Spanish Civil War, or a film director, or even an idea. When I wrote my book on happiness, I organized my research around the history of happiness as an idea; only then could I see where the fissures had appeared, allowing

---

[7] *Provocations*, 381.

me to focus more intensely on the essential change in its meaning.[8]

Paglia notes that pop culture has replaced robust history surveys, making education the hostage of whatever is frivolous, faddish, and merely reactive.[9] Anyone who has been a teacher in the past thirty years has felt the pressure from the students to include material they are consuming, whether it's pop music, music videos, superhero movies, or what's hot on TV. Reference to the present culture no doubt belongs in the classroom—there's no avoiding it and no reason to do so—but these should be treated as pedagogical devices, not ends in themselves.

E. D. Hirsch

No one in the United States has done more to reform education than E. D. Hirsch. Hirsch began his career as a literary scholar with books on romantic poets, critical interpretation, and composition, work which lead to an endowed chair in literature at the University of Virginia. The focus of his research and writing changed when he started "feeling guilty" about UVA's freshman writing course, which he thought inadequate.[10]

To gain further insight, he divided a group of students into two groups for a reading comprehension exam: one with students already possessing a broad knowledge of

---

[8]   Deal W. Hudson, *Happiness and the Limits of Satisfaction* (Lanham, MD: Rowman & Littlefield Publishers, 1995).

[9]   *Provocation*, 406.

[10]   Sol Stern, "E.D. Hirsch's Curriculum for Democracy," *City Journal*, Autumn, 2009, www.city-journal.org/html/e-d-hirsch's-curriculum-democracy-13234.html.

history and the humanities, the other of students lacking that knowledge, many of whom came from homes of poverty and neglect. The first group performed far better than the second, leading him to find "a way to measure the variations in reading skill attributable to variations in the relevant background knowledge of audiences."[11]

As Hirsch began to share his findings and his concerns about what kind of knowledge many students lacked, he published his seminal essay "Cultural Literacy" in *American Scholar*,[12] followed by his best-selling 1987 book *Cultural Literacy: What Every American Needs to Know*.[13] The latter continues to be a reference point in the debate over what people need to know.

As a young college professor at the time, I recall the controversy that Hirsch aroused. Hirsch had exposed a flaw in mainstream American education, and the reaction from the establishment was predictable. Critics accused him of imposing European culture on students while ignoring racial and class diversity. Cultural conservatives, not those he believed his natural allies, embraced him. Hirsch was not intimidated or discouraged. Hirsch did not belong to the conservative camp: he was a lifelong Democrat, a progressive whose goal was to benefit those from disadvantaged backgrounds.[14] The

---

11   Ibid.
12   E. D. Hirsch, *American Scholar*, Spring, 1983: A portion of the article can be found here: https://3o83ip44005z3mk17t31679f-wpengine.netdna-ssl.com/wp-content/uploads/2018/03/From_Cultural_Literacy_1983.pdf.
13   E. D. Hirsch, *Cultural Literacy: What Every American Needs to Know* (New York, Vintage Books, 1988).
14   Eric Liu, "What Every American Should Know: Defining common cultural literacy for an increasingly diverse nation,"

next year, with the help of two co-authors, Hirsch published a response to his critics, *The Dictionary of Cultural Literacy,* which sold over one million copies.[15]

Hirsch wrote in the 1980s, before the problems posed by increasing internet use discussed by Daisy Christodoulou. His arguments, however, prepared later scholars to recognize the dangers of over-reliance on technology. Hirsch's immediate concern was the turn towards teaching practical skills in preparation for the world of work, while "social studies" reduced history and classics to a tiny portion of the curriculum. What the teachers failed to notice, however, according to Hirsch, was that students are better prepared to acquire skills with more background knowledge.

In other words, to use the formal setting of school to teach skills without any connection to some body of knowledge doesn't work. For example, I could teach a young boy to hit a baseball, but to play baseball, he would have to learn the rules and much more. To play well requires the kind of knowledge held so deeply it seems instinctual: you are playing third base, a power hitter steps to the plate. To anticipate where he will hit the ball requires an awareness of how the pitcher is throwing that day; where in the field a hitter typically hits the ball; whether anyone is on base; watching each pitch as it comes to the plate; how the batter leans, and so on. The same can be said of all skills and practices; all require

---

The Atlantic, July 3, 2015, https://www.theatlantic.com/politics/archive/2015/07/what-every-american-should-know/397334/.

[15]   E. D. Hirsch, Joseph F. Kett, and James Trefell, *The Dictionary of Cultural Literacy: What Every American Needs to Know* (Boston: Houghton Mifflin Harcourt; Revised, Updated edition, 2002). First published in 1988 and revised in 1993.

a large body of long-term memory to inform the present moment.

Take a step further and ask yourself what general knowledge is required to be a parent or a citizen. A person who is "literate" can pick up, say, Hemingway's *Old Man and the Sea*, read it, and grasp its basic meaning. Hirsch broadens the notion of literacy to apply to a person's entire life within a culture and a nation. Shared literacy enables human solidarity, mutual understanding, and responsible citizenship. The last is not a trivial concern—knowledge is necessary for the citizens of a democratic republic to protect their freedoms and avoid totalitarianism.

Now, this is a substantial claim that I will expand and defend in later chapters. The lack of cultural literacy is the only way to explain—except for determined ignorance—the number of people who continue to believe that the call to freedom for all means perfect egalitarianism, a kind of ideal state. There are many examples by now that give the lie to that notion, examples of egalitarian prophets turning to totalitarianism and using imprisonment and mass killings by dictatorial fiat to ensure that their version of "equality and justice" wins the day. Paul Johnson's *Modern Times: The World from the 20s to the 90s* describes in jarring and precise detail how the twentieth century became the bloodiest in world history due to the prophets of equality.[16]

Although Johnson's case is fully supported by historical fact and analysis, it is sadly no longer well-known: younger people remain enamored of various forms of collectivism in

---

[16] Paul Johnson, *Modern Times: The World from the 20s to the 90s* (London, Weidenfeld & Nicolson, 1983), 413–31.

large part because they have not been taught any history, including the history of their own country and its founding documents. More recently, the call by some to end the electoral college has proceeded without any reference to the fierce debates among the Founders over the reasons why less populous states should be protected from domination by the biggest ones. Government, not politics, is perhaps the most crucial area where cultural literacy is lacking because it directly affects the reasons why citizens cast their vote.

A year before he published *Cultural Literacy*, Hirsch created the Core Knowledge Foundation with the assumption "that every child in a diverse democracy deserves access to enabling knowledge."[17] The curriculum recommended by the foundation stressed the importance of providing the background knowledge to understand how the United States is governed.

Emotional Minds

The concern for educational reform continues. Greg Lukianoff and Jonathan Haidt, self-professed "old-style liberal" professors, published a critique of American education, which, surprisingly, received widely positive reviews. In *The Coddling of the American Mind: How Good Intentions and Bad Ideas Are Setting Up a Generation for Failure*, the co-authors attack the three "Great Untruths" at large in education—"fragility," "emotional reasoning," and "us versus them" mentality.[18] It's obvious that the assumption

---

[17]   https://www.coreknowledge.org.
[18]   Greg Lukianoff and Jonathan Haidt, *The "Coddling of the American Mind: How Good Intentions and Bad Ideas Are Setting Up*

of fragility leads to lower teacher's demands, and less difficulty—less memorization, shorter reading assignments,
sprinkles of pop culture, and avoidance of direct intellectual
challenges. The authors take the opposite view: Young people are "antifragile"; therefore, "prepare the child for the road
not the road for the child."[19]

The authors' cure for student fragility is cognitive behav-
ioral therapy, the goal of which is to reframe your feelings
so that they seem less fearsome. Examples are typical, such
as losing an important sports event but picking oneself up
by reframing it as "a learning experience" or "I will be better
prepared next time."

The core of emotional reasoning, on the other hand, is
the assumption that one should "always trust your feelings."
College campuses are fueling emotional reasoning by disin-
viting speakers who cause some students anxiety or offering to counsel anyone who is so traumatized by the visit of
a particular speaker. The attitude of "us versus them" per-
meates the culture and is endemic among member of the
media, to whom the authors propose the following advice:
"Give people the benefit of the doubt. Use the principle of
charity."[20] In other words, make an effort "to interpret other
people's statements in their best or most reasonable form,
not in the worst or most offensive way possible."[21] Identity
politics, they add, should be monitored in schools, which
can lead to a form of groupthink they call "common-enemy

---

a Generation for Failure (New York: Penguin Press, 2018), 4.
[19]   Ibid., 237.
[20]   Ibid., 243.
[21]   Ibid., 243–44.

identity politics."[22] All of these "untruths," as they call them, constitute obstacles to a rigorous, challenging education that requires memorization and the tackling of difficult material, especially that which challenges a student's core assumptions.

Camille Paglia urges the addition of two areas of study to historical surveys—military history and history of religions.[23] Religions, of course, should be a no-brainer since they serve as the foundations of all civilizations, without exception. In my education, religion received some consideration, and military history stopped at the Revolutionary War and the Civil War. Coverage of both was cursory. It's odd, is it not, that students never ponder why millions of men charged directly up a hill where machine guns, mortars, artillery, and rifles were entrenched in bunkers and trenches. On the first day of the Battle of the Somme, July 1, 1916, there were 57,470 British casualties, 19,240 dead, including 60 percent of the officer corps. After 141 days of fighting, there were 1.1 million casualties on both sides. After 150 days, the British had advanced six miles.[24]

How does one respond upon becoming aware of the shortcomings of his or her education? The starting point can be to become proficient in a single subject matter—perhaps a period or person that already piques your interest. My reason for making this recommendation is straightforward: Anyone who has become knowledgeable enough to become conversant in any subject knows that it takes time, diligence, and

---

[22]   Ibid., 244.
[23] · *Provocations*, 398.
[24]   Jörn Leonhard, *Pandora's Box: A History of the First World War,* trans. Patrick Camiller (Cambridge, Massachusetts: The Belknap Press of Harvard University, 2018), 414.

patience. Perhaps the reader has already acquired in-depth knowledge in some area. If so, you know the kind of exercise I have in mind. What's important is that knowledge is pursued *for its own sake* and not for pragmatic purposes.

Choose something that intrigues you so much that your curiosity will pull you along through times of distraction, exhaustion, and confusion. In my case, I have written two books prompted by intense interest—a book on the history of happiness[25] and one on the intersections of religion and politics since the 1960s.[26] One thing that each project taught me was how little I know. Some of the insights I thought were my own, I came across in books published long before.

As you may already realize, digging deep enough to become proficient is not a simple task, but believe in yourself. You have chosen a project, and the last thing that should get in the way is your fear. It's natural to feel uncertain when you face a new and demanding task. If you decide to run a marathon, do one-hundred push-ups, learn a language, learn how to golf, or learn how to play a musical instrument, plunge in, putting aside all the reasons it can't be done.

Embracing difficulty is no longer a habit gained in most schools and universities. As we have seen, Greg Lukianoff and Jonathan Haidt have chronicled how American education is guilty of "coddling" students and "setting up a

---

[25] *Happiness and the Limits of Satisfaction.* What piqued my curiosity was reading how Aristotle equated happiness with a virtuous life and not with the kind of feeling state. I went looking for the reasons happiness became dissociated with a moral life.

[26] Deal W. Hudson, *Onward Christian Soldiers: The Growing Political Power of Catholics and Evangelicals in the United States* (New York: Threshold Editions, 2010).

generation for failure."[27] Facing an intellectual challenge is how the mind grows, how understanding takes on more complexity and nuance. As the mind's power grows through exercise, so does one's ability to see more deeply into texts and art.

"All reading is rereading," one professor told me. To write the book you are now reading, I reread all the texts I discuss, some of which I had not touched for decades. But in all honesty, I've never enjoyed them as much, or learned as much from them, as I did this past year while doing my research. Think about that as you start digging through boxes to find your old books.

---

[27]   *The Coddling of the American Mind*, 9.

CHAPTER 9

Finding the Lever Point: The Battle Over Human Nature

Over the past fifty years, we have lived through what is called the "post-truth" world.[1] This world has a name—*postmodern*. The term *postmodernism* has been used to describe changes in architecture, painting, music, or literature. What's far more critical is the postmodern rejection of the classical Western notions of truth, objectivity, and human nature. Postmodernism did not appear without warning—it had been in development over centuries. With the Renaissance and the Reformation, the certainties of the ancient and medieval words began to be challenged by skeptics such as Michel de Montaigne, Giordano Bruno, Francis Bacon, Pierre Gassendi, Rene Descartes, and, most importantly, Thomas Hobbes.[2] Their skepticism and its deeper implications did not become part of the mainstream until

---

[1]   Julian Birkinshaw, "The Post-Truth World - Why Have We Had Enough Of Experts?" *Forbes*, May 22, 2017, https://www.forbes. com/sites/lbsbusinessstrategyreview/2017/05/22/the-post-truth-world-why-have-we-had-enough-of-experts/#7e19a0d154e6.

[2]   The best account, I know, of these periods is Friedrich Heer, *The Intellectual History of the West*, trans. Jonathan Steinberg (Cleveland and New York: The World Publishing Company, 1966), chapters 15–17.

the nineteenth century primarily in the work of Friedrich
Nietzsche and his announcing "the death of God."

God is dead, Nietzsche claims, "because we have killed
him."[3] Nietzsche is not a detached observer of the decline in
religious belief; he mounts an intellectual assault on the idea
of any Absolute. Nietzsche disavows any need for the false
comforts of an eternal world. His task is to eradicate religion, to act as an "axe laid to the root of men's 'metaphysical
need.'"[4]

Thus, the exponents of postmodernism[5] roll their eyes
at notions of truth, including categorization by definition.
Merriam-Webster defines the term both as appropriately if
unhelpfully "the era after modernism" and "of, relating to, or
being a theory that involves a radical reappraisal of modern
assumptions about culture, identity, history, or language."
If you consider that less than helpful, you're not alone. To
understand better how we got to the point where so many
people think all truth is relative, understanding postmodernism is crucial.

Ordinary people believe there is truth and live their lives
accordingly. Two plus two equals four, don't stand on the
tracks as the train approaches, and so on. If you show up

3   Friedrich Nietzsche, *The Gay Science: with a prelude of rhymes and
      an Appendix of Songs*, #125, trans. Walter Kaufmann (New York:
      Vintage Books, 1974), 181.

4   Friedrich Nietzsche, *Human, All Too Human: A Book for Free
      Spirits*, #37, trans. Marion Faber and Stephen Lehmann (Lincoln,
      NE: University of Nebraska Press, 1984), 42.

5   A reasonable starting date for postmodernism's arrival in the US is
      the 1969 lecture by French philosopher Jacques Derrida at Johns
      Hopkins University entitled "Structure, Sign and Play in the
      Discourse of the Human Sciences."

late to work enough times, your boss has a right to fire you, despite what might be your advanced theories of time and space. And it's not that those who live a simple, reality-based life don't know that what they encounter can be understood in different ways. A high-school graduation can simultaneously be a necessary public event and a time to recognize achievement, a moment of profound joy for a family whose first child graduates and the end of an era for a group of friends.

Disagreements over the interpretation of things and events does not lead normal people to conclude that there is no truth. Reality holds, and we can know a great deal about it. Regular people rely on truths of various sorts in everything they say or do: Imagine a life where you could not trust maps, clocks, thermometers, yardsticks, physicians, teachers, engineers, car mechanics, the directions on your medication, and so on. Regardless of how original and exciting your ideas about "place" may be, the police officer will still give you the ticket for doing fifty in a thirty-five.

'Goodbye' to Truth

The postmodernists, of course, are not concerned about such things—they have to trust the markers of reality just like everyone else. They are more concerned with reinterpreting truths regarding human nature, morality, social norms, and values. In other words, they want to revisit and reconstruct what it means to be human. From the postmodern perspective, the traditional accounts of human nature and meaning no longer apply. Truth claims about right and wrong cannot be universalized: they belong to the age and society that articulated them. Truth, like all knowledge, is created, not discovered. Knowledge itself has no objective value since it is determined by those in power from age to age.

Why go down this rabbit hole, one might ask? For "justice" and "freedom," of course. Since Western culture is primarily the product of white males, mostly heterosexual, for postmodernists its tradition is an expression only of the *point of view of those in power*. They see claims to truth as expressions of power, the attempt by one group to define truth for others who are not white, male, or heterosexual. Wealth and social class are an overlaying factor as well.

Postmodernism began roughly in the middle of the twentieth century in universities, those unique places, protected from the free market of ideas and moral scrutiny, where theories and concepts that deny reality can be incubated. Its eruption into the public sphere is seen in the Sexual Revolution that began in 1967 and which continues to this day; its more recent manifestations, including "gender ideology," a set of beliefs that has corrupted the academy and is transforming almost all institutions in the West. On this view, gender is not only, as it was historically, a feature of languages that have masculine and feminine features. Postmodernists in the academy have for decades been taking this linguistic construct and trying to apply it to actual human sexuality, claiming that even biological gender is a construct. And if this is true, then the traditional, biological sex binary of male and female is itself a construct, one created by the white male powers to keep people from discovering the full range of gender and sexuality, a tool of oppression.

It is not difficult to see how postmodernism led to such a theory and why it was confined to universities until early in the twenty-first century when it escaped quarantine in the academy and started affecting institutions and public discourse. It was striking how an obtuse, obscure theory so quickly became such an important moral cause, to the point where already in 2015, the city of New York officially recognized thirty-one genders.[6] Early in 2019, a wide variety of sources place the number of genders somewhere between 2 and 121, but it appears that few major publications are prepared to offer a specific number.

In his 1998 encyclical *Fides et Ratio* (Faith and Reason), Pope John Paul II addressed the postmodern denial of truth and whether or not we can know reality. "Whether we admit it or not, there comes for everyone the moment when personal existence must be anchored to a truth recognized as final, a truth that confers a certitude no longer open to doubt."[7] We have to be able to know basic truths with some "certitude" (a high degree of certainty) to live, says the pope. To some, it may seem ironic that it would take a churchman to remind the world that the Church affirms the capacity of the human mind to know reality, to a greater or lesser degree. This encyclical makes a further point about the consequences for culture: Because truth itself is integral to the creation of culture, a culture without truth loses its

---

6   Bushrod Washington, "NYC Just Released a List of Officially Recognized Genders," May 24, 2016, https://thefederalistpapers. org/us/nyc-just-released-a-list-of-officially-recognized-genders.

7   Pope John Paul II, *Fides et Ratio*, September 14, 1998, https:// w2.vatican.va/content/john-paul-ii/en/encyclicals/documents/ hf_jp-ii_enc_14091998_fides-et-ratio.html.

connection to the past, its piety, and separates the present generation from the wisdom accumulated by its ancestors.

Regardless of your faith, looking around today, does this not describe what has happened to us in the Western world?

The postmodern historicist assumption, coupled with its use of deconstructive techniques, set the work of the humanities in a new direction—to dissect great literary works and reduce them to their historical, cultural, sexual, and other limited contexts. Doing so will liberate us from the shackles of the structures and linguistic norms of the past (post-structuralism), opening up new vistas of human knowledge and endeavor. Practitioners of these types of postmodernism see meaning as culturally-bound. Shakespeare was not the greatest playwright (and perhaps poet) in the history of Western civilization; he was merely a white, heterosexual, and probably Catholic male whose seductive prose has enslaved generations with its oppressive sexism, racism, et cetera. The same deconstruction has been applied to the works and persons of the creators of most of the canon, leaving humanities departments full of graduate students with little more to do than to read their sexual proclivities into the classics and re-condemn the creators in ever-more harsh terms.

Bear in mind that what I describe here not only dominates higher education but it has made its way into public school education at all levels. Students studying a poem, play, novel, theory, science, customs, or laws are being told to regard them as products of the social class who created them. Within the dominant social class, other factors are to be considered as well, particularly race, gender, sexuality, education.

Postmodern Spawn

In what has rightly been called the "second wave,"[8] postmodernism spawned other areas of research and writing, which have become privileged in the academy: multiculturalism, ethnocentrism, postcolonial studies, queer studies, women's studies, feminist studies, and LGBTQ studies. All of these represent not simply scholarship but forms of political activism aimed at addressing inequality and injustice. The postmodern voice heard most often by the general public is aptly described in the following passage. Good-willed people who ask why the solution to identity politics is not an appeal to "all of us being human beings," can find the answer to that question here: "The postmodern epistemic shift which took place within these movements has changed the focus from universal liberalism—everyone deserves equal rights and freedoms regardless of their race, sex, sexuality, gender identity, nationality, creed, physical ability—to identity politics—individuals are part of various collectives based on race, sex, sexuality, gender identity, nationality, creed, physical ability who all experience things differently and action against inequality must be filtered through these identities."[9] In other words, since persons have experienced injustice because of their identity as female, Latino, or homosexual, they demand that their "grievances" need to be addressed in the same terms.

---

[8] Helen Pluckrose, "No, Postmodernism is not Dead (and Other Misconceptions)," *Areo*, Feb 7, 2018, https://areomagazine.com/2018/02/07/no-postmodernism-is-not-dead-and-other-misconceptions/.

[9] Ibid.

Harold Bloom calls the various branches of postmodernism the "School of Resentment."[10] Their practitioners, he explains, resent the greatness that came before them and demand their attention as scholars. Virgil, Dante, and Shakespeare are judged great, *if* they are, based upon their aesthetic values alone. Postmodernist scholars' resentment springs from their being expected to respect, teach, and write about that form of greatness, which they do not recognize. "Either there were aesthetic values, or there are only the overdetermination of race, class, and gender. You must choose," says Bloom.[11]

Before postmodernism, scholars did not ignore cultural, historical, and biographical factors when studying the past. Take the French Revolution, for example. You could fill a small library with the books about the myriad factors and figures that brought on the downfall of Louis XVI and the French Republic and led to the Terror.[12] One direct influence on the revolution was the American Declaration of Independence, written thirteen years earlier, which contained the remarkable statement, "We hold these truths to be self-evident, that all men are created equal, that they are endowed by their Creator with certain unalienable Rights, that among these are Life, Liberty and the pursuit of Happiness." In 1789, "The Declaration of the Rights of Man" was read in the National Constituent Assembly. Article One begins, "Men are born and remain free and equal in rights."

---

[10]   *The Western Canon*, 492.

[11]   Ibid., 487.

[12]   Pierre Darmont, *Damning the Innocent: A History of the Persecution of the Impotent in Pre-Revolutionary France*, trans. Paul Keegan (New York: Viking Penguin Inc, 1986).

Many of us take such declarations to be common sense, paying little attention to their novelty in the context of the eighteenth century when monarchies still held sway. Yet, what do the historicists and their intellectual descendants, the postmodernists, make of them? Are equality and human rights self-evident fundamental truths about human existence? In his seminal book *On Grammatology*, Jacques Derrida denies the traditional understanding of rationality and truth. "The 'rationality'... which governs a writing thus enlarged and radicalized, no longer issues from a logos. Further, it inaugurates the destruction, not the demolition but the de-sedimentation, the de-construction, of all the significations that have their source in that of the logos. Particularly the signification of *truth*."[13] By "logos," Derrida means the classical assumption that the world can be known though reason as an overarching whole. Postmodernism does not regard the world or human existence as having a coherence or purpose.

How then can they defend human rights if all truth is relative and bound to the era in which it was declared? The second wave of politically-active postmodernists appeal to human rights and principles of equality and justice. But how, given their premises, can they regard conceptions of equality and rights morally or legally binding? Postmodernists deny self-evident truths. On both sides of the Atlantic, the declarations were written by white men from middle or upper classes. How can such thoughts be directly relevant to men and women everywhere and at any time?

---

[13]   Jacques Derrida, *Of Grammatology*, trans. Gayatri Chakravorty Spivak (Baltimore: John Hopkins Press, 1976), 10.

Today, at a popular level, we witness people using expressions such as "my truth" and "your truth." As the philosopher Julian Baggini comments, "To disagree with someone risks hindering their right to personal truth. Truth has become personalized, with the individual sovereign over their interpretation of reality."[14] Or, who are you to oppress me with your "objective truth?" Truth used to be an independent standard sought by all to judge different opinions about the same subject. Now if you challenge someone's "own truth," you will be judged guilty of "judging" them—the entire conversation becomes a kind of weaponized absurdity, the only resolution of which is to give in to the angry offended one.[15]

Many of us know George Santayana's dictum hanging above the door of the Nazi concentration camp Dachau: "Those who cannot remember the past are condemned to repeat it."[16] If you're a postmodernist, you might as well take that sign down. Historical knowledge, and concepts of virtue such as justice, have no meaning or claims to truth that transcend time and place. One of the founders of postmodernism, Jacques Derrida,[17] had to contradict his own teaching

---

[14]   Julian Baggini, *A Short History of Truth: Consolations for a Post-Truth World* (London: Quercus, 2017), 71.

[15]   Jillian Kay Melchior, "Fake News Comes to Academia," October 5, 2018, https://www.wsj.com/articles/fake-news-comes-to-academia-1538520950.

[16]   George Santayana, *The Life of Reason: The Phases of Human Progress,* 1905. The original sentence and context can be found here: http://www.gutenberg.org/catalog/world/readfile?fk_files=169068&pageno=115.

[17]   Jacques Derrida, *The Other Heading*, trans. Pascale-Anne Brault and Michel B. Haas (Bloomington: Indiana University Press, 1992), 70–83.

to discuss justice as a universal goal that stands apart from postmodern and historicist assumptions. The postmodernists and their many activist disciples, however, continue to demand justice. What do they mean by justice? Be careful if you ask: you're likely to be attacked for demanding an oppressive definition, as well as for racism and sexism. Theirs is not the justice of Socrates, Plato, Aristotle, Aquinas, or any other dead white male. It is a demand for submission to a pure Will to Power. It is Nietzschean justice.

We Are All Different!

Setting the inconsistency aside, let's notice what becomes exposed by the ethical implications of postmodern assumptions. Human nature is no longer a "nature" as it is ordinarily understood, a fixed and unchanging reality. There is no nature common to all, no common good to direct human lives, only understandings of the social and moral preferences that differ from age to age, culture to culture, nation to nation. Historical knowledge provides only *constructions* of the truths believed in a given era. No other Truth lies beyond that.

I've repeatedly referred to a classical view of human nature. Rather than taking it on faith from me that such a view exists, I want to describe the understanding that's been challenged by postmodernism and, in particular, feminist theory.

Let's start with Carl Linnaeus. I would bet you've never heard of him, but you have heard of *homo sapiens*, or "thinking man," the species of which everyone reading this is a member. *Homo sapiens* is a phrase so well-known it is natural to think it has ancient origins. Well, yes and no. Linnaeus was an eighteenth-century Swedish biologist who first coined *homo sapiens* to identify human beings as a part of his system of naming organisms.[18]

His method, binomial nomenclature, was simple enough. Using Latin words, Linnaeus created categories for different biological beings, assigning the first part of the name according to an organism's *genus* and the second part, its *species*; that is, the species within the genus. In this case, the Latin noun *homō* means "man" or "human being," while *sapiēns* denotes something that thinks.

When a species is specified within a genus, it is based upon a *difference* within the genus. In other words, thinking man is differentiated from our ancestors by our thinking (*homo erectus* referred to the generations that first walked upright). More importantly, thinking man is the only organism within the entire world of organisms deemed *sapiens*. This is an *essentialist view* of human nature, meaning that the essence, the distinguishing mark, of a human being is his or her thinking.

The question then arises—what difference does thinking make? The answer is everything; it changes everything. Thinking—that is, the ability to consider and conceptualize one's environment—frees men from the determinism of physical instinct and reaction. This natural, essential characteristic allows human beings to choose between different actions, between the values that prompt those actions. It

---

[18]   An excellent source of information on Carl Linnaeus is found on the website of the Linnean Society of London: https://www.linnean.org/learning/who-was-linnaeus.

also entails a natural ethics and morality: Freedom makes us responsible for those choices and, at least in part, for their consequences. Note my qualification: "at least in part." Only a thinking being can consider levels of responsibility and the factors that qualify responsibility.

It is this intellectual ability of human beings that makes culture and civilization possible. The often-startling contrast between different societies is due to the unique freedom human beings have in actualizing their nature, which is always conditioned by their response to their environment. The freedom of our rational human nature bestows variability and diversity between and within societies, across history, and around the globe. This is not to discount the role of "nurture"—that is, the extent to which we thinking beings care for and shape one another within a culture. But the freedom implicit in nurture does not destroy or alter the fundamental needs of human nature, which explains the transcultural values discernible across different eras and societies.

We recognize that certain species of animals have higher levels of intelligence, yet it remains true that only humans can conceptualize, for example, what a moral argument would be for a given action. With our intelligence, how we encounter natural phenomena is radically different from non-thinking animals, although we retain our animalistic qualities (physical needs, biological reactions, et cetera). A unique feature of our intelligence is our ability to recognize and respond to natural phenomena with wonder—that moment when something inspires awe in us, prompting us to ask the "big questions." That moment that helps us realize that philosophy—the love of wisdom and the desire to understand—is also a natural and unique feature of humanity.

Among the "big questions" are questions about purpose—why am I here? And about basic ethics—is this action right or wrong, and why? Within moral thinking, questions arise about whether something is true just for oneself or for others. The question of justice asks: Is it right that some have more than others? Is it right that the government can demand I pay taxes? And love: Is it loving to punish a child? Must I always forgive wrongdoing? Just what is love after all?

Science is born of the same impulse, the same response of wonder at noticing an event in nature and *wondering*: Why do apples fall to the ground? What is the relation of the earth to the sun? How can sound be delivered wirelessly? And beauty: What makes some works of art more beautiful to me than others? Why does beauty give me such sudden joy? What makes artists create?

No other living beings on this earth grapple with these questions. Cultures and societies are the cumulative results of age after age seeking answers. Answers change as the cultures change, but they do not change in one crucial respect: *the fundamental questions are always the same, and the answers always resemble those of previous ages.*

Postmodernists are fixated on differences; they believe the full range of human experience cannot be reconciled with a fixed human nature. The classical view, by contrast, can explain both difference and the remarkable sameness between cultures and peoples. The latter, those things that point to true human nature, share an understanding of *the potentialities that are common to all individuals in the species,* regardless of the many variations. These potentialities are not chosen but are given. *Nature stands for what is given, not made.* An individual being cannot choose to be what it is; we do not decide to exist. In the case of human beings, who can reflect upon existence, we are faced with the fact that we both have a nature and belong to a nature.

What an individual does with those potentialities constitute a "second nature," according to St. Thomas Aquinas.[19] *A person's second nature is merely what he or she has made of those potentialities possessed at birth, the use made of the freedom bestowed by having a rational intellect.* When we contrast "nature" with "nurture," we make this distinction, but it does not exhaust the distinction. Nurture is how an individual's life is shaped by the environment he is born into—most of all, how his parents raise him. After nurturing, our second nature is created by our choices—what we do with the potentialities of our first nature. Nurture does not *determine* an individual's choices later in life, although it may limit them. If a child is not taught grammar, how to use language, for example, his linguistic capacities will be limited.

Without a second nature, it would be difficult to distinguish one person from another. But behind even vast discernible differences between individuals and groups, we find always that shared set of capacities belonging to their human nature.

---

[19]   *Summa Theologica* I-II.32.2.

Beyond Male and Female

Let's begin by distinguishing feminist theory from the feminist movement. Feminist scholars, such as Vivian Gornick,[20] identify three "waves" of the feminist movement. The women's suffrage movement started with Lucretia Mott, Elizabeth Cady Stanton, and Susan B. Anthony at the Seneca Falls Conference with the "Declaration of Sentiments" and grew into the formalized "first wave" of feminism. "Second wave" feminism that gave birth to feminist theory—a confluence of scholars and leaders from science, literature, history, psychology, philosophy, and politics—all focused on understanding "the insecurity behind society's need to agree that women would live a half-life in order that men might gain the courage to pursue a whole one."[21] What Ms. Gornick calls the "visionary years" of feminism lasted until the late 1980s when feminism was narrowed "down to single-issue organizing, the issue now being abortion instead of suffrage."[22] Abortion rights were unifying for women during the sexual revolution who didn't want sex to result in children, as that would limit their recently gained "freedom."

"Third wave" feminism set aside its single-issue focus on abortion, and as a result, it lost its coherence as a movement, as Gornick says, and came to resemble "the young

---

20   Vivian Gornick was a reporter for the *Village Voice* from 1969–1977; has published eleven books; written for the *New York Times*, *The Nation*, and *The Atlantic Monthly*; and has taught writing at the New School and University of Iowa.

21   Vivian Gornick, "Good Feminist," *Boston Review*, December 8, 2014, https://bostonreview.net/books-ideas/vivian-gornick-good-feminist-solnit-rhode-cobble-gordon-henry.

22   Ibid.

women who called themselves free women in the 1920s."[23] Ms. Gornick does not hide her disappointment at descriptions of modern feminists, who organize "slutwalks," dress provocatively to prove their empowerment, and celebrate the freedom to have sex without an emotional connection or procreation. She concludes, "Right now women's liberation is in a holding pattern—not likely to recover its visionary impetus in my lifetime."[24]

While the feminist movement may have fizzled, feminist theory has become standard fare among intellectuals. The problem with an essentialist account of human nature, according to feminist theory, is its theory of knowledge. Feminist theorists, like good postmodernists, argue that all knowledge comes from a standpoint, by which they mean that a male understands things from a male point of view, the dominant view of Western history. Males use concepts associated with patterns of subordination using terms like nature, rationality, and hierarchy. Essentialist theories of human nature, beginning with (those men!) Plato and Aristotle, understand human existence without taking history or culture into consideration. Neither factors change human nature. They both believed that reality was knowable and that there is a "nature" to certain things that did not depend on a particular time or place.

The worst offenders, according to feminist theory, were these Greeks, who viewed the female as inferior to the male. On this, they have a point: the inferiority of the feminine was based on the association of rational knowledge with

---

23   Ibid.
24   Ibid.

masculinity and the natural world with femininity. Think Zeus, king of the gods, and Hera, goddess of earth. What does reason do? It transforms, orders, and controls natural forces. Femaleness is identified with what male reason needs to overcome with its power of abstracting essences.

This part of the feminist critique is, as indicated above, fair. Throughout the ancient Greek world, women were subordinated to men. In Hesiod's *Theogony,* the first generation of humans was exclusively men; women were created later as a punishment because of Prometheus's theft of fire. Pythagoras, the pre-Socratic philosopher and mathematician, illustrated this with his association of femaleness with badness, multiplicity, and darkness. For Pythagoras, maleness implied unity, goodness, and light.[25]

In Aristotle, during conception the active form is male, and the passive matter is female. Women are likewise assigned the character traits appropriate to human beings who are more bodily than intellectual—more subject to the whims of the passions. They are compassionate, sentimental, jealous, argumentative, wrathful, despondent, despairing, shameless.[26] Man is by nature the superior ruler, and woman, having a disadvantage in the realm of practical wisdom, should not be relied upon to rule.[27] Women, therefore, are naturally subordinate to men, just as the mind should rule the body, and the master his slave.

---

[25]   Aristotle, *Metaphysics,* I, 50, 986a22-35, 21.

[26]   Aristotle, *History of Animals, IX, 1, 608b9-l3, The Basic Works of Aristotle,* 637.

[27]   Aristotle, *Politics,* I, 5, 1254b6-14, *The Basic Works of Aristotle,* 1132.

Feminists also reject the Judeo-Christian view of the female. They reject the implications in what the Book of Genesis says about Eve being made from a rib of Adam (Gn 2:22). But they despise how the theologians of the Patristic and Middles Age fused the Greek view of woman as lacking reason with Scripture's creation story. For this, I don't blame them. Christian theologians viewed the creation account as corroborating the philosophical accounts of the Greeks. For the scholastic philosopher Peter Abelard, famous for his relationship with Heloise, not only do females lack intellect, but they are also lacking in the very image of God.[28] Somehow Abelard interpreted Genesis 1:27 as only applying to Adam: "So God created man in his own image, in the image of God he created him; male and female he created them."

St. Thomas Aquinas softened this subordination without rejecting it entirely. Unlike Peter Abelard, he teaches that both man and woman are equally *imago dei* but, interpreting St. Paul (I Cor 11:3), adds a qualification: "for man is the beginning and end of the woman."[29] He also rejected the association of marriage and procreation with the Fall; each was a part of God's original purpose and do not result from original sin.[30] Every major stream of influence in the West, from the ancients and the medievals to the Renaissance and the Enlightenment, offered a consistent portrait of woman as naturally subordinate to man. The feminist consensus on

---

[28] Elisabeth Gössman, "The Image of the Human Being According to Scholastic Theology and the Reaction of Contemporary Women," *Ultimate Reality & Meaning*, 11, 1988, 187–88.

[29] Ibid., I.93.4.

[30] Ibid., I.98.2.

the history of ideas is that rationality has been conceived as an overcoming, a transcending, of the feminine.

Feminist scholars have done valuable scholarship in uncovering the philosophical and theological bias against women. Also, texts that have been largely ignored in traditional scholarship are being made known. For example, women of the Middle Ages, many of them mystics, are emerging as important figures: Hildegard von Bingen, Mechthild von Magdeburg, Beatrice of Nazareth, Hadewijch of Antwerp, Marguerite of Porete, Hrosvitha of Gandersheim, Elisabeth of Schonau, and Margery Kempe. We are learning about women who were Renaissance painters,[31] Renaissance writers,[32] or previously unknown or little-known composers.[33]

By insisting that interpreters acknowledge how Western culture has regarded women as inferior to men, feminist scholars made our understanding of the past more truthful; that is, closer to reality. Feminist theory, however, tears sex apart from gender, making one a biological and the other a cultural construct. It's become the first principle of feminist thinking, leaving many young women and men uncertain of their gender. They've been taught to believe gender is a matter of choice that doesn't need to comport with their natural bodies. Like any first principle, the sex-gender distinction

---

[31]   Elena Martinique, "10 Brilliant Female Artists of the Renaissance," January 9, 2018, https://www.widewalls.ch/famous-female-renaissance-artists/levina-teerlinc/.

[32]   Elaine V. Beilin, *Redeeming Eve: Women Writers of the English Renaissance* (Princeton: Princeton University Press, 1987).

[33]   Maggie Mulloy, "Women in (New) Music: Timeline of Women Composers," October 11, 2016, http://www.classical-music.com/article/10-female-composers-you-should-know.

lays the groundwork for the whole spectrum of feminist thought.

The practical implications of the classical view of human nature are these: *a common human nature establishes the foundation for understanding the moral and political life of human beings.* As Mortimer J. Adler writes, "Nothing else but the sameness of human nature at all times and places, from the beginning of *Homo sapiens* 45,000 years ago, can provide the basis for a set of moral values that should be universally accepted."[34] To have a common good requires a universal nature. The well-being of the individual and the state can only be known when human nature is regarded as the same for everyone. Without that acknowledgment, society will be ruled by an elite network of educators, media leaders, judges, financial leaders, police, and the military.

One of the first American postmodernists, Richard Rorty, argued against the concept of a shared human nature: "There is nothing deep down inside us except what we have put there ourselves, no criterion that we have not created in the course of creating a practice, no standard of rationality that is not an appeal to such a criterion, no rigorous argumentation that is not obedience to our own conventions."[35]

Rorty and other prophets of postmodernism, like Jacques Derrida and Michel Foucault, bring the legacy of relativism and radical individualism to its logical conclusion. In its most extreme version, they argue that the way in which

---

[34]   Mortimer J. Adler, *Haves Without Have-Nots* (New York: Random House, 1996), 230.

[35]   Richard Rorty, *Consequences of Pragmatism* (Minneapolis: University of Minnesota Press, 1981), xiii.

individuals interpret their experience is the source of all meaning and value.

Once upon a time, it would have been considered axiomatic that an acknowledged "common good" grounded in the basic facts about human nature was considered necessary to have a conception of justice at all. This is, sadly, no longer the case. To even suggest as much is, in some circles, considered oppressive, one more belief that somehow benefits those in power. The case for this view is, to put it kindly, less than convincing. Those who believe in the reality of human nature recognize that different human communities and societies are capable of actualizing their human potentialities in differing ways. The "babel" of different languages itself attests to this diversity. But those who are overly invested in the celebration of cultural diversity and who embrace an exaggerated concept of individualism can easily blind themselves to the more important point that these languages themselves are unique to the human species and bespeak a uniquely human potential differing in *kind* rather than *degree* from other animals.

CHAPTER 10

Exposing Untruth:
Multiculturalism and
the Therapeutic

The first word we heard about the changes going on in the educational establishment was "multiculturalism." At the surface, there seems nothing objectionable in learning about other cultures. But this was never the sole intention of multiculturalists: the chant, "Hey, hey, ho, ho, Western Culture's got to go!" from Stanford students in 1987 expressed the intent clearly. The media reported that veteran activist Jesse Jackson led the chant, but an eyewitness has been trying to correct the record for years. Jackson did not lead the chant, although he led the march. When the chanting started, according to the eyewitness, Jackson replied, "No, we don't want to get rid of Western Culture. We want to expand it and bring in new voices."[1] That was the attitude I held as a young college professor, but like the Rev. Jackson, I

---

[1]   John Reider, Letter to the Editor, *Chronicle of Higher Education*, November 21, 2016, https://www.chronicle.com/blogs/letters/jesse-jackson-didnt-lead-chant-against-western-culture/.

was naive enough to think the chanters represented a fringe group.

What began as a chanted slogan became part of the multiculturalist agenda that started in higher education but made its way down to the public schools—all in the name of "new voices." How did this happen?

In the 1980s, educational theorists lead by James A. Banks, known as the "father of multiculturalism," began to press for changes in school curricula to include texts from minority groups and other cultures.[2] In short, he and others held that we should seek knowledge that surpasses the limitations of our own culture. As Banks put it:

> The main goals of presenting different kinds of knowledge are to help students understand how knowledge is constructed and how it reflects the social context in which it is created and to enable them to develop the understandings and skills needed to become knowledge builders themselves. An important goal of multicultural education is to transform the school curriculum so that students not only learn the knowledge that has been constructed by others, but learn to critically analyze the knowledge they master and how to construct their own interpretations of the past, present, and future.[3]

---

[2]   James A. Banks, "The Canon, Knowledge Construction, and Multicultural Education," *Educational Researcher*, vol. 22, n. 5 (Jun.–Jul., 1993), 12.

[3]   Ibid.

If any of this sounds familiar, it is because we discussed postmodernism already—multiculturalism is just one derivation of the overall ideology. As Camille Paglia describes it, multiculturalists quickly politicized the curricula, putting aside any questions of quality. Instead of the promised mutual understanding and reconciliation across cultures, they created divisiveness.[4]

In the beginning, Banks and fellow multiculturalists won approval among scholars and institutional leaders by appealing to the *Western* idea of *toleration.* Let's take a quick look at when and where this ideal emerged to offer an example of how multiculturalists bite their own tail. Toleration was born out of post-Reformation religious struggles engulfing Europe and America in the seventeenth century. The Letter on Toleration of 1689 by the philosopher John Locke led to the British Parliament passing the Act of Toleration the same year. Since the Act did not apply to Catholics, there was still a way to go. It took a century for toleration to include Catholics, which tells us how serious a division remained between Reformers and the Roman Church. The American colonies during this period were rife with anti-Catholicism.

The Declaration of Independence implied a tolerance that included all religious faiths, but it was not made explicit until the passage of the First Amendment in 1791. The French Declaration of the Rights of Man (1789) talked a good game. Article 10 reads, "No-one shall be interfered with for his opinions, even religious ones, provided that their practice does not disturb public order as established by the law." But Catholic priests and nuns were slaughtered

---

[4]   *Provocations,* 408.

alongside other human obstacles to "Liberté, égalité, fraternité," their blood running from Madame Guillotine down the Champs-Élysées. Within five years, the Catholic faith had been replaced by the God of Supreme Being, one of the strangest moments in Western history.

The true philosophical prophet of toleration was the Jewish philosopher Baruch Spinoza (1632–1677). In the last chapter, "Freedom of Thought and Expression," of his *Tractatus Theologico-Politicus* (1670) he writes, "Men must be so governed that they can openly hold different and contrary opinions, and still live in harmony."[5] Spinoza expressly extends this to religious opinion: Rulers who try to control the beliefs of their subjects are attempting the impossible—"no one can surrender that even if he wants to."[6]

What makes Spinoza particularly relevant to this conversation is obvious: he advocates complete freedom of belief and opinion, which necessarily broadens a society's pool of knowledge. Multiculturalists, whether intending to or not, used a bait-and-switch tactic: *Let's widen knowledge, then we will tell you what's important and what isn't.*

It is ironic that multiculturalists gained even more approval by appealing to the need for *empathy*, insisting that it isn't enough to know *about* other people, we should also know what those people think *about themselves.* By the 1980s, American culture had embraced "emotivism," a philosophical perspective from the early twentieth century that

---

5   Benedictus de Spinoza, *The Collected Works of Spinoza*, vol. 2, III/245 20-21, trans. Edwin Curley (Princeton: Princeton University Press, 2016), 351.

6   Ibid., III/238 19, 344.

equates statements of morality and value with expressions of feelings.[7] Unlike toleration, emotivism was not a step in the right direction. This was the decade when men were being called to explore their feminine side and so forth. Emotivism unleashed the habit of expressing thoughts forcefully and dramatically, rather than logically through the use of argument, to influence people. Mere assertion is all that is required.

The Triumph of the Therapeutic

Philip Reiff called this *The Triumph of the Therapeutic*, a book whose description of our cultural future has been proven eerily accurate: "I expect that modern society will mount psychodramas far more frequently than its ancestors mounted miracle plays."[8] He saw that the "psychologizers" had freed the culture from the moral restraints of its religious teaching grounded in Scripture and expressed throughout the Western tradition. That culture was once rooted so deeply that it bound "even the ignorants of a culture to the great chain of meaning."[9]

Whereas the moral tradition of the West had taught the necessity of the virtues, what Reiff calls "instinctual renunciation," our culture has made its ultimate concern the satisfaction of individual desires. Instead of valuing an individual's ability to contain and channel desire, our culture

---

[7]   Emotivism is most often identified with a book by the philosopher A. J. Ayer, *Language, Truth and Logic* (London: Victor Gollancz Ltd, 1936).

[8]   Philip Reiff, *The Triumph of the Therapeutic: Uses of Faith After Freud* (New York: Harper Torchbooks, 1968), 26.

[9]   Ibid., 3.

applauds the freedom of "impulse release." What used to be regarded as "wants" are now deemed "needs."[10] Reiff was describing what he observed happening in the academic culture of the 1960s. This adds an important dimension to the understanding of why multiculturalism took root so quickly. The intellectuals had already lost faith in the past, in the ideals and texts that had been the cornerstone of their education. It's useful to recall here that Adler and Hutchins's Great Books were published in 1952, anticipating the curriculum battles and culture wars to come. Philip Reiff, born in 1922, witnessed what happened in academia after World War II, commenting, "The death of a culture begins when its normative institutions fail to communicate ideas in ways that remain inwardly compelling, first of all to the cultural elites themselves."[11] Reiff truly was "the prophet of anti-culture."[12]

Want more proof that Reiff predicted the future? In 2016, education researcher Ashley Thorne mapped out the change in education after the adoption of multicultural goals. She points out that in 1964, fifteen of the fifty premier universities in America required students to take a survey of Western civilization.[13] But all fifty offered the Western civilization survey, and forty-one offered it as a way to satisfy some requirement. By 1988, not one of those same top fifty

---

[10]   Ibid., 17.

[11]   Ibid., 18.

[12]   David Glenn, "Prophet of the 'Anti-Culture,'" *The Chronicle of Higher Education,* November 11, 2005, https://www.chronicle.com/article/prophet-of-the-anti-culture/19703.

[13]   Ashley Thorne, "The drive to put Western civ back in the college curriculum," March 29, 2016, *New York Post,* https://nypost.com/2016/03/29/the-drive-to-put-western-civ-back-in-the-college-curriculum/.

universities required Western civilization, and thirty-four of them did not offer the course at all. The multiculturalists demanded inclusion of new voices while demanding the exclusion of those who had been part of classical education in the United States since the establishment of its first colleges and universities.

They destroyed what the classicist Mary Beard has described as "the dialogue with those who have gone before us who were themselves in dialogue with the classical world."[14] Beard mentions those writers and artists regarded as great: Dante, Raphael, Shakespeare, Gibbon, and Picasso, among others. For many people, the common sense of our past remains the common sense of the present. However, for many this kind of sense is no longer common; for them, default attitudes have changed, in particular, what constitutes an argument, a reasoned approach to addressing differences of opinion.

The drastic change is ironic and duplicitous. Western learning has always been multicultural. As Bernard Knox puts it, classical Greek texts "[have] always been innovative, sometimes indeed subversive, even revolutionary."[15] Knox offers the example of an ancient historian, Herodotus (484–425 BC), the first great historian and author of the *Histories.*[16] He chronicled the histories of Greek and Persian

---

[14]   Mary Beard, *Confronting the Classics: Traditions, Adventure, and Innovations* (New York: Liveright Publishing, 2013), 11.

[15]   Bernard Knox, *The Oldest Dead White European Males and Other Reflections on the Classics* (New York: W. W. Norton & Company, Inc., 1993), 15.

[16]   Herodotus (484–425/413 BC) is regarded as the first important Western historian. His *Histories* have been translated many times into English and are still considered generally reliable.

empires, the cultures of Egyptians, Lydians, Babylonians, Massagetae, Indians, Arabians, Scythians, Libyans, Thracians, and Paeonians, along with the lives of Cyrus, Darius, Xerxes, and Cambyses. Knox asks whose work "is more multicultural than Herodotus?"[17] Plutarch even accused Herodotus of being "too fond of foreigners."[18]

In my own experience as a high school and college student, I read texts from the ancient worlds of the Middle East, Mesopotamia, Greece, the Roman Empire; from the distinctive medieval cultures of what came to be called Europe; from the emerging nations of young Europe. The history of the Americas was included, North, Central, and South, along with the study of their indigenous peoples. What was lacking during those years was serious instruction about the history and culture of Japan, China, and the rest of Asia, which would have made the Vietnam War more comprehensible. It would come as a great surprise to me later on when my son informed me that a "novel" had been written in Japan long before the first European novel, Cervantes's *Don Quixote* (1605–1615). Murasaki Shikibu wrote *The Tale of Genji* in the early eleventh century.[19]

False Promises

If multiculturalists had kept their promises, school and college curricula would have been enriched by the inclusion of the literature, ideas, values, and history of societies relatively

---

17   *The Oldest Dead White European Males*, 20.
18   Ibid.
19   Murasaki Shikibu, *The Tale of Genji*, trans. Royall Tyler (New York: Penguin Classics, 2001).

ignored in Western education. As Camille Paglia puts it, "Multiculturalism is in theory a noble cause that aims to broaden perspective in the U.S. which, because of its physical position between two oceans, can tend toward the smugly isolationist."[20]

Instead, of course, the multiculturalists have used their agenda not only to broaden our knowledge but to denigrate the texts and traditions that form Western civilization. The inclusion of ethnic content was not enough; schools required deep structural change. If all multiculturalists wanted was for schools to cast a wider net, then there would be no need for multicultural curriculums to match the ethnicity of students sitting in American classrooms.

Multiculturalism is much more exclusionary and prejudicial than any form of education the West has ever known. Both curricula and pedagogy are being tailored to serve the political purposes of a bureaucratic elite. This elite, meanwhile, distracts students from noticing the education they are missing with loud protestations of concern for their psychological well-being. Paglia once again: "In this first decade of the new millennium, I have yet to be persuaded that college students are graduating even from elite schools with deeper or broader knowledge," though "they are certainly well-tutored in sentiment."[21]

When multiculturalism merged with the therapeutic, the demand arose for a new form of segregation, self-segregation. For example, the designation of "safe spaces" on college campuses, black-only or women-only college events, and lectures

---

[20]   *Provocations*, 407.
[21]   Ibid., 409.

about "white privilege" and "toxic masculinity" at freshman orientations. It's one thing for a grown up to hear this nonsense being thrown around, but an eighteen-year-old can be easily intimidated into believing it. For many years, stories have been spilling out from the media that have made me wonder, only for a moment, if I was losing my mind. The culture that tolerates and encourages postmodern thinking bears no resemblance to the post-war world into which I was born and grew to adulthood. As described by Camille Paglia: "America is presently suffering from an effete, cynical pseudo-intellectuality in the universities, a manic rotation of superficial news cycles in the media, and a generalized hypochondria in the professional middle class, as shown by its preoccupation with stress-related ailments and disorders, buffered by tranquilizers."[22]

We live in a time when freedom of speech is denied and university professors sponsor segregated activities while condemning an entire race for its "white privilege." Though challenged on a daily basis by various opinion writers,[23] these attitudes are embraced so tightly by the cultural bosses that counter-arguments pass by unnoticed. As I mentioned earlier, mass culture is the school we go to every day. Colleges and universities continue to offer degrees in humanities, liberal arts, and sciences, but these traditional brands have been turned inside out by postmodern identity politics—multiculturalism, gender theory, and ethnocentrism.

---

[22]   Ibid., 414.

[23]   I'm thinking of conservative writers at the *New York Post,* the *Washington Times,* the *American Spectator,* the *New Criterion,* and *National Review,* among others.

Take a look at the list of publications found on a professor's personal page, especially you who are paying for your child or grandchild's education.

There are notable exceptions: there are professors, departments, and a few colleges that have not succumbed. It is also true that clever and nimble students can pick and choose their way through four years of college to minimize contact with the madness of ideology gone wild.

Those of us beyond, perhaps well beyond, those student days encounter these ideas packaged throughout the media from news reporting and political speech to our central forms of entertainment—television, movies, music, magazines, and books. Militant feminist, gay, lesbian, and transgender characters abound, rarely depicted as anything less than serenely happy and far superior to white males and married women with children.

These duplicitous practices carry messages about morality, politics, traditions, religion, and our nation. Some messages are embedded; others are blatant. Once these messages gain traction, they give birth to more of what Socrates and Plato called "sophistry," the reliance on fallacious arguments.[24] Plato's dialogues record how Socrates exposed the fallacies and moral shallowness of the prominent teachers of fifth century BC. Many of these Sophists, as they were called, were good teachers or rhetoricians. But all of them risked being publicly humiliated by an encounter with the "gadfly" of Athens. The mounting number of humiliations among the more

---

[24] Keep in mind many of the Sophists were distinguished teachers and neither blowhards or egotists. Thus, the term *sophistry* can be misleading by subsuming all the Sophists under a pejorative.

prominent Sophists eventually sparked an outrage that put Socrates on trial for his life and convicted. It is instructive to remember Socrates's fate. When sophistry is unmasked, it becomes personal. The reaction is not *I see your point* or *I stand corrected*, but rather an attack against the person who did the unmasking. Socrates's fate illustrates how far an *ad hominem* response can go.

CHAPTER 11

Unmasking the Gurus:
Despots and Dictators

Parents in recent decades have become increasingly concerned about the effect of post-secondary education
on their children's core beliefs. When their son or daughter comes home for the holidays repeating their professors'
jargon about multiculturalism, deconstruction, and feminist
theory, proclaiming the lack of an intelligible order in reality,
and rejecting any truths or facts derived from white male
authors, parents are understandably alarmed. This has been
happening long enough, however, for younger parents to
recognize what they were taught.

All the classics are now grist for the mill of criticism motivated by concern about race, gender, ethnicity, and social
class—different forms of *identity politics*. The term was
coined in the 1970s to identify groups who, it is claimed,
have been victims of deliberate oppression as well as social
and economic inequality. Now it is more common, however, for the concept itself to be used as a sort of intellectual
"club" with which to beat your adversaries, the invocation by
someone of one particular race or gender to settle a dispute:
"You say that because you're a wealthy white woman," and
so forth. How you use "identity politics" depends on how

163

much you believe that those factors, such as race, determine our values and opinions.

This ideology has become the leading edge of cultural indoctrination. What is often introduced as a kind of relativism—the idea that values and morality have no objective status, but are merely relative to various situations—quickly becomes absolutist: the values of certain groups are meaningless or worse, depending on the race or sex of the one holding them. These damaging assumptions about our most basic ideas, including human nature, morality, justice, et cetera, have been adopted and promulgated by most educational institutions to the point that any claim they make to offer an "education" is dubious. When choosing a college, it is advisable to find out what the professors in the core courses (if there are any) assign their students. Do identity politics dominate classroom discussions? Fifty years ago, a student could sit down in a class about Plato's *Republic* and not be lectured on his "phallocentrism."

Identity politics only serves to reinforce the platitudes of one side of the debate or another. The use of labels is just another form of "preaching to the choir" by insinuating mental and moral error to the person on the other side of the debate. Ironically, it is the mirror image of past racist caricatures of certain groups based on their skin color, sex, or implied moral inferiority, and just as baseless.

However, the promotion of identity politics explicitly *encourages the use of power rather than reason.* In other words, it has given rise to despotism in education, culture, and politics. As is often said, an educated citizenry is required to avoid totalitarianism. At the cultural level, we have neither provided the former nor prevented the latter. These abuses of power are usually kept concealed by both the perpetrator and the victim; the former not wanting to tarnish his moral high ground and the latter not wishing to suffer any further for his disobedience. Abuses of this power have sent fears throughout our nation that a refusal to bend to these assumptions will put careers, reputations, and finances in jeopardy.

This power has resulted in the acceptance of the *ad hominem* argument. Meaning literally "against the man," *ad hominem* attacks have become so common that they are no longer recognized as the logical fallacy that they are. An *argument ad hominem* is an argument "directed against the arguer rather than against his argument or against the conclusion of his argument" states the description from the textbook I used to teach informal logic.[1] There is an important distinction to be made here. For example, if we were watching a program with two people debating air traffic safety and one asks the other to explain their expertise on the subject, that would be reasonable. Now, if on the same program one of the interlocutors pointed out the other had once crashed his private plane, that's *ad hominem*—a rhetorical move meant to embarrass and silence the opponent. Most *ad hominem* attacks these days are based upon the factors held so dear by postmodernists: gender, race, nationality, political party affiliation, wealth, religion, and even residential location.

Cultural despots may not be able to control you with personal intimidation or the threat of bad grades, but they can

---

[1]   Robert J. Fogelin, *Understanding Arguments: An Introduction to Informal Logic* (New York: Harcourt Brace Jovanovich, 1982), 96.

create a social climate where specific opinions and attitudes are morally unacceptable. The power of rejection and shaming takes a toll even on our most hardened sensibilities. It can cause a painful loss of friendships and exclusion from once-welcoming communities. The same climate can create divisions where we work, worship, and play. The despots do not disagree, they condemn. *Ad hominem* arguments are effective but for reasons having nothing to do with the issues.

I should pause to say that I do acknowledge that one's sex, race, ethnicity, and other traits will undoubtedly influence how he thinks and acts, but they do not determine his thoughts and actions to the degree that the identity politics crowd insists.

Ad hominem attacks often go unchallenged in public because those dominating public opinion accuse one of hatred and ignorance if he opposes, say, teaching transgenderism (the idea that a person may have a "gender identity" that is different from his biological sex, and may choose any form of such identity) to grade school children. If race is involved, racism can be imputed, even if race isn't an issue at all.

In this perverse view, only someone lacking an enlightened, compassionate, moral sensibility would challenge the wisdom of requiring eight-year-olds in public schools to question their gender. Such a troublemaker must have a character deficiency and needs to be re-educated, perhaps ordered to attend some "training." There are few things more powerful in a community than publicly shaming one of its members—recall Hester Prynne's scarlet "A" in Nathaniel

Hawthorne's *The Scarlet Letter*. The threat of moral shaming is supposed to keep all of us quiet or compliant.

A true education prepares and allows students, especially children, to think freely, without the constraint of ideology or fear of prejudice from the teacher. As much as the faculties of colleges and universities force postmodernism and identity politics upon their students, they disable freedom of thought. The pursuit of knowledge for its own sake is denied outright. Nothing has meaning apart from the categories employed by postmodernists, and these are likely to change monthly. Their judgments only reinforce their assumptions about the decisive factors of gender, ethnicity, and so on, demanding compliance from everyone, or else. There is no knowledge *per se*, for its own sake.

It is one thing to reject these ideologies out of hand, another to understand them critically. As I said earlier, multiculturalism—defined as a general appreciation for cultures other than one's own—should have enriched learning by expanding the range of cultures studied in the classroom. This kind of enlightened education is not what multiculturalism has delivered: we now live instead in a culture where all disagreements are immediately chalked up to a person's race, ethnicity, and class, and from there to their supposed moral standing.

If this discussion leaves you dazed, know it's inevitable in a culture like ours. After all, like *Alice in Wonderland*, we have given birth to a culture that is topsy-turvy and in which what passes for intellectual discourse is, more often than not, complete and utter nonsense. The changes in our culture seem to have appeared suddenly, but they developed slowly under cover of false promises. The intellectual take-over of the university and other institutions by postmodernists over the past five decades was largely concealed from donors and alumni until their dominance made objections passé. Once these scholars and school administrators had the power, they could hire who they wanted, change the curriculum as they wished, and name board members who would not challenge them.

History and Truth

History teaches that people's convictions can change quickly. The Russian aristocracy and bourgeoisie were blindsided by what happened after Lenin returned from exile on April 16, 1917. They had felt compelled to support the formation of the first Russian Republic on September 1, 1917, under Alexander Kerensky. The supporters of the Czar assumed the creation of a Republic would be enough to quiet the social upheaval. Lenin immediately challenged the liberal government and called for more radical action to return government to "the people." Within six weeks, the October Revolution started, the Republic ended, the Bolsheviks took charge, and, on Lenin's order, the Romanov family was murdered by armed peasants.

This complete undoing of a powerful nation by revolution occurred only a century ago. Going back further, imagine being a French Catholic priest on July 7, 1790, when the National Assembly ratified the "Civil Constitution of the Clergy," declaring the Church subordinate to the state. All Church properties had been confiscated the year before. The following December, the assembly declared that all priests and bishops were required to swear an oath of allegiance *before the altar* to the republic or suffer dismissal, deportation, or death.[2] Only a few bishops swore the oath, but one half of the active clergy complied.[3] In just over a year after the fall of the Bastille, Catholic clergy went from being highly regarded as figures of authority and wisdom to employees of a godless state. In the chaos that followed, thousands of priests and nuns were killed, thousands more were forced to marry or fled the country. By the time the "Cult of the Supreme Being" was announced in May 1794, only a few parishes remained open.

Who saw this coming in a nation with ancient Catholic roots and a Catholic monarchy? Why wasn't the French Church prepared for it? Do *we* see what's coming?

French philosopher Bernard-Henri Levy reminds us how what seem to be insignificant little groups of malcontents can become very powerful. Levy recalls how the crowds that hung out in the beer houses of Munich in the 1920s were mesmerized by the ravings of a failed artist named Hitler. "It starts with a group, a sect, and, within that sect, a local aberration, the tiniest novelty, which at first no one imagines it will ever go past the stage of accident, or of freak abnormality, or both—and which thanks to a quick reinforcement, because of a strange but irresistible attraction, soon affects all world history."[4]

---

[2] John McManners, *The French Revolution & The Church* (New York: Harper Torchbooks, 1969), 38, 47.

[3] Peter McPhee, *Liberty or Death: The French Revolution* (New York: Yale University Press, 2016), 124.

[4] Bernard-Henri Levy, *Left in Dark Times: A Stand Against the New Barbarism,* trans. Benjamin Moser (New York: Random House, 2008), 208.

Both the French and Russian Revolutions have a similar provenance. Levy assures us that we in the United States are not soon to experience a similar seizing of power by those previously marginalized. His implied caution is to take ideas seriously no matter how silly or deranged they seem.

When did the German Jews realize what the Nazis had in mind? Among them were artists, intellectuals, teachers, artisans, families, and institutions that had flourished for centuries. The rise of the Nazis had taken place slowly at first. Hitler was jailed in 1924 for the failed "Beer Hall Putsch"—a failed attempt to overthrow the German government. But he wisely used that year to write *Mein Kampf,* which brought him greater notoriety and wealth. Less than ten years later, Hitler became chancellor of Germany. Dachau, the first concentration camp, opened the same year. Hitler became far more than chancellor; he became a dictator. By passing the 1933 Enabling Act,[5] the Reichstag gave Hitler and the Nazi Party the power to enact laws without Reichstag approval.

One of Germany's leading writers from the period before 1933 was Joseph Roth. His 1932 novel, *Radetzky March,* is considered the best fictional portrayal of the Hapsburg Empire in decline under Emperor Franz Joseph.[6] He penned several successful novels before that—*Hotel Savoy* (1924),

---

[5]   Volker Ullrich, *Hitler: Ascent 1889-1939*, trans. Jefferson Chase (New York: Alfred A. Knopf, 2016), 440–41. The Enabling Act of 1933, passed in both Reichstag and Reichsrat, was an amendment to the Constitution of the Weimar Republic, signed by President Paul von Hindenburg, former commander of the German army during WWI. Thus, the German political leadership *gave away* the freedom of the German people and created a *de facto* dictatorship.

[6]   Joseph Roth, *Radetzky March*, trans. Michael Hoffmann (London: Granta Books, 2003).

Flight Without End (1929), and *Job* (1930)—all while working as a journalist. Roth's family was Jewish, and he cut off his
education to fight on the Eastern front in WWI. His newspaper work began when he returned to Vienna. According
to his English translator, Michael Hoffmann, he worked as a
journalist while living between Berlin and Paris.[7] From these
vantage points, he watched Europe trudge towards the next
world war. Roth was the first journalist to mention Adolph
Hitler in print, in 1924, the year he spent in prison.

In 1933, Roth wrote an essay from Paris, "The Auto-da-Fé
of the Mind."[8] The Nazi book burnings began in Berlin forty-
three days after the Enabling Act, on May 6 with 20,000
burned and five days later with another 25,000. Books by
Jewish authors were the highest priority. Roth called it an
auto-da-fé, meaning a public burning usually reserved for
criminals and heretics, an instrument of the Spanish Inquisition. Those who resisted the rise of Hitler watched as the
mind of the nation became "the first defeat." Roth traces
the cause of the book burning back to the Prussian mindset, represented by Otto von Bismarck, which gave prece-
dence to everything material over the life of the intellect.
The military, engineers, chemists, and professors all join in,
but among these the professor "is in fact the most dangerous (the most dogmatic) enemy of European civilization,

7   "European Dreams; Rediscovering Joseph Roth," *The New
       Yorker,* January 19, 2004, https://www.newyorker.com/magazine/
       2004/01/19/europeandreams.
8   Joseph Roth, *What I Saw: Reports from Berlin: 1920-1933,* trans.
       Michael Hoffmann (New York: W. W. Norton & Company,
       2003), 207–17.

the inventor of the philological equivalent of poison gas."[9] Roth's condemnation of professors was based on his experience of how so many were absorbed, willingly or not, into the Nazi killing machine. Roth is alluding to the extraordinary capacity intellectuals possess for rationalization, especially on the basis of serving abstract ideals such as those of the German Reich.

At the same time, however, Roth recognizes the opposite problem of sheer ignorance, the result of the materialism represented by Bismark. Paul von Hindenburg, the president who signed the Enabling Act and handed power to Hitler, publicly confessed that "he had never read a book in his life."[10] Roth saw this coming in 1925: "Is a people that elect as its president an icon that has never read a book all that far away from burning books itself?"[11] Roth further comments that Hitler would not have been so fulsome in his praise of Benito Mussolini if he had "studied his Roman history more closely!"[12]

Roth ends his essay with gratitude for being Jewish: Even if he had tried to collaborate—had moral weakness got the better of him—the Nazi's revulsion towards Jews would have ended that effort. Joseph Roth died at age forty-four, an early death brought on by ravages of drinking and keeping his watch on the death of civilization as he knew it.

---

[9]   Ibid., 209.
[10]   Ibid., 211.
[11]   Ibid., 212.
[12]   Ibid., 213.

Lessons of the Past

Despots come in all varieties. They can take the form of violent protestors who succeed in keeping some speakers off college campuses, as has become common in the last decade. Physical violence has become common at such protests, and this criminal activity has not been discouraged by politicians and police commissioners who order the police to stand down. More recently, left-wing senators playing to TV cameras viciously shamed a Supreme Court nominee for unsubstantiated accusations of sexual assaults to keep a perceived conservative from a seat on the court.

For now, the reader can get a general idea by observing how the use of power is justified by those who claim greater enlightenment and moral purpose than the rest of us. One example is how LGBTQ programs in public education are implemented over the objections of parents and church groups.[13] Polling supplies the numbers to justify these programs: According to a 2013 survey by GLSEN, a national nonprofit focused on providing safe educational spaces for LGBTQ students, just 5 percent of LGBTQ students reported having health classes that included positive representations of LGBTQ-related topics.[14]

It doesn't matter if parents don't want "positive representations" of LBGTQ relationships because it contradicts their religious values. Whatever occurs at the top of society among the leaders in the academy, media, politics, and

---

[13] Jeanne Sager, "The Power of Inclusive Sex Education," *The Atlantic*, July 17, 2017, https://www.theatlantic.com/education/archive/2017/07/the-power-of-inclusive-sex-ed/533772/.

[14] Ibid.

business can happen at any level below, all the way down to the family and various relationships. The temptation to dictate how others should think and act is promoted by forms of education that attempt to crush our freedom of mind.

In 1953, the playwright Arthur Miller (1915–2005) wrote *The Crucible* in reaction to the McCarthy hearings, the government harassment of people accused of having been members of the Communist Party. The hearings had led to a "Hollywood Blacklist," an agreement among major studios to not knowingly employ a Communist or anyone associated with a group trying "to overthrow of the government of the United States." As a result, prominent actors, directors, and screenwriters lost their income and their future. The revered Charlie Chaplin was forced to leave the United States in 1952 and vowed never to return. In retrospect, we can see McCarthy was exactly right about the infiltration of Soviet spies into the US government, even if his tactics went well beyond what was necessary and people were unnecessarily hurt.[15]

Miller's play compares anti-Communists with those caught up in the Salem witch trials of 1692. Miller's sympathies at the time were with the Communists. Regardless of the ideologies of Miller or McCarthy, *The Crucible* depicts how hysteria can sweep through a community fueled by this man's envy or that man's ambition. Miller's characters are modeled on figures taken from Salem's historical accounts:

---

[15]   Nicolas von Hoffman, "Was McCarthy Right About the Left?" *Washington Post*, April 14, 1996, https://www.washingtonpost. com/archive/opinions/1996/04/14/was-mccarthy-right-about-the-left/a0dc6726-e2fd-4a31-bcdd-5f352acbf5de/?utm_term=. a1321b99a626.

a frustrated, lonely clergyman tries to discover why his daughter will not eat and stumbles upon an incident that will ignite the witch hunt: Four teenage girls dancing in the dark woods, each trying to deny it, cover it up, and blame others for being there. In the late 1600s, the people of Salem believed in witches, and the woods surrounding their towns and villages were where they lived. Thus, the tree line was literally a boundary line between Christians and pagan forces. As the investigation gets closer to exposing them, the young women start making vague accusations of witchcraft, even altering their appearance and behavior to suggest an evil influence. Quickly, these accusations are taken up passionately by locals who in the name of God pursue the source of the evil tormenting those afflicted.

A clergyman is called in to examine the accused teenagers to see if exorcism is required. He doesn't notice what several prominent citizens have quickly realized, that is that the epidemic is being used to settle old scores, get revenge, and acquire land, all driven by envy and resentment. Arrests are made, and the deputy governor arrives to preside at the trial. He attempts a balanced inquiry, but once challenged, his pride leads him to fall in with the false accusers. Several of the prominent citizens whose integrity remained intact are executed themselves because it was from them the accusers wanted to steal.

This play is shattering to read and more so to watch. Miller is better known for his classic *Death of a Salesman* from 1949, but *The Crucible* has grown in relevance to American culture—we regularly see episodes of group hysteria, prompted by nothing reasonable, but capable of ruining lives by shouting the loudest.

Shoah

The one who wants to know where despotism leads would do well to watch *Shoah*, a nine-hour documentary about the Holocaust. Director Claude Lanzmann took eleven years to make the remarkable film, shooting 350 hours of interviews with witnesses, survivors, even perpetrators, and visits to extermination camps. Lanzmann created a masterpiece, but more than that, he created the closest thing we have to a definitive record of the greatest evil in human history. If you asked me how I could watch it for nine hours, I would tell you that I couldn't stop watching *Shoah*, the film wouldn't let me. The Criterion Collection has issued a completely restored version of the film.[16] Watching it is, in a sense, like reading *Les Miserables*—the reader hungers for justice. Unlike the Hugo novel that inspired the famous musical play, in *Shoah,* justice never comes, there is no relief. The only satisfaction comes when someone takes the time to remember and tell the story, like Lanzmann, without blinking or looking away.

A film like this is not made without risk. Germany did not like its Nazi past pieced together so revealingly. Much of his material was collected by using hidden cameras. There were death threats, and one interviewee attacked Lanzmann after discovering a hidden microphone. Lanzmann spent a month in the hospital recovering.

---

[16]   *Shoah*, dir. Claude Lanzmann (1985: New York: The Criterion Collection, Inc., 2013), DVD.

There's one scene that still haunts me: A Czech Jew, Filip Muller, was assigned to work at the doors of the gas chambers. In return for his work, Muller survived. Lanzmann asked him to describe what he saw:

> Muller: You see, once the gas was poured in, it worked like this: It rose from the ground upwards. And in the terrible struggle that followed—because it was a struggle—the lights were switched off in the gas chambers. It was dark, no one could see, so the strongest people tried to climb higher. Because they probably realized that the higher they got, the more air there was. They could breathe better. That caused the struggle. Secondly, most people tried to push their way to the door. It was psychological; they knew where the door was; maybe they could force their way out. It was instinctive, a death struggle. Which is why children and weaker people and the aged always wound up at the bottom. The strongest were on top. Because in the death struggle, a father didn't realize his son lay beneath him.
>
> Lanzmann: And when the doors were opened?
>
> Muller: They fell out. People fell out like blocks of stone, like rocks falling out of a truck.[17]

"Because in the death struggle, a father didn't realize his son lay beneath him": I've never forgotten that line since the first

---

[17]   Claude Lanzmann, *Shoah: An Oral History of the Holocaust, The Complete Text of the Film*, preface by Simone de Beauvoir (New York: Pantheon Books, 1985), 125.

time I heard it. I have to wonder what went on inside of a man like Filip Muller, after the war, who has conscience enough to make that observation. Most of Lanzmann's interviewees confess to knowing what was going on but kept on "doing my job." This was the same excuse used by the Nazi war criminals at the Nuremberg Trials[18] and by Hitler's architect, Albert Speer, in his memoirs.[19]

Shoah has been called, deservedly, the best documentary of all time and can only be compared to Marcel Ophüls's 1969 The Sorrow and the Pity.[20] Ophüls's two-part, four-hour documentary on the collaboration of the Vichy government in France with the Third Reich was a breakthrough in documentary filmmaking, and it's apparent that The Sorrow and the Pity served as the model for Lanzmann. But Shoah is a film different in kind, not degree, from The Sorrow and the Pity.

If This Is a Man

There have been many notable books about the Holocaust. Among them, one has a special place—Primo Levi's Auschwitz memoir If This Is a Man (1947). It is such a horrifying

---

18   The Nuremberg Trials, held 20 November 1945 and 1 October 1946, tried twenty-four leaders of the Third Reich before an International Military Tribunal. All the official proceedings of the Nuremberg trials can be found here: http://avalon.law.yale.edu/imt/imtmin.asp.

19   Albert Speer, Inside the Third Reich, trans. Richard and Clara Winston (New York and Toronto: Macmillan, 1970). The German edition, Erinnerungen, was published in 1969.

20   The Sorrow and the Pity, dir. Marcel Ophüls (1969; Hertfordshire, UK: Arrow Academy. 2017), Blu-ray.

expose of the human condition that it also stands alone.[21] Born in 1919 in Turin, Italy, Levi was raised in a cultured Jewish family. His early life was entwined with the growing Fascist movement in which he participated in a nominal way, preferring to ski rather than practice marksmanship. He became a chemist after graduating from Turin University.

When Benito Mussolini fell from power, Italy aligned itself with the Allies. The German army moved in quickly to occupy Northern Italy. Levi, in spite of his aversion to war, joined the Italian resistance but was captured by Fascist militia working with the Nazis. He was going to be shot as a partisan, but when Levi told his captors he was Jewish, they sent him to an Italian internment camp. When the Nazis took over the camp, they sent Levi and other Jewish prisoners on trucks to Auschwitz. He was an inmate at Auschwitz for one year until the Soviets liberated the camp in 1945. Of the 650 Jews who arrived with him, only twenty survived. One of the twenty, Primo Levi went on to tell the story.

His account focuses on the prisoners themselves, how they struggled to adapt to their captivity, their hunger, their slave labor, the constant beatings, and fear of death. He calmly saves his words of condemnation for only the most egregious acts of inhumanity. Levi's account is detached in places, speaking like a scientist describing a specimen, until what he sees removes all distance and his voice cries out in lament.

---

[21]   Primo Levi, *If This Is a Man*, trans. Stuart Woolf, *The Complete Works of Primo Levi*, vol. 1 (New York: Liveright Publishing Company, 2015).

The train from the internment camp stops; Levi is put into a truck loaded with other Italian prisoners and driven to Auschwitz, where they are led to a large bare room. They are ordered to form rows of five and undress. Their shoes are swept into a pile, then swept away through an open door and freezing wind fills the room. Four men with razors enter wearing striped trousers and jackets with numbers sewn on them. After being shaved, the new arrivals are put into a wet shower room with no place to sit down. They are given no water to drink after traveling for five days. They are left standing and shivering. Another man in stripes enters speaking Italian telling them they must be disinfected. A bell sounds waking up the camp, then five minutes of a hot shower. Still wet, they are handed clothes and shoes. With no time to dress, they are herded out into the ice and snow, where they run to a barracks. They dress and stand around the walls—no one looks at each other. Levi writes:

> Then for the first time we became aware that our language lacks words to express this offense, the demolition of a man. In a moment, with almost prophetic intuition, the reality was revealed to us: we had reached the bottom. It is not possible to sink lower than this; no human condition is more miserable than this, nor could it conceivably be so. Nothing belongs to us anymore; they have taken away our clothes, our shoes, even our hair; if we speak, they will not listen to us, and if they listen, they will not understand. They will even take away our name: and if we want to keep it, we will have to find ourselves the strength to do so, to

manage somehow so that behind the name something of us, of us as we were, still remains.[22]

The witness of Primo Levi, found in *If This Is a Man* and his other writings, reminds us what can happen when an unmet threat is allowed to advance. He committed suicide in 1987, jumping from an interior landing of his apartment building and falling to his death on the ground floor. It was well-known among his friends that he suffered from depression. A few friends believe he lost his balance, arguing that as a chemist Levi would have devised an easier way to die. A fellow Holocaust survivor Elie Wiesel understood it best, perhaps, when he said, "Primo Levi died at Auschwitz forty years later."[23]

Symphony of Sorrowful Songs

In 1976, the Polish composer Henryk Gorecki (1933–2010) composed his Third Symphony, *The Symphony of Sorrowful Songs*. In each of its three movements, a solo soprano sings lyrics from carefully chosen texts. In the first movement, Gorecki chose a Silesian folk song describing a mother's lament for her son killed in the war. The second movement was inspired by a text found on a Gestapo prison cell wall in 1944 written by the eighteen-year old Helena Wanda Blazusiakowna: "No, Mother, do not weep, most chaste Queen of heaven Help me always. Hail Mary." The melody from a Silesian folk song is sung in the third movement, to the

---

22   Ibid., 22–23.
23   Diego Lambetta, "Primo Levi's Last Moments," *The Boston Review*, July 1, 1999, https://bostonreview.net/diego-gambetta-primo-levi-last-moments.

text of the Virgin Mary speaking to Jesus on the cross, "O my son, beloved and chosen, Share your wounds with your mother."

This symphony is a beautiful, haunting, mesmerizing tribute to the victims of WWII in Poland: the soldiers killed, the mothers in grief, the search for spiritual solace in the Catholic faith. The symphony premiered in 1977 and was considered a failure.[24] This wasn't the only negative reaction to the work, which shows you how entrenched the *avant-garde* among the artistic elite was at the time. One of the leading figures of that elite was the French composer and conductor Pierre Boulez who was sitting next to Gorecki. His only comment was "merde."[25] Gorecki was challenging not only the twelve-tone establishment but also the anti-religious attitude that prevailed there. Attempts to dismiss the symphony as reactionary failed because of a commercial recording released in 1992.[26] The Nonesuch recording featuring soprano Dawn Upshaw made Gorecki's symphony world famous. The recording sold over a million copies, which was unprecedented for a modern classical composer. The producer thought he would be lucky if it sold twenty to

---

[24]   Luke B. Howard, "Laying the Foundation: The Reception of Górecki's Third Symphony, 1977-1992," Polish Music Journal, vol. 6, n. 2, https://polishmusic.usc.edu/research/publications/polish-music-journal/vol6no2/gorecki-third-symphony/.

[25]   Ibid., 216.

[26]   After a concert of the Atlanta Symphony Orchestra in 1986, I asked principal guest conductor Louis Lane what he thought of the Gorecki Third Symphony. Lane dismissed it with a wave of his hand. This was before the Nonesuch recording. I had the luck to buy an Erato LP of a 1985 French film, *Police*, that used the Third Symphony as its soundtrack.

thirty thousand.[27] If you've heard *The Symphony of Sorrowful Songs*, you understand its popularity, and if you haven't, you have quite a treat in store.[28] When I first heard it, I felt as if it pushed back the limits of what I understood as beautiful. The music critic Nicholas Kenyon, after a live 1989 performance in London, wrote, "It was as if a spark had been lit. The evening had all the signs of an event which could change the course of our musical taste."[29]

I've included *The Symphony of Sorrowful Songs* because it's one example of a remarkable artistic creation being dismissed by the cultural elite because it did not conform to their expectations. The lesson here is that Gorecki's symphony won people over with its originality and beauty. There wasn't any pressure put on the Catholic audience to "support" it for non-musical reasons. Gorecki chose to compose for the human ear and not for the approval of the gatekeepers of high art. They trashed music of great beauty, lest it enter into the wider world. Elite power failed, and all the music that was composed for their approval has failed with it. It does matter, as it turns out, whether audiences cheer because they're expected to or because they were moved by the music they heard. Gorecki demonstrates that what the elite tell us we should like cannot compete with art that reveals beauty on human terms.

---

[27] William Robin, "How a Somber Symphony Sold More Than a Million Records," *The New York Times*, June 9, 2017, https://www. nytimes.com/2017/06/09/arts/music/how-a-somber-symphony-sold-more-than-a-million-records.html.

[28] This video is a stunning performance of the Gorecki Third Symphony with soprano Zofia Kilanowicz, conductor Anton Wit, and the National Polish Radio Symphony Orchestra in Katowice: https://www.youtube.com/watch?v=v_pn_cVqGJQ&t=8s.

[29] Nicholas Kenyon, "Jump Up and Shout," *Observer*, April 9, 1989.

CHAPTER 12

Assigning Blame: Barbarians and Straw Dogs

A uthor and literary scholar Harold Bloom has described reading as the way "to enlarge solitary existence."[1] Some readers might assume much more is at stake. They may consider it part of restoring a *civilization* that has been lost. Or they may equate classical education with moral benefit. There are good reasons for such associations, but a word of caution is in order. It is commonplace to read about someone giving credit to Greek and Roman education for saving the West from barbarism. But, taken at face value, this statement is false.

Scholars point out that the ancient Greeks first applied the barbarian label to those who could not speak Greek well due to stammering.[2] So "bar-bar" was a way of mocking those who stammered, which became a label for anyone who could not speak the language. Following suit, the Romans labeled anyone living outside the borders of its empire as barbarians. It didn't matter to them that the great barbarian tribes often lived more or less the same lives as Romans,

---

[1]   *The Western Canon*, 484–85.
[2]   *The Oldest Dead White European Males,* 13.

although in less comfortable circumstances. From ancient times on, people were considered barbarians if they spoke a strange language, lived in an unfamiliar culture, or threatened the lives of other groups.

Once labeled as barbarians, these persons were often subjected to dehumanizing cruelty by those who considered themselves the guardians of civilization: the French in Vietnam, the Belgians in the Congo, the Germans in East Africa, the British in India, the Spanish in Mexico and South America, the Americans in the United States with their African slaves and horrific treatment of native peoples.

This is not to say that all cultures are equal in objective terms—one could imagine that a horde of Germanic tribes facing Roman columns would evoke images beyond a mere difference in language and geography. It is, rather, to distinguish between such objective differences and the way in which certain cultures used their advantages, often to dehumanizing effect.

The Heart of Darkness

No writer has portrayed the reality of life under colonial rule with the ruthless insight of Joseph Conrad. In *Heart of Darkness*,[3] Conrad's character Marlow tells the story as captain of a dilapidated steamer traversing far up an African river into the Congo to contact a man named Kurtz. Marlow excelled in delivering coveted elephant tusks back

---

[3]   Joseph Conrad, *The Heart of Darkness and Selected Short Stories* (New York: Barnes & Noble Books, 2008). Conrad began his serialization of *The Heart of Darkness* in 1899 before publishing it as a book in 1902.

to The Company in England. Although he is a sailor who has seen much of the world, Marlow is sickened by what he sees being done to the African natives working in the mines: "They were dying slowly—it was very clear. They were not enemies, they were not criminals, they were nothing earthly now—nothing but black shadows of disease and starvation, lying confusedly in the greenish gloom. Brought from all the recesses of the coast in all the legality of time contracts, lost in uncongenial surroundings, fed on unfamiliar food, they sickened, became inefficient, and were then allowed to crawl away and rest."[4]

Halfway up the river, Marlow meets the manager of the Central Station, who explains that "each station should be like a beacon on the road toward better things, a centre of trade of course, but also for humanizing, improving, instructing."[5] In fact, Kurtz, the chief of the next station, Inner Station, deeper in the Congo, is described by the manager as an ideal person for this mission, "an emissary of pity, and science, and progress," a man sent to provide "guidance of the cause entrusted to us by Europe, so to speak, higher intelligence, wide sympathies, a singleness of purpose."[6]

Coming closer to his destination, Marlow watches along the river banks and suddenly sees "a burst of yells, a whirl of black limbs, a mass of hands clapping, of feet stamping, of bodies swaying, of eyes rolling." Then realizes, "No, they were not inhuman. Well, you know, that was the worst of it—the suspicion of their not being inhuman. It would come

---

[4]   Ibid., 53.
[5]   Ibid., 72.
[6]   Ibid., 62.

slowly to one. They howled and leaped, and spun, and made horrid faces; but what thrilled you was just the thought of their humanity—like yours."[7]

Who Are the Barbarians?

The setting of Conrad's dark, vivid fictional tale was real enough. By the beginning of the twentieth century, the colonization of Africa was at its peak: the massive continent was divided among European powers. The Congo belonged to the Dutch Empire and suffered under the inhumane demands of Leopold II for rubber production. The British Empire claimed huge swathes of Africa: Sierra Leone, Gold Coast, Nigeria, South Africa, Basutoland, Swaziland, North and South Rhodesia, Kenya, Uganda, Sudan, and Egypt. The mistreatment of native peoples was made possible by the assumption that one nation was "civilizing" another. It's lost on me how you can civilize a people by treating them as less than human. The motive behind the organized, militaristic occupation of various regions was profit, though legitimate explorers, scientists, and missionaries often led the way. While some went to understand, know, or save, others went to take; the "barbarians" were seen as either obstacles or as a sub-human resource to be exploited along with the other natural resources.

French philosopher Alain Finkielkraut sums up the reason one group labels another as barbarians: "Everyone wants to rule over everyone else and is therefore everyone's enemy."[8]

---

7   Ibid., 76.
8   Alain Finkielkraut, *In the Name of Humanity: Reflections on the Twentieth Century*, trans. Judith Friedlander (New York: Columbia University Press, 2000), 18.

The barbarians, on this view, are not the conquered, but the conquerors. He quotes from a speech given to UNESCO by French anthropologist Claude Levi-Strauss: "The barbarian is first and foremost a man who believes in barbarism."[9] Ironically, Finkielkraut argues, with great force, the barbarians are those who describe others as barbarians.

Readers may recall that in the twentieth century, it was the intellectuals who celebrated the rule of Lenin and then Stalin as the leaders of "progress." A number of them continued their adulation even after proof of Stalin's purges, concentration camps, mass executions, and the Ukrainian famine—5.5 million were killed in the years 1932–1933[10]— were made public. As early at 1927, Julian Benda had chronicled the self-deception of European intellectuals who supported Stalin in Benda's influential *La trahison des clercs* (1927), translated as *The Betrayal of the Intellectuals*.[11] To this day, Lenin and Stalin do not receive their due condemnation due to the continuing influence of the political Left in our culture. Every eighth-grade student knows about the evils of Hitler and the Holocaust, but almost none know that on the list of most murderous dictators, Hitler is ranked third, after China's communist Mao Zedong and Stalin, and just before

---

[9]   Ibid., 16.

[10]   Timonthy D. Snyder, *Bloodlands: Europe Between Hitler and Stalin* (New York: Basic Books, 2010), 55.

[11]   Benda's *La trahison des clercs* was first published in 1927 and published in 1928 in a translation by Richard Aldington. The book has been reprinted with an introduction by Roger Kimball, https://www.amazon.com/Treason-Intellectuals-Julien-Benda/dp/1412806232/ref=sr_1_1?keywords=julien+benda&qid=1552501637&s=books&sr=1-1.

Lenin. Meanwhile, Soviet symbolism is openly embraced by current "anti-fascist" violent rioters.

Matthew White has cataloged the worst slaughters in human history and eighteen of his Top Fifty "Deadliest Multicides" occurred in the twentieth century.[12] Apart from the death tolls of WWI, WWII, and Vietnam, that century produced forty million dead in China due to the will of Mao Zedong. Joseph Stalin's reign from 1928–1953 resulted in twenty million deaths, all deliberate. That was after ten million died in the Russian Civil War itself. Another ten million died at the beginning of the century in the war over the Congo Free State.

The Judeo-Christian view is that human nature has not changed since the Fall, though Christians believe the incarnation of Christ began the process of restoring human nature. The practical evidence of such restoration, however, is scant. We think ourselves more civilized than previous epochs, even as we descend into paganism that denies such basic scientific facts as the genetic origins of male and female differences. We hold in our hands technological devices that make us feel smart, hyper-aware, and in control of our lives, even as we find ways to ignore the silent genocide of legalized abortion. This human factor—what Christians refer to as "original sin"—is always present lurking under the patina of civilization. Entering the last century, the elite believed progress was inevitable, that the modern world promised enlightenment and peace. It was instead the era of the worst

---

[12]   Matthew White, *The Great Big Book of Horrible Things* (New York: W.W. Norton & Company, 2012), 528–29.

genocides in human history. A reassessment about how far we have progressed beyond "barbarism" is overdue.

Why should we assume the twenty-first century will be any better? We've already witnessed 9/11, mass atrocities, terrorism, wars, nuclear threats, bankrupt nations, the reemergence of authoritarianism in Russia, and the rise of an economically powerful China that retains its authoritarian government and has regional military ambitions. Meanwhile, the Middle East continues to stir into flames ancient hatreds, coming closer and closer to exploding into a world conflict. If you ask why I bring up twentieth-century atrocities, such as the fourteen million killed by Hitler and Stalin between 1933 and 1945, it is because I agree with historian Timothy D. Snyder, "Today there is widespread agreement that the mass killing of the twentieth century is of the greatest moral significance for the twenty-first."[13]

In the United States, social conflict is escalating, and sides have formed for battle over immigration, abortion, climate change, marriage, sexuality, and the Constitution itself. These conflicts are not confined to the public stage—they have become part of daily life.

The conflict is not merely global—it has been made very personal. For example, elementary school children are being treated as pawns in the battle. The educational establishment now dictates that certain values and attitudes must be impressed upon students. Thus, parents discover their children are being taught values opposed to their own, not only in public schools, but also in faith-based schools supposedly founded on religious orthodoxy.

---

13   Bloodlands, x.

Social media has made this battle everybody's business, accelerating the long march through the institutions into a sprint. Social "apps" occupy tens of millions of people every day as they scan their screens at all times and all places. With the rise of digital interaction, manners and basic kindness have been mostly forgotten. Online digital actors and "com-box warriors" act like drivers weaving and honking through traffic, not caring about their rudeness because they are anonymous. And then, there are those who proudly put their names next to their latest obscene diatribe.

Those who consider themselves "well brought up" are faced with a dilemma: Their attempts to engage these debates by taking the "high road" are met with scorn. Gentlefolk find out that manners get in the way of engaging the enemy on social media. What to do? Many have given up on having an intelligent conversation about differences. Some have capitulated by adopting the tactics of the TV bully— name-calling, moral outrage, and verbal battery.

Does education make a difference? I have observed in myself a tendency *not to see* aspects of a work of art that directly challenge my deepest convictions and inclinations. Perhaps a better way of putting it is that I came to notice that I was scanning for agreement, leaning away from what I didn't want to see. When I first read Kurtz's lament, "The horror, the horror," I didn't get it. The same thing happened when I saw Francis Ford Coppola's masterpiece *Apocalypse Now*, based upon the Conrad novel, when Marlon Brando as Kurtz uttered Kurtz's line.[14] In both instances, I couldn't

---

14   Francis Ford Coppola's *Apocalypse Now* was released in 1979. Roger
       Ebert writes, "'Apocalypse Now' is the best Vietnam film, one of

fathom the "heart of darkness" because at the time it didn't mesh with my understanding of human nature. I had known since I was a boy about the fall of Adam and Eve but had not yet fully appropriated its meaning. "The horror" took on meaning later as I grew older and realized my resistance was rooted in a lack of self-understanding.

The Flowers of Evil

Charles Baudelaire (1821–1867) was, according to T. S. Eliot, the greatest Christian poet since Dante.[15] The French poet's life, however, would not withstand the scrutiny of a Christian moralist, nor would much of his poetry, wherein sinners far outnumber saints. It is for this very reason that moral thinkers seldom appreciate the spirituality of poets. In the case of Baudelaire, his book of collected works, which he called *The Flowers of Evil*, begins with a poem, "To The Reader," which reverses the first impression given by the title. Far from glorifying evil, the poet is holding up a mirror to the reader. It begins:

> Folly and error, avarice and vice,
> Employ our souls and waste our bodies' force.
> As mangey beggars incubate their lice,
> We nourish our innocuous remorse.

---

the greatest of all films, because it pushes beyond the others, into the dark places of the soul. It is not about war so much as about how war reveals truths we would be happy never to discover." Roger Ebert, "Apocalypse Now," November 28, 1998, https://www.rogerebert.com/reviews/great-movie-apocalypse-now-1979.

[15]   T. S. Eliot, "Baudelaire," *Selected Essays*, trans. Roy Campbell, (New York: Harcourt, Brace, & World, 1964), 373.

Our sins are stubborn, craven our repentance.
For our weak vows we ask excessive prices.

Anyone looking for cheap thrills has come to the wrong place—Baudelaire is addressing the reader below his surface pretensions, behind the face he presents to the world, beyond the lies he tells himself about being a "good person." The poet does not let up, does not pull his punch; his reader who hides behind his tears, in fact, is in league with the devil:

Trusting our tears will wash away the sentence,
We sneak off where the muddy road entices.
Cradled in evil, that Thrice-Great Magician,
The Devil, rocks our souls, that can't resist;
And the rich metal of our own volition
Is vaporised by that sage alchemist.

This might appear to some readers as a kind of violent relativism, a way of saying, "I'm so bad that you must be too!" Looking at the passage closely, one sees Baudelaire's Augustinian frankness about the weakness of human will. To whom, precisely, is he speaking, even if the poem is addressed "to the reader?" And those who think the poet is merely rhapsodizing metaphorically about the Evil One only need to read on:

The Devil pulls the strings by which we're worked:
By all revolting objects lured, we slink
Hellwards; each day down one more step we're jerked
Feeling no horror, through the shades that stink.
Just as a lustful pauper bites and kisses

The scarred and shriveled breast of an old whore,
We steal, along the roadside, furtive blisses,
Squeezing them, like stale oranges, for more.

Lusting for a "shriveled breast" is compared to forcing juice from "stale oranges"—why does the reader keep reading this poem? Why not throw the book against the wall? The reader doesn't because he recognizes the truth in the poet's portrayal. There is another dimension to our being, something supposedly hidden:

Packed tight, like hives of maggots, thickly seething
Within our brains a host of demons surges.
Deep down into our lungs at every breathing,
Death flows, an unseen river, moaning dirges.
If rape or arson, poison, or the knife
Has wove no pleasing patterns in the stuff
Of this drab canvas we accept as life —
It is because we are not bold enough!

Yes, the reader has had violent urges, impulses to break rules, void laws, and live immorally. The poet incites the reader who is wondering to himself, "Am I as bad as all that?" That is what the poet hopes his words will elicit. But then Baudelaire surprises the reader: even worse than all this wretchedness there is an evil that would "swallow up existence with a yawn."

Amongst the jackals, leopards, mongrels, apes,
Snakes, scorpions, vultures, that with hellish din,
Squeal, roar, writhe, gambol, crawl, with monstrous shapes,

In each man's foul menagerie of sin —
There's one more damned than all. He never gambols,
Nor crawls, nor roars, but, from the rest withdrawn,
Gladly of this whole earth would make a shambles
And swallow up existence with a yawn . . .
Boredom! He smokes his hookah, while he dreams
Of gibbets, weeping tears he cannot smother.
You know this dainty monster, too, it seems —
Hypocrite reader! — You! — My twin! — My brother![16]

There are two surprises in the final lines of this poem. The reader neither anticipates that "Boredom" be at the root of the moral uproar nor does he expect the fraternal embrace of the poet:

Hypocrite reader! — You! — My twin! — My brother!

The poet does not speak *ex-cathedra* as a pope, but as a person who shares fully, perhaps more, in the reader's sinfulness. But this accusatory poem adds a kind of creedal context for all that follows. The writer and reader inhabit the same circle of hell, so to speak. Whatever is said about barbarians, despots, or frauds, none of us can assume that we live on a higher moral ground. In the end, we want to see and that includes seeing ourselves.

---

[16] Roy Campbell, *Poems of Baudelaire* (New York: Pantheon Books, 1952). Read it here: https://lyricstranslate.com/en/au-lecteur-reader.html-0.

Straw Dogs

Philosopher John Gray uses the evocative descriptive "Straw Dogs" to stand for the failure of education to create a better, more moral, society.[17] "Anyone who looks to classical liberal thinkers to deliver the West from its present difficulties is fixated on an irretrievable past."[18] Humans, Gray argues, are not that much different from other animals. He reports that humans now are less well-off nutritionally than in the Stone Age.[19] The prevalent belief in human progress is a myth—history only tells the same story again and again. Living freely in a nation ordered by the rule of law is what Gray calls "liberalism" (which has nothing to do with the contemporary use of the word in a political context). What he means is that our present way of life will someday be regarded as only one era in world history, an era created by monotheistic belief, the Ten Commandments, and the Sermon on the Mount. Enlightenment philosophers tried to find a non-religious basis for morality for an increasingly secular world, but since then liberal values have slowly lost their hold in Western nations. With full knowledge of the carnage of the last one hundred years, Gray remarks darkly,

---

[17]   "In ancient Chinese rituals, straw dogs were used as offerings to the gods. During the ritual they were treated with the utmost respect. When it was over and they were no longer needed they were trampled on and tossed aside. . . . If humans disturb the balance of the Earth they will be trampled upon and tossed aside." John Gray, *Straw Dogs: Thoughts on Humans and Other Animals* (New York: Farrar, Straus & Giroux, 2007), 33–34.

[18]   John Gray, "Deluded liberals can't keep clinging to a dead idea," *Unherd*, October 3, 2018, https://unherd.com/2018/10/deluded-liberals-cant-keep-clinging-dead-idea/.

[19]   *Straw Dogs*, 157.

"We may well look back on the twentieth century as a time of peace."[20] Empires never last forever.

Given the reality of a declining civilization, Gray suggests that education should serve contemplation, a more modest goal than a search for absolutes: "Simply to see" should be the task.[21] I have faced this argument before. As a young man, I had assumed a sound education was necessary to establish moral character and continue to build our civilization. Then, in graduate school, I read an essay, "To Civilize Our Gentlemen," by literary scholar George Steiner, which has haunted me ever since.[22] Steiner points out that the Nazis' SS officers were products of the German gymnasium, arguably one of the most rigorous educational systems in the world, liberal education *par excellence*. Noting the apparent contradiction, Steiner poses the question, "We must surely ask ourselves: are the humanities humane and, if so, why did they fail before the Holocaust?"[23] Steiner, one of the most learned men of our time, further asks "whether the study and delight a man takes in Shakespeare makes him any less capable of organizing a concentration camp."[24]

The ovens of Auschwitz were designed and often administered by highly educated men who read Goethe and listened to Bach in the evening after their day's work. Highly educated men and women have committed some of history's greatest crimes. It would not be difficult to compile a long

---

[20]   Ibid., 181–82.
[21]   Ibid., 199.
[22]   George Steiner, "To Civilize our Gentlemen," *The George Steiner Reader* (New York: Oxford University Press, 1984), 25–36.
[23]   Ibid., 35.
[24]   Ibid.

list of men and women who read the ancients in both Greek and Latin but became traitors, sadists, torturers, thieves, and murderers. Both Lenin and Stalin had classical educations. Lenin studied as the son of a school inspector, and Stalin, who was particularly fond of Victor Hugo, learned at the hands of the Jesuits.[25]

That it came to be that so many exquisitely educated men and woman collaborated in the Holocaust willingly, even enthusiastically, needs to be kept at the back of one's mind.

In spite of this, Steiner has resisted the path taken by many contemporary intellectuals, who have opted for the postmodern view that behind any claims to a hierarchy of values stands a willing oppressor. In his recent appeal to affirm a meaning that transcends the relativism of cultural boundaries and interpretative standpoints, Steiner holds fast to the Enlightenment principle that meaningful communication about existence is possible in the first place: "I am wagering, both in a Cartesian and a Pascalian vein, on the informing pressure of a real presence in the semantic markers."[26] Steiner uses the phrase "real presence" to borrow from the Catholic meaning of Christ's presence in the Eucharist. Steiner's wager, as he puts it, is that language possesses meaning.

Without a language of "real presence," as Steiner puts it, basic moral and ethical claims lose their ontological (essential reality) basis and become pragmatic (a matter of mere

---

25   Daniel Kalden, *Dictator Literature: A History of Despots Through Their Writings* (London: Oneworld Publications, 2018), 4 (Lenin) and 40–43 (Stalin).

26   George Steiner, *Real Presences* (Chicago: The University of Chicago Press, 1989), 215.

choice). Unless there is a shared understanding of both reality itself and the reality of moral claims from which legitimate moral outrage springs, outrage against injustice or atrocity can be met with blithe dismissal: "mind your own business." More than Descartes or Pascal, Steiner is arguing in a Thomistic vein here. With Aquinas, following Aristotle, he is saying that there are truths about the human person that we ignore at our peril, truths underlying any moral argument.

Cooperation between nations cannot be realized without some philosophical agreement on human nature, even if it only amounts to a practical consensus on a list of human rights. Such an approach to cross-cultural dialogue and organization has become necessary to excise the deepening skepticism about a universal human nature which has developed since the eighteenth and nineteenth centuries. During this period of "progress" beyond "antiquated" views of a universal human nature, we have seen the greatest genocides of history. Now, human nature is denied, and a person is reduced to his race, sex, ethnicity, and cultural context. With the rise of nationalism, dictator-led nations sought to justify their desire for domination by distinguishing themselves as a people [*Volk*] from the less-human. From the barbarians.

What makes education in the classics so important if it does not make us better persons? The answers are relatively simple and, I think, persuasive: First, we should recast the question with the proper qualification: An education in the classics *does not by itself guarantee* the possession of virtue and sound judgment. For the one who would engage the culture and pass authentic culture to the next generation, the study of the classics is essential. That said, this kind of education is *necessary, but not sufficient*, to defeat the destructive ideas of this or any age.

Second, classical education is also invaluable for freeing one's mind from the prejudices of an age or ideology. Without freedom of mind, thinking remains servile, force-fed by whatever messages are shaping a person's thoughts and stimulating their passions. For the most part, persons don't think for themselves—their thoughts depend on the thoughts of others, they take on the passions of the moment, they become, what Søren Kierkegaard called, part of the "crowd."[27]

Third, virtue cannot be downloaded, to use a modern metaphor. Every individual who consistently chooses to act rightly will develop the virtues. What a virtue *is* can be taught by studying classics, but I don't see much evidence that knowing them, or any moral system, necessarily leads to a virtuous life.

If we follow John Gray, a study of the classics enables one *to see*. And, it could be argued in turn, in *seeing*, the rationale for the virtues become apparent, and a model can take shape in the mind. When we see various kinds of lives, we are presented with choices, whether to prefer one kind of life over another. We also have the choice of doing nothing.

---

[27]   Kierkegaard describes the crowd as being only an abstraction and that "it does not take long before this abstraction becomes God." Søren Kierkegaard, *The Sickness Unto Death: A Christian Psychological Exposition for Upbuilding and Awakening* trans. Howard V. Hong and Edna H. Hong (Princeton: Princeton University Press, 1980), 118.

The vices, too, are met throughout literature, film, TV, and other media. In our post-truth world, what have been traditionally regarded as vices go largely unrecognized. I qualify this observation for the following reason; lust, avarice, and, to some extent, gluttony are recognized, but those more easily hidden—sloth, wrath, envy, and pride—roam our world freely. Another possible aspiration arises, and it's perverse. The classics as a whole portray human acts in a morally ordered world but one subject to tragedy. In other words, bad things happen to good people. Alternately, good fortune comes to those who are undeserving. But we at least *know* who they are. The classics introduce us to different ways of life, but they remain grounded to the same classical Western worldview given birth by the historical meeting of Christianity with Greece and Rome.

So what can we say about the benefit of education in the classics? One outcome, at least, is plausible—freedom of mind. Those who possess freedom of mind are not servile. But freedom of mind requires the world be fundamentally *intelligible*, which, as we have seen, is denied by the dominant form of philosophy, postmodernism.

PART 3

Goodness: Love Is the Crux

CHAPTER 13

Parental Love

W hen I first read *The Four Loves* by C. S. Lewis, I was amazed by what seemed Lewis's effortless wisdom found on every page. One of the most respected medieval and Renaissance scholars of his age, Lewis wore his learning lightly. He had the unique gift of writing the mind-grabbing essay, which, in the space of twenty-odd pages, could leave the reader astounded.

He first read the essays in *The Four Loves* on 1958 BBC radio broadcasts.[1] The book itself was first published in 1960 and since then has rightly become regarded as a classic. The only twentieth-century books about love I would place beside it on my bookshelf are by Josef Pieper, Denis de Rougemont, Jean Guitton, Dietrich von Hildebrand, and Hans Urs von Balthasar.[2]

Lewis takes his framework for the four loves from the ancient Greeks: Storge (love between parent and child), Philia (friendship), Eros (desire), and Agape (charity, or divine love). The chapter that caught me most by surprise

---

[1] "Lewis on Love," *The Official Website of C. S. Lewis*, http://www.cslewis.com/lewis-on-love/.

[2] These are listed under "Recommended" at the end of the chapter.

was Storge—the natural affective connection between parents and their children. Before reading Lewis, I had never encountered a serious treatment of this type of love apart from commentaries on the birth of Christ.

He characterizes Storge as "the humblest and most widely diffused of loves, the love in which our experience seems to differ *least* from animal."[3] At first, I flinched at reading this but then remembered how fiercely, and to the death, both animal and human mothers fight for their children. Throughout the chapter, Lewis translates Storge as "affection, especially of parents to offspring," according to his Greek dictionary. Lewis can evoke the same feeling he writes about: "The image we must start with is that of a mother nursing her baby, a bitch or a cat with a basketful of puppies or kittens, all in a squealing, nuzzling heap together, purrings, lickings, baby-talk, milk, warmth, the smell of young life."[4]

Telemachus

Discussions of Storge understandably tend to focus on the love of mothers and their young children. The fierceness of Storge, however, cannot be limited to this clear manifestation of parental love.

Homer's *The Odyssey* contains a powerful depiction of Storge. When this perennial classic appears in modern culture, it is usually to recall the trials endured by King Odysseus upon his return to Ithaca (after the Trojan War and other

---

[3]   *Four Loves*, 42, emphasis added.
[4]   Ibid.

adventures), and the years of trials he was made to endure. The first three books of Homer's second epic (after *The Iliad*) are about Odysseus's son Telemachus, and Telemachus's love for both his father and his mother, Queen Penelope.

The Odyssey opens with an invocation of the Muse to sing of "the man of twists and turns driven time and time again off course." After complaining to Zeus about Odysseus's trial and his fate, the goddess Athena "fastened the supple sandals, ever-glowing gold, that wing her over the waves and boundless earth" to Ithaca, his kingdom (1:114–16). Telemachus is the first to notice her presence: "Greetings, stranger! Here in our house you'll find a royal welcome." She sits among the "swaggering suitors" (1:124) who, in the absence of the king and uncertainty about his fate, have taken control of the court and over the years have freely consumed the wealth and material resources of the royal family. Telemachus confides to the goddess in disguise his anger towards the men who "feed on another's goods and go scot-free" (1:187). Like everyone else, he doesn't know whether his father is alive or dead and asks the stranger for news of his father.

Athena tells him that Odysseus is not dead and tells of a prophecy that he will return soon. Still concealed, she says it is "Shameful!" that he has done nothing about the suitors, reminding him of how his father would have vanquished them. The powerful stranger advises Telemachus to fit out a boat and spend one year in search of his father: "You must not cling to your boyhood any longer—It's time you were a man" (1:341–42). A stung Telemachus knows the truth when he hears it, and immediately agrees.

He declares to his mother, "I hold the reins of power in this house" (1:414), which means he is going to become the man of the house and confront the suitors. The suitors shrug off his demand to leave and threaten Telemachus when he announces he is leaving to find his father. Ignoring their threats, Telemachus finalizes his plans to leave the next day. By now he has realized the stranger had been "the immortal goddess" (1:479). In less than twenty-four hours, the helpless son had taken on the bearing of his famous father:

> When young Dawn with her rose-fingers shone once more
> the true son of Odysseus sprang from bed and dressed,
> over his shoulder he slung his well-honed sword,
> fastened rawhide sandals under his smooth feet
> and stepped from his bedroom, handsome as a god. (2:1–5)[5]

Before leaving, he defends his mother Penelope against the suitors who blame her for their plundering, basically accusing her of being a tease. Telemachus tells the suitors his mother is not to blame for their shameful behavior, adding, "How can I drive my mother from our house, the one who bore me, reared me too?" (2:143–44). Here Telemachus, now a man, declares his Storge for his mother. Here the *man* vows to set sail in spite of the suitor's threats to stop him. Athena helps once again by putting them all into a deep sleep, allowing the ship to leave for the mainland of Greece without a fight.

---

[5]   Homer, *The Odyssey*, trans. Robert Fagles, Intro. Bernard Knox (New York: Penguin Books, 1996).

Telemachus, still in the company of the disguised Athena, first visits King Nestor, one of the wisest and bravest of the soldiers who fought at Troy alongside Odysseus. He learns how Nestor arrived home safely but little about his father's fate. Nestor urges him to visit their foe, King Menelaus of Sparta: "Press him yourself to tell the whole truth" (3:168). When Telemachus arrives, he finds Menelaus and Helen are reconciled after the years of fighting recounted in *The Iliad*. He addresses the royal couple about his father: "More than all other men, that man was born for pain. / Don't soften a thing, from pity, respect for me—tell me, clearly, all your eyes have witnessed" (4:365–66). The son has learned that Storge requires him to endure any suffering necessary to find his father and free his mother.

This moment illustrates what Lewis says about Storge as a combination of "need-love" and "gift-love." The former is love motivated by the self's need, the latter a love freely given by the self toward others and God. In the case of Telemachus, his love for his parents contained all the needs of a baby growing to adulthood, including, as we have seen, reaching maturity. His gift-love expands far beyond the affection of embraces and becomes a firm resolve to save both their lives.

Storge, as it appears in the *Odyssey*, highlights an aspect of parental love that Lewis struggles to explain; namely, how a mother needs the love of her child: "The Need and the Need-love of the young is obvious; so is the Gift-love of the mother. She gives birth, gives suck, gives protection. On the other hand, she must give birth or die. She must give suck or suffer. That way, her Affection too is a Need-love. There is the paradox. It is a Gift-love but it needs to be needed."[6]

As I reread Lewis, I noticed how his word for parental love, *affection*, can be construed so broadly; it's not quite adequate to describe the love shared between parents and their children. Lewis spends much of this chapter talking about the affection that "extends far beyond the relation of mother and young."[7] When he returns to distortions of a mother's love, the word *affection* cannot do justice to what Lewis portrays in the character of "Mrs. Fidget." Poor Mrs. Fidget. Her death did not sadden her family but released them from custody. Lewis dissects the late Mrs. Fidget. It's not pretty to watch, but it's true. I'm sure readers are familiar with a mother who in the name of "living for her family" watched over them like a prison guard. "She always sat up to 'welcome' you home if you were out late at night; two or three in the morning, it made no odds; you would always find the frail, pale, weary face awaiting you, like a silent accusation."[8] Here's an example of the "need to be needed" becoming paramount, disconnected from the good of the child. Mrs. Fidget wants her children to remain dependent but is foiled by death.

Lewis does not limit need-love to selfishness, though, as he points out, it can become that. As a Christian apologist, he recognized human persons are born in need and remain so their entire lives. The need for friendship, the need for Divine love, is integral to our nature. Each arises out of the

---

6   *Four Loves*, 43.
7   Ibid.
8   Ibid.

most fundamental of all loves, our natural Eros, the desire that drives our journey, our search towards human fulfillment, what St. Thomas Aquinas called the natural desire for God.[9]

But at times Lewis seems on the edge of separating need-love from gift-love, making concern for the self always suspect. It is at moments like this that Lewis's Protestantism is manifest: the deep suspicion that fallen human nature cannot act benevolently without divine help.

In *Love's Sacred Order: The Four Loves Revisited*, Erasmo Leiva-Merikakis develops a more complete view of Storge than Lewis's framework allows. Leiva-Merikakis remarks that "in the beautiful order God established in nature, the family is the foundation of every other human relationship, including that between God and man."[10] He explicitly ties Storge to God's love, but that connection falls under the principle articulated by St. Thomas Aquinas, "Grace does not destroy nature but perfects it."[11] This point about grace has been a sticking point between Catholic and Protestants since the Reformation, the true relation between the natural and the supernatural order in a single reality. As Leiva-Merikakis puts it, regarding Storge, "[The] heavenly Father does not supplant but builds upon the experience of an earthly father's and mother's love for their child."[12]

---

[9]   *Summa contra gentiles* III.I.48, 162–67.

[10]   Erasmo Leiva-Merikakis, *Love's Sacred Order: The Four Loves Revisited* (San Francisco: Ignatius Press), 50.

[11]   *Summa Theologica* I.1.8.

[12]   *Love's Sacred Order,* 51.

As a theologian, Leiva-Merikakis uses Scripture to support his argument, finding Storge and Philia conjoined in the word *Philostorgoi*. In the twelfth chapter, verse 10, of his Letter to the Romans, St. Paul is, according to Leiva-Merikakis, "straining his Greek" to describe the unique quality of Christian love.[13] On this view, God's grace is bringing the human loves towards perfection *in their own order*. In other words, "the more it divinizes, the more it humanizes."[14]

That a person's perfection in grace is described as being fully human has enormous consequences for depictions of the Christian life in the arts and humanities. It means an artist or philosopher can follow the growth of persons *as human*, not as a supernatural add-on. The problem with many attempts at creating a specifically Christian art is the artist cannot be content with telling a story—he insists on telling the moral as well. Any work of art, like every human person, must be treated as an end-in-itself, not turned into a megaphone for evangelization. Preaching ruins art and dries the deep wells of beauty.

Siegfried Idyll

Richard Wagner was an awful man and a virulent anti-Semite. He treated his friends terribly; his wife Cosima had been the wife of his friend and the most important conductor of Wagner's music, Hans von Bulow. That von Bulow acquiesced and allowed Wagner to take Cosima as his mistress and future wife makes the betrayal no less cruel. Indeed, the

---

13   Ibid., 56.
14   Ibid., 57.

composer was so accommodating that he adopted the first of their illegitimate children, Isolde. Cosima herself was the third illegitimate child of the pianist and composer Franz Liszt, who eventually became a close friend of Wagner.

As is often the case, an artist's creations are better than their creator. Despite his narcissism and betrayals, Wagner's *Siegfried Idyll* remains one of the most direct expressions of Storge in music. Composed for his wife's thirty-third birthday, *Siegfried Idyll* was first performed by fifteen musicians on Christmas Eve on the stairway under her bedroom at Tribschen, their villa home outside Lucerne overlooking the Vierwaldstattersee (Four Cantons Lake). The work's pure beauty puzzles listeners familiar with the composer's life and wretched personality. As music critic Anthony Tommasini comments, "How did such sublime music come from such a warped man? Maybe art really does have the power to ferret out the best in us."[15]

But what if it wasn't art that inspired Wagner? What if it was the love for his newborn combined with his passion for Cosima? Due to financial problems, Richard and Cosima had agreed not to exchange gifts that Christmas in 1870. Their first four years at Tribschen had been happy ones. Their Siegfried, nicknamed "Fidi," their third and last child, had been born at Tribschen on June 6 of the previous year. All the Wagner children, including Isolde (1865) and Eva (1867), were born out of wedlock—their parents didn't marry until August 25, 1870, the year our story begins.

---

[15]   Anthony Tommasini, "Richard Wagner, Musical Mensch," *New York Times*, April 10, 2005.

On Christmas morning, Cosima was awakened by the sound of music from outside her bedroom door. As she writes in her diary:

> *Sunday, December 25, 1870* When I woke up I heard a sound, it grew even louder, I could no longer imagine myself in a dream, music was sounding, and what music! After it had died away, R. came in to me with the five children and put into my hands the score of his "Symphonic Birthday Greeting." I was in tears, but so, too, was the whole household; R. had set up his orchestra on the stairs and thus consecrated our Tribschen forever![16]

Opening the door, Cosima saw the musicians from the Zurich Tonhalle Orchestra arranged on the staircase and her husband, baton in hand, conducting the beautiful piece of music she had never heard, which came to be known as *Siegfried Idyll*. Lasting about twenty minutes, *Siegfried Idyll* was always intended to be a private composition for his beloved. Wagner had been prompted to compose the work immediately after his son's birth, making use of an unpublished string quartet and leitmotifs from his then-forthcoming (and renowned) *Ring* cycle.

Its melody came from the sound of a bird who sang in the morning as the sun made its appearance. Siegfried was born at four, while the bird started singing at three thirty. "It was

---

[16]   See the program notes by Phillip Huscher, "Richard Wagner - Siegfried Idyll," https://cso.org/uploadedFiles/1_Tickets_and_Events/Program_Notes/ProgramNotes_Wagner_SiegfriedIdyll.pdf.

Siegfried's bird, which had announced his arrival and now came to inquire after him," said Wagner.[17]

Though composed for only fifteen players, *Siegfried Idyll* can pack a punch. Music historian Robert Philip describes it as a "symphonic poem for chamber orchestra."[18] Recorded performances vary a great deal, depending on the conductor's interpretation: some want to treat it as a chamber piece for a smaller group, others want to release its fullest sonorities.

Even on first hearing of *Siegfried Idyll*, one grasps Wagner's ecstatic intention.[19] Beginning with a rocking theme in its opening bars, we hear bird songs scattered throughout, and the use of a German lullaby midway through the piece. There is also a "slumber" motif borrowed from his *Ring* opera cycle, *Die Walkurie*, and a woodwind theme, a variation of the earlier rocking theme, taken from the opera *Siegfried*, "O Siegfried, Herrlich! Hort der Welt!" ("O Siegfried glorious one. Treasure of the world").[20] The structure of *Siegfried Idyll* can be heard clearly in legendary pianist Glenn Gould's transcription, who recorded it shortly before his death in 1982.[21]

Wagner's tribute to his son and wife is tender, gentle, soothing, and, finally, peaceful. It's the creation of a man who truly earned his ghastly reputation. Still, faced with a

---

[17]   https://web.archive.org/web/20071211050734/, http://francisba rnhart.com/projects/siegfried-idyll/.

[18]   *Classical Music Lover's Companion*, 882.

[19]   I recommend the recording made by Herbert von Karajan with the Vienna Philharmonic in 1988: https://www.youtube.com/ watch?v=f0QsSCPoa0w.

[20]   Ibid., 883.

[21]   Audio of Gould playing his transcription of *Siegfried Idyll* can be found here: https://www.youtube.com/watch?v=FIjesjmMq_g.

newborn son and a wife with whom he was madly in love, his natural love for his child emerges and is beautifully expressed in music.

Autumn Sonata

Many films, both good and great, strip the veneer away from family life. One that comes immediately to mind is the painfully honest film *Ordinary People* (1980), the first film directed by Robert Redford. Mary Tyler Moore's depiction of the grieving, angry mother, Beth, was mind-blowing given her reputation as a comedian. The trigger of *Ordinary People* is the death of Buck, the eldest son, who is killed in a boating accident, while his younger brother, Conrad, survives the event. Beth's preference for Buck over her younger son Conrad disables her from consoling him, exacerbating his guilt, which leads to his attempted suicide. Beth's inability to recognize anyone else's point of view, or empathize with the suffering of her husband and son, causes her to leave altogether.

Ingmar Bergman reveals family suffering at an even deeper level in *Autumn Sonata* (1978). Seeing it for the first time left me emotionally shattered. Subsequent viewings have not softened the blow. It is the kind of film, I suspect, many would find "depressing" and turn it off. Bergman's achievement as screenwriter and director in *Autumn Sonata,* however, is to uncover the subterranean lava flow of childhood memories that remain red hot below the encrusted surface.

The entire movie, except for a few exterior shots, takes place within the home of Viktor (Halvar Björk), the village pastor, and his wife, Eva (Liv Uhlmann), who plays the organ at church and the piano at home for pleasure. Eva sends a letter of invitation to her mother, Charlotte (Ingrid Bergman), a famous concert pianist whom she has not seen for seven years. Given her mother's constant traveling and performing, Eva and Viktor are surprised when she accepts their invitation to visit. Also living at the parsonage is Eva's young sister, Helena (Lena Nyman), who since birth has suffered from a disability that keeps her in a wheelchair and a bed. Unwilling to care for her, Charlotte placed Helena in an institution and in the years following never visited. Two years before the invitation to Charlotte, however, Eva and Viktor had brought Helena home from the hospital to live with them. In the invitation letter, Eva did not tell Charlotte that Helena would also be there.

In the opening shot of the film, we see into a room where Eva is writing the invitation to her mother. Viktor turns and addresses the camera directly, telling us about his marriage and his wife's difficulty accepting love: "Cannot find the right words to tell her she is loved wholeheartedly." Although he doesn't say so, he lets us know we're headed for stormy seas if Charlotte accepts. He knows that Eva wants to reconcile with her mother, but that it will not happen: Eva has invited pain and trouble. He doesn't seem surprised when, listening from the top of the stairs, mother and daughter square off in a lengthy quarrel which exposes Eva's raging hate of her mother and the mother's icy hatred of her daughter.

Typical of Bergman's mastery at portraying the subtlety of mother-daughter relationship is a scene in which Charlotte realizes after arriving that she has only been talking about herself and had not asked her daughter about her life. When Charlotte asks, Eva replies that she recently did an organ recital for the village children. Her mother's quick reply is breathtaking in its callousness: "Yes, I just played five concerts in LA with three thousand children at each concert." Eva is understandably hurt but chooses that moment to tell her mother that Helena lives with them. "You should have told me!" Charlotte barks, but Eva reminds her that she was told in a letter sent two years ago. Charlotte, it is clear, had never read it: her face turns ugly and she excuses herself, "I had no choice, some people are so naïve."

"Me?" Eva asks. "If the shoe fits," comes the angry reply.

Charlotte wants to see Helena right away, apparently to get the unpleasantness over as quickly as possible. The mother does her best to show affection for the child she has not seen in twenty years since she was sent to live at a "home." Helena is overjoyed, reaching out for her mother: "Mama! Mama!" She shows more joy and recognition than her mother shows her. Helena's jubilation causes her physical pain as Eva explains that her sister wants to be touched. It's Charlotte who seems to be in pain bending over to touch Helena. She asks her daughter if she is in pain. "No," Helena replies. At what should be a tender moment, Charlotte looks down at her daughter's wrist and seeing no watch, takes hers off, and puts it on her daughter's arm. Standing up, Charlotte's face has the look of a debt having been paid, as if the gift of an expensive watch absolves her of all shame regarding Helena. Eva is astonished at her mother's pretense.

This is Storge twisted into innumerable knots, undoing one of which only leads to the next; they never seem to end, nor do they. In C. S. Lewis's terms, one could say that Charlotte gave birth to two children, but without being touched by the miracle of birth, the gift of life she has given, or her daughters' subsequent need for love. Charlotte's detachment makes her look hollow and unnatural; the only affection she feels is towards her manager, past lovers, and, most of all, her memories of performing.

Film scholar Farran Smith Nehme comments that in *Autumn Sonata*, Bergman's last theatrical film, "With Charlotte, Ingmar Bergman got the fully human and ultimately tragic monster that he wanted."[22] I'm not sure "fully human" is the best way to express what I think Nehme means to say. Since 1936 when she made her American debut in *Intermezzo*, Ingrid Bergman performed magnificently in all film genres, no role seemed to be beyond her range. But except for some films made in the 1950s with director Jean Renoir and her husband Roberto Rossellini, Bergman's characters, even her Joan of Arc, shone with the patina of Hollywood glamour. In *Autumn Sonata*, Bergman left Hollywood far behind. Her Charlotte seems more "fully human" in the sense that the dark complexity of her inner life is revealed on the screen. Her virtual nakedness shocks us because nothing is left hidden and all her secrets are exposed. Yes, Charlotte is a kind of moral monster, but writer and director Ingmar Bergman does not condemn her. Instead, his direction evokes our feelings of sympathy for a self-absorbed woman whose cruelty has deeply scarred the lives of her two daughters.

---

[22]   Ibid., 199.

The Bicycle Thieves

Film critic Jonathan Rosenbaum captures what I believe is the essence of the great film *The Bicycle Thieves* (1948), directed by Vittorio de Sica: "This is possibly the greatest depiction of a relationship between a father and son in the history of cinema, and it's an awesome heartbreaker. If you set it alongside something like [the successful 1997 Italian film] *Life Is Beautiful* you get some notion of how much mainstream world cinema and its relation to reality have been infantilized over the past half century."[23]

De Sica's masterpiece has been highly prized since its release, being awarded an Oscar for Best Foreign Film in 1949. In 1952, when Sight & Sound published its first poll of filmmakers, *The Bicycle Thieves* ranked first[24] and has remained in the top fifty ever since. In 2014, film critic J. Hoberman called it "surely the most universally praised movie produced anywhere on planet earth."[25] It tells a simple story of a family dealing with poverty in post-World War II Italy. De Sica uses non-actors in a technique which became known as neorealism, a label used to describe many of the major Italian films from the late forties and early fifties. These are films stripped of all cinematic glamour. They display all the impoverishment of life in bombed-out Italian

---

[23]   Jonathan Rosenbaum, "The Bicycle Thief," *Chicago Reader*, March 1, 1999, https://www.jonathanrosenbaum.net/2017/06/the-bicycle-thief-2/.

[24]   Roger Ebert, "Bicycle Thieves," March 19, 1999, https://www.rogerebert.com/reviews/great-movie-the-bicycle-thief--bicycle-thieves-1949.

[25]   Kenneth Turan, *Not To Be Missed: Fifty-Four Favorites From a Lifetime of Film* (New York: Public Affairs, 2014), 100.

cities, with people living under the Nazi occupation and amidst the rubble of what was left behind.

These are films about survival. In Roberto Rossellini's *Rome, Open City* (1945), the image of a mother (Anna Magnani) who runs down the street to retrieve her son from a Nazi truck, once seen, is unforgettable and has deservedly become iconic in the history of film. Eric Rhode sees De Sica's neorealist classics, such as *Umberto D* (1952), *Miracle in Milan* (1951), and *Shoeshine* (1946) as "someone hungering for love in a loveless world."[26]

The Bicycle Thieves pits the love of family, particularly the love shared by the father and the son, against the backdrop of a world that doesn't give a damn. Shooting on the streets of Rome, De Sica also creates images that stay with you long after seeing them. This is not a film that can be summarized by quoting important dialogue; it's all told visually, reminiscent of the silent movies.

The plot is simple: the father, Antonio Ricci (Lamberto Maggiorani), needs a job. Maggorini is quite handsome in a classically Italian way, but his handsomeness doesn't distance the viewer because it exudes kindness. Out of work for two years, he stands in line day after day until his name is finally called, and he is offered a job putting up posters along the streets. He needs a bicycle, however, which he doesn't own, but takes the job promising to get one. His young son Bruno (Enzo Staiola) stays close to his father, watching him with eyes filled with love, a look which his father returns again and again. Kenneth Turan describes Staiola, whose

---

[26]   *A History of Cinema*, 443.

parents were owners of a vegetable cart in Rome, as having "one of the most expressive childhood faces in the history of cinema."[27]

The viewer can feel the love that binds them. Without telling her husband, his wife, Maria (Lianella Carell), takes her dowry of fine linen to the pawn shop and returns with the money for the bicycle. Antonio buys the bike, but on the first day of work, it is stolen while he is on a ladder putting up a poster of a Rita Hayworth movie, *Gilda*. He pursues the thief, who evades him with the help of partners who send him the wrong direction. Together with Bruno, the father continues to search but is humiliated in front of his son by a crowd who sourly turns on him when he apprehends the thief. Bruno's heart, if not broken, is severely bruised. His father is ashamed for what he sees in his son's eyes. This brings Antonio close to panic, and he tells Bruno to leave; he will meet his son later. The father has seen an unattended bicycle and plans to steal it. It is a shock to the viewer that such a good man would take such a step. Good men, after all, make bad thieves, and Antonio is caught immediately by the police, while Bruno looks on. The owner notices Bruno standing near and asks the police to release the father.

This unexpected moment of kindness from a stranger contrasts sharply with the indifference of his employer and the ill-treatment Antonio has received on the streets. Now free, Antonio looks at his son and begins to weep. The son takes his hand, and they walk away from the camera, mixing into a crowd. Was this merely a stroke of good fortune, a

---

[27]   *Not To Be Missed*, 103.

matter of luck? Or did the face of Bruno convey a message, like a sudden light that bursts through a typical street scene in a large city? The bicycle owner only glances, not hesitating a moment to tell the police to let the father go. The love shared between parents and children creates a lot of wattage.

When a love this powerful faces death, all systems go down. In "Special Treatments Ward,"[28] the poet Dana Gioia depicts the nightmare of every parent, facing the death of a child. When a child dies, it's an event that is met with something close to wordlessness. Gioia, who lost a young child himself, puts words to the unimaginable grief. As a reader, I almost expect it can't be done. But the poet finds the words and more.

Special Treatments Ward

I

So this is where the children come to die,
hidden on the hospital's highest floor.
They wear their bandages like uniforms
and pull their IV rigs along the hall
with slow and careful steps. Or bald and pale,
they lie in bright pajamas on their beds,
watching another world on a screen.

The mothers spend their nights inside the ward,
sleeping on chairs that fold out into beds,
too small to lie in comfort. Soon they slip
beside their children, as if they might mesh

---

[28] Dana Gioia, *99 Poems: New & Selected*, reprint edition (Port Townsend, WA: Graywolf Press, 2017), 69–71.

those small bruised bodies back into their flesh.
Instinctively they feel that love so strong
protects a child. Each morning proves them wrong.

No one chooses to be here. We play the parts
that we are given—horrible as they are.
We try to play them well, whatever that means.
We need to talk, though talking breaks our hearts.
The doctors come and go like oracles,
their manner cool, omniscient, and oblique.
There is a word that no one ever speaks.

No parent or friend wants to be in the place "where the children come to die." The "Special Treatments Ward" is "hidden" away on the top floor: hidden perhaps because of an unconscious desire to protect the rest of the hospital from the rending grief of the parents and their children. It's an intensely private horror—the death of a beloved child. The parents who need to talk but are thwarted by the staff who stay in character. The doctors play out the conceit, they "come and go like oracles, / their manner cool, omniscient, and oblique." And to complete the pretense, the word *death* is never uttered. But death is why everyone is here. The pretense is shattered by images of children in "bright pajamas" who "pull their IV rigs along the hall."

Rarely has the love of a mother for her child been depicted with such immediacy, "Instinctively they feel that love so strong / protects a child." Here is parental love at its most naked and vulnerable. Mothers sleep in chairs, never leaving. Each mother inevitably slips into the bed beside her sleeping child. She wants to give life again as she did before, "But, in the morning, all is in vain."

Twelve years pass before Gioia completes the last sections of the poem.

II

I put this poem aside twelve years ago
because I could not bear remembering
the faces it evoked, and every line
seemed—still seems—so inadequate and grim.

What right had I, whose son had walked away
to speak for those who died? And I'll admit
I wanted to forget. I'd lost one child
and couldn't bear to watch another die.

Not just the silent boy who shared our room,
but even the bird-thin figures dimly glimpsed
shuffling deliberately, disjointedly
like ancient soldiers after a parade.

Whatever strength the task required I lacked.
No well-stitched words could suture shut these wounds.
And so I stopped . . .
But there are poems we do not choose to write.

Gioia feels the burden of survival, "What right had I, whose son had walked away, / to speak for those who died?" But he cannot shake the memories of the boy who shared rooms with his own son and deathly-looking "bird-thin figures dimly glimpsed" walking the halls. He had doubted his ability to write this poem and knew his words would heal no one, "But there are poems we do not choose to write."

III

The children visit me, not just in dream,
appearing suddenly, silently—
insistent, unprovoked, unwelcome.

They've taken off their milky bandages
to show the raw, red lesions they still bear.
Risen they are healed but not made whole.

A few I recognize, untouched by years.
I cannot name them—their faces pale and gray
like ashes fallen from a distant fire.

What use am I to them, almost a stranger?
I cannot wake them from their satin beds.
Why do they seek me? They never speak.

And vagrant sorrow cannot bless the dead.

He still sees the children who passed away, "not just in dream." These are not nocturnal visions dimmed by the night; he sees "the raw, red lesions they still bear." They come to him "unprovoked, unwelcome" because there is nothing he can do for them; he sees they "are healed but not made whole." He cannot heal them: "What use am I to them." As a poet and father, one who has also lost a child, his "vagrant sorrow cannot bless the dead."

Storge is the human love closest to Agape. It's the most reliable, the most sacrificial, the most vulnerable. Unlike lovers and friends, parents and children know each other too well to get away with wearing a mask. No matter how old each becomes, there's an intuitive knowledge between them that cannot be fooled, the same happens between siblings who grew up together. It's a love that can be broken but never entirely severed. Between family members, their blood will cry out (Gn 4:10).

Recommended

Books

Sophocles, *Antigone*, 441 BC.
William Shakespeare, *King Lear*, 1623.
Jane Austen, *Sense and Sensibility*, 1811.
Mary Shelley, *Frankenstein*, 1818.
Gustave Flaubert, *Madame Bovary*, 1856.
Leo Tolstoy, *War and Peace*, 1867
Giovanni Verga, *The House by the Medlar Tree*, 1881.
Thomas Hardy, *The Mayor of Casterbridge*, 1886.
Junichiro Tanizaki, *The Makioka Sisters*, 1936.
Arthur Miller, *The Death of a Salesman*, 1949.
Jean Guitton, *Human Love*, 1951.
Eugene O'Neill, *Long Day's Journey Into Night*, 1956.
Han Urs von Balthasar, *Love Alone: The Way of Revelation, 1970.*
Joseph Pieper, *About Love*, 1974.
P. D. James, *The Children of Men*, 1992.

Music

G. W. F. Handel, *Messiah*, 1741.

Robert Schumann, *Kinderszenen*, 1838.
Hector Berlioz, *L'Enfance du Christ*, 1854.
Carl Nielsen, *Saul and David*, 1901.
Gustav Mahler, *Kindertotenlieder*, 1905,
Herbert Howells, *Hymnus Paradisi*, 1951.
George Rochberg, *Symphony No. 5*, 1986.

Film

Charlie Chaplin, *The Kid*, 1921.
Buster Keaton, *Steamboat Bill, Jr*, 1928.
King Vidor, *The Champ*, 1931.
Leo McCarey, *Make Way for Tomorrow*, 1937.
Yasujirō Ozu, *Late Spring*, 1949.
Yasujirō Ozu, *Tokyo Story*, 1953.
John Ford, *The Searchers*, 1956.
Ingmar Bergman, *Wild Strawberries*, 1957.
Piero Pasolini, *Moma Rosa*, 1962.
Francis Ford Coppola, *Godfather II*, 1974.
Robert Redford, *Ordinary People*, 1980.
Jean-Pierre and Luc Dardenne, *The Son*, 2002.

CHAPTER 14

Friendship

I read Aristotle's *Nicomachean Ethics* for the first time at the age of thirty. I wish I had read it much earlier. Aristotle would have saved me from much emotional twisting and turning over the loss of people who were significant to me.

Think of persons you thought were close friends in high school, college, or in places you lived or worked, but who have fallen out of your life. When you try to contact them, they respond tepidly, if at all. Friends, classmates, coworkers, neighbors, teammates—all people who shared significant parts of your life, with whom you could let down your guard and let yourself be seen—no longer feel any connection with you. It can be painful to find only apathy upon reaching out to one for whom you still have affection.

Nicomachean Ethics

Reading book 8 of the *Ethics*, I found a way of understanding these losses. Nearly four decades later, I still refer to Aristotle's description of the three types of friendship, based on what motives bring friends together.

The first type of friendship is based on usefulness, in which "the partners do not feel affection for one another per se but in terms of the good accruing to each other."[1] In other words, each finds advantages in knowing one another. The second type is also a form of mutual advantage, or utility, but is based upon "the pleasure they get out of it."[2]

This was my "Aha" moment: Since both usefulness and pleasure between two people can be lost, so can the friendship itself. How these are lost is the stuff of countless stories told in every age. But I've never read a novel or seen a film in which any character pulls Aristotle off the shelf and figures it out. Imagine a film where that happened: A woman tries to reconnect with her college roommate but receives only terse and cool replies. Frustrated and upset, she wonders whether they were ever friends. She doubts the authenticity of her fond memories of college and the character of her roommate. Then she spies Aristotle's *Ethics* on the bookshelf and remembers it contained something about friendship. She picks it up and starts reading book 8, following her own penciled markings and underlined passages. Then she sees a line she had put a checkmark beside: "The affection ceases as soon as one partner is no longer pleasant or useful to the other."[3]

I'm not a screenwriter, obviously, and have no idea where to go from here. I doubt she would send the passage to her roommate, but she might ask herself questions about the friendships that have lasted for years, appreciating them in a new way and perhaps more alert to the potential, or lack thereof, for other relationships.

---

[1]   *Nicomachean Ethics*, 1156a1013, 218.
[2]   Ibid., 1156a15. 220.
[3]   Ibid., 1156a20-21, 218-219.

The neighbor who moves away, the classmate who graduates, the teammate who gives up the sport, the coworker who changes jobs, the lover who dumps you for another, the friend who turns to heavy drinking and drugs, or the friend who simply gets married—very often these relationships lose their immediacy, distance and time set in, until there is nothing left but a memory. Aristotle's focus on the motives that create friendship led me into an inventory of all those I had grieved to lose, except now I understood the reason why. No one was to blame. It was not what I lacked, or they lacked, necessarily; it came down to circumstance, proximity, and chance.

Aristotle adds that it is typical of young people to form friendships based upon pleasure because their lives are guided by emotion: "Young people make and lose friendships within the same day."[4] What then is true friendship, according to Aristotle?

The perfect form of friendship is that between good men who are alike in excellence or virtue. For these friends wish alike for one another's good because they are good men, and their friendship is a good in itself.[5]

Aristotle is arguing that their goodness is something intrinsic, not incidental. Their friendship will endure. The philosopher does not, however, leave us thinking that such friendships consist of a dull mutual admiration society. True friends are both beneficial and pleasurable.[6] Their mutual usefulness and pleasure do not, however, imply the

---

4   Ibid., 1156b2-3, 219.
5   Ibid., 1156b7-10, 220.
6   Ibid., 1156b12-18, 220.

precariousness of lesser friendships, because the utility and pleasure are based upon the "actions of good men." Thus, what true friends have in common is what Aristotle calls excellence and virtue. Virtues are firm dispositions toward excellence, toward various sorts of action, such as seeking justice, thinking and judging prudently, facing danger head-on with courage, displaying temperance in the enjoyment of pleasure.

As excellent as the philosopher's account of friendship is, it still has flaws. On his account, true friendship could not happen between a man and a woman, since he considers women to be less rational. The female is a defective male, and, as Aristotle claims, just as animals are better off when trained by a human being: "Again, the male is by nature superior, and the female inferior; and the one rules, and the other is ruled."[7] Free women fare better than male slaves, however, as the latter have no rational ability at all.[8] Other barriers to true friendship include class, wealth, fortune, and reputation. Men whose lives differ markedly on any of these do not possess the equality which is the precondition for their virtues to meld into friendship.

Taking a step back from Aristotle's discussion of friendship, it remains to think further about what he gets right and what he does not. Even the best teachers are often limited by the time and place in which they live, as we find with the philosopher's uncritical acceptance of slavery and inequality of the sexes.

---

[7]   Aristotle, *Politics*, 1.4, 1254 b10-14, *The Basic Works of Aristotle*, 1132.

[8]   Ibid., I, 13, 1260a12-14, *The Basic Works of Aristotle*, 1144.

Symphony No. 9

Ludwig van Beethoven disliked individual men but loved the ideal of "universal friendship." Unburdened by humility, the great composer knew himself to be a genius and, isolated by deafness, didn't care much for the people around him, with few relationships that could be characterized as friendships. Yet, he dedicated his greatest work, one certainly among the greatest in music history, to the ideal of "All men becoming brothers." The lyric was taken from a poem by Friedrich Schiller, "An die Freude," or "Ode to Joy."

Beethoven was not alone in considering himself a genius. Early nineteenth-century Europe is characterized by a fascination, if not obsession, with the "greats"—Napoleon leading the way. The general populace wanted heroes and found them not only in generals but in artists and writers. Johann Wolfgang von Goethe (1749–1832) was the German genius of the literary world, while in England, George Gordon (Lord) Byron (1788–1824) may not have been the best writer, but he cut the most Romantic figure. Aristotle would have been at home in such a society where a specific class of men—necessarily men—were regarded as existing above the masses. But it's doubtful Aristotle would have placed the laurel wreath on the head of an artist, no matter how great. Artists, after all, did not contemplate; they made. Had the philosopher been at the premiere of the Ninth Symphony, however, he might have reconsidered the connection between contemplation and the creation of art.

New York Times music critic Anthony Tommasini argues that the gradual dimming of the prestige of classical music

among audiences makes it easier for us to approach Beethoven's "swaggering works" rather than treating them as
"messages from an oracle beamed down to concert halls."[9]
Nonetheless, the Ninth Symphony has a life of its own, as
seen when it is performed on such momentous occasions as
Leonard Bernstein's concert celebrating the fall of the Berlin
Wall.

In asking my readers to listen to Beethoven's Ninth, I realize it may already be very familiar, like Handel's *Messiah,*
which is perhaps seen as even more iconic by those generally
unfamiliar with the rest of the composer's music. However,
when listening to such well-known works, it is best to put
all expectations aside, especially questions about whether "I
will get this," and listen to the music naively as if hearing it
for the first time.[10] As the BBC music critic Robert Philip
puts it, "What you find, once you get to know the whole
symphony, is that it has a sense of inevitability in its progress, which arises from the way that Beethoven has related
the themes of the different movements. Once you spot this,
you find that the 'Ode to Joy,' when it finally arrives, is not
just a random tune plucked out of nowhere, but the logical
outcome of what has gone before."[11]

If Beethoven's listeners have followed with any attention
"what has gone before" the famous choral triumph in the

---

[9]   *Indispensable Composers,* 173.

[10]   A good place to do that is by watching a video of Bernstein's
       Berlin concert on Christmas Day, 1989 which is quite remarkable:
       https://www.youtube.com/watch?v=IInG5nY_wrU.

[11]   Robert Philip, *The Classical Music Lover's Companion to Orchestral
       Music* (New Haven: Yale University Press, 2018), 81.

final movement, they are in no danger of hearing it either as an add-on or a saccharine flourish of a stone-deaf and sickly eccentric composer. No, the miracle is that the climactic final movement reaches that level of idealization *in spite of all* that has come before in the first three movements. In these, the composer expresses a range of raw human emotions—fear, anger, longing—that defeat many. Yet he pushes on to the moment when the baritone enters on with the word *Freude* (Joy)!

As if to underscore the point of what must be overcome, the baritone sings, "Oh friends, *not these sounds!* Let us instead strike up more pleasing and more joyful ones!" In the few bars before he enters, the orchestra returns to the opening bars of the symphony, an "ominous sound"[12] as described by music scholar Harvey Sachs. He continues, "the rawness, hollowness, fragmentariness of the Ninth's opening bars, their amoral brutality or brutal amorality." Within the first movement are two musical themes that thrust and parry through the work. Robert Philip describes them as a struggle between the "jagged rumbling motif and the smooth rising and falling motif."[13] These jagged and smooth themes, evident to the one who listens for them, recur through the second and third movements.

This often dark, anxious, and turbulent first movement carries in it a reflection of the composer's misery, which he inflicted on others. Beethoven was a difficult man, rude to others, even those close to him, a failing which was

---

12   Ibid., 133.
13   Ibid.

aggravated by his deafness. As the years passed and his hearing worsened, he grew more and more isolated and irritated by any demands of sociality. Those who knew him did their best to be patient, realizing that the music flowing from Beethoven's pen was extraordinary.

The second movement, a scherzo, marked "very lively," is more confident and less encumbered by doubt about where the music is going. There are outbursts, as Sachs describes them, of menace, fury, and anger that dissolve into a gorgeous legato melody that "blend into a stunning, wordless, organ-like paean."[14] The sudden ending of the movement, however, reminds the listener that more, much more, is to come.

About the third movement, Sachs writes, "Nothing more beautiful than this movement has ever been written for the symphony orchestra."[15] One might close Sachs's book at this point, thinking his passion for his subject has gone too far and he has become, as it were, an unreliable guide. After all, isn't the great choral movement what everyone reveres so highly? But reconsidering the third movement's aching loveliness, one is tempted to sympathize with Sachs's summation: "A life could end beautifully as this movement diminishes tranquilly into nonexistence. Beethoven is at peace; the world is at peace."[16]

What comes next had never been heard in the history of music—a symphony with words, a text set to music for four soloists and a full chorus. It could be argued that of all the

---

[14]   Ibid., 143.
[15]   Ibid., 145.
[16]   Ibid., 149.

innovative breakthroughs in the piece, this is the greatest. But it would not be just for its innovative use of Schiller's text but for Beethoven's outrageous intention to change the world.

Why did Beethoven choose this particular text? As might be expected, there is far more behind this choice than the words themselves convey. Beethoven was twenty-four years old when Schiller published his best-known work, *Letters on the Aesthetic Education of Man* (1794). For modern readers, the title is misleading—Schiller's idea of aesthetic education is based upon beauty "because it is only through Beauty that man can make his way to freedom."[17] Working within the tradition of the German Idealism of Kant and Hegel, and the poetics of Goethe, Schiller argues that beauty can harmonize the tension between flesh and spirit, between nature and culture, without succumbing to rigid rationalist authoritarianism—which places the artist between the demands of the monarchy on one side and mere amusement on the other. For Schiller, to be in an entirely "aesthetic state" is to reach full human potential.[18]

Thus, Schiller's use of *aesthetic* has little to do with the cultivation of taste. The aesthetic represents an integration of the human being—body, reason, and will—resulting in the freedom to become "citizens of the world."[19] Artists must lead the way, he wrote, by putting aside all notions of utility: "This kind of art must abandon actuality, and soar with

---

[17] *Friedrich Schiller, Essays*, ed. Walter Hinderer and Daniel O. Dahlstrom (New York: Continuum, 1998), 90.

[18] Ibid., x–xi.

[19] Ibid., 89.

becoming boldness above our wants and needs; for art is the daughter of freedom, and takes her orders from the necessity inherent in minds, not from the exigencies of nature."[20] This describes what Beethoven is seeking in his music, especially his last and most magnificent symphony. Because music was Beethoven's language, his paean to world friendship took musical form, with the text of a poem he thought apt to the moment.

The last movement opens with a "call to arms," which is one of the most radical things Beethoven ever wrote, "literally stopping the symphony in its tracks and flinging back our horizons in one fell swoop."[21] After a review of the first three movements, there occurs an overwhelming outpouring of beauty when the chorus returns to the baritone's opening words, "*Freude, schöner Götterfunken*" (Joy, beautiful spark of the gods) reveals Beethoven's deepest spiritual urgings, elevating the soul of the listener as only the greatest art can. Indeed, we are inevitably drawn in, perhaps wanting to sing "Freuden" with the choir as well.

At that moment, it appears that the "jaggedness" of the earlier movements, and all their misery, have been overcome—a victory has been won. But not so fast, the symphony is not

---

[20]   Ibid., 88.

[21]   These comments about the Ninth Symphony were sent to me in a private email from the Irish composer John Kinsella on March 24, 2019. John Kinsella's eleven symphonies possess more creative use of tonal beauty than any other composers writing in the same period. He composed his Symphony No. 1 in 1984, the year he turned 52. His powerful *Elegy for Strings* (2011) is an excellent place to start becoming familiar with Kinsella's work: https://www.youtube.com/watch?v=t_RBv6P6ejA.

over yet. Philip writes, "The last notes the orchestra hammers out are not the smooth lyrical theme but the jagged fifths that began and ended the first movement. Beethoven has brought these two elements together: the lyrical and the peaceful may be triumphant, but the 'aggressor' has been brought into the fold: All humanity shall be brothers, not just the peace-lovers."[22]

Just what is the universal friendship the composer had in mind? Aristotle had personal friendship in mind, while Beethoven was thinking in terms of an impersonal "friendship" of social equality before law and authority. As a committed Republican and quiet revolutionary, Beethoven, like Schiller, wanted to tear away the traditional social barriers to exalt the paradigm of "world brotherhood," a precondition of widening the spectrum of relationships at a personal level. In other words, Beethoven held the popular contempt of his day for the types of class distinctions that divided people, the distinctions that Aristotle's Greece embraced and his theory on friendship required.

Beethoven had in mind the condition of Europe after the French Revolution, specifically the restoration of the monarchy in France and the commanding presence of Europe's royal families at the Council of Vienna (1815) after the defeat of Napoleon. The rejection of *Liberté, égalité, fraternité* and its revolutionary spirit left Beethoven in an awkward place. He relied on commissions and stipends from the aristocracy and electors, but he had been eighteen years old when "The Declaration of the Rights of Man and of

---

[22]   Ibid.

the Citizen" was published by France's National Constituent Assembly (1789).

He was a man of the Enlightenment, but like Diderot and the other *philosophes,* Beethoven viewed the revolution in France as the era's natural outcome and waited for its spirit to spread throughout Europe. Napoleon, who was elected first consul of the French Republic in December 1799, seemed to be bringing a new freedom to Europe, beginning with his defeat of the Austrian army in 1800, the Concordat of 1801 with Pope Pius VII, the new French constitution of 1802, and the Civil Code of March 1804.

Of course, as is the case with so many great revolutions throughout history, succeeding generations suffered for the sins and errors of its early advocates. The French Revolution not only gave birth to a spirit of new equality, it drenched that equality in the blood of tens of thousands from the Champs-Élysées to the Vendee, and hundreds of thousands more across the battlefields between France and Russia. When Napoleon was proclaimed emperor two months later, Beethoven famously scratched out his name on the title page of his Third Symphony, *Eroica* ("Heroic").

As music historian Harvey Sachs explains, there is a "hidden thread" that connects Beethoven with other British and European romanticists of his generation, such as Byron and the German poet Heinrich Heine: "this quest for freedom: political freedom, from repressive conditions that then dominated Europe, and freedom of expression, certainly, but above all freedom of mind and spirit."[23]

---

[23]   Harvey Sachs, *The Ninth: Beethoven and the World in 1824* (New York: Random House Trade Paperback Edition), 95.

These are questions Aristotle never faced directly. As the teacher to the young Alexander the Great, he did influence his student to treat the foreign peoples he met with respect for their own traditions. But Aristotle never questioned the absolute rule of his kingship. Neither did Aristotle's teachers—Socrates and Plato. Plato's ideal Republic is neither republican or democratic: the social stratification remains firmly in place. Socrates was imprisoned for embarrassing the prestigious and influential sophists: his so-called "subversive political opinions" had nothing to do with political revolution. Aristotle wrote at a time when and in a place where friendship was possible only among a select group of people—those free persons of the male gender with the leisure time enough to allow not merely for contemplation but time enough to become a contemplative.

What can a philosopher and a composer like Aristotle and Beethoven possibly have to say to each other about the true nature of friendship, given their different fields, nationalities, and the periods in which they lived and worked? Differences in time, place, and media make little difference when creative minds explore the human condition, whatever the medium. Reflection on, and expressions of, these fundamental truths will never end—they are revisited and encountered in the classics throughout the centuries.

Huckleberry Finn

There are many memorable friendships in literature that put Aristotle to the test: Didi and Gogo in *Waiting for Godot*; Robinson Crusoe and Friday; David and Jonathan in *The Book of Daniel*; Gilgamesh and Enkidu in *The Epic of Gilgamesh*; Homer's Achilles and Patroclus in *The Iliad*; Shakespeare's Horatio and Hamlet; Jane Austen's Elizabeth Bennett and Charlotte Lucas in *Pride and Prejudice*; Emily Bronte's Cathy and Heathcliff in *Wuthering Heights*; Cervantes's eponymous protagonist and Sancho Panza in *Don Quixote*. Given Aristotle's view of slavery, however, let's look at Mark Twain's characters, Huck and Jim.

Large claims are made about the influence of Mark Twain's classic *The Adventures of Huckleberry Finn*, first published in 1885 in the United States. Perhaps the boldest praise comes from Ernest Hemingway: "All modern American literature comes from one book by Mark Twain called *Huckleberry Finn*. American writing comes from that. There was nothing before. There has been nothing as good since." High praise, indeed, coming from one considered to be among the greats himself. Given changing sensibilities, I imagine many who have read *The Adventures of Huckleberry Finn* would be hesitant to admit as much these days. Controversies sparked by its inclusion in the syllabi of high school and college literature courses—for its use of the N-word—appear with frequency.

The novel remains beloved and, more importantly, read. There are at least three reasons for *Huckleberry Finn*'s lasting appeal beyond its status as a classic. First, the story immediately grabs the reader—we care about what happens to Huck and Jim. Second, the dialogue sparkles, especially Huck's ramblings on meaning-of-life matters. And, finally, the appearance, at least, of a growing friendship between the runaway white boy and the runaway black slave.

Huck and Jim know each other as acquaintances living with Miss Watson, who is determined to "civilise" Huck. Jim is Miss Watson's slave, her "property." They unexpectedly meet up on an island in the Mississippi River where Huck is hiding after faking his death to get away from his violent, drunken father. Jim is in hiding too, to avoid being sold to someone in the South, a transaction which would take him away from family. At first, Jim is afraid of Huck, "Doan' hurt me—don't! I hain't ever done no harm to a ghos."[24] He had been accused of the killing that Huck staged. It took some explaining to make Jim realize he is glad to see him. "I warn't lonesome, now."[25] They welcome each other as companions, finding the camaraderie *useful*, each escaping from the town, and both cold and lonely. That utility is multiplied when they decide to adventure down the river together on a raft. Huck, however, is acutely aware of the difference between his own plight and that of Jim, who has broken the law to escape Miss Watson, the one person who had shown Huck kindness. He constantly grapples with himself about the morality of helping Jim escape from Miss Watson. Huck firmly believes Jim is the property of Miss Watson—it was a clear-cut matter of doing the right thing to help capture Jim. Finally, he writes Miss Watson a letter, telling her where she can find her runaway slave.

> It was a close place. I took it up [the letter to Miss Watson], and held it in my hand. I was a-trembling,

---

[24] Mark Twain, *The Adventures of Huckleberry Finn* (Amazon Classics Edition, 2016), loc. 591 of 4604, Kindle.
[25] Ibid.

> because I'd got to decide, forever, betwixt two things, and I knowed it. I studied a minute, sort of holding my breath, and then says to myself: "All right, then, I'll go to hell"—and tore it up. It was awful thoughts and awful words, but they was said. And I let them stay said; and never thought no more about reforming.[26]

For most of the trip, Huck and Jim are no doubt friends linked by mutual usefulness even as they increasingly find pleasure in each other's company. Their friendship is constantly evolving during their adventures floating down the Mississippi, and they are forced to make choices, each of great consequence, such as Huck's decision whether or not to turn Jim in.

By the end of chapter eleven, it is quite clear that Huck and Jim are true friends. For example, as soon as Huck hears Jim is being suspected of murder, he quickly warns Jim. He also identifies closely with Jim because they are in the same predicament, escaping.

> And got to thinking over our trip down the river; and I see Jim before me all the time: in the day and in the night-time, sometimes moonlight, sometimes storms, and we a-floating along, talking and singing and laughing. But somehow I couldn't seem to strike no places to harden me against him, but only the other kind. I'd see him standing my watch on top of his'n, 'stead of calling me, so I could go on sleeping; and see him how glad he was when I come back out of the fog;

---

[26]   Ibid., loc. 3376 of 4603, Kindle.

and when I come to him again in the swamp, up there
where the feud was; and such-like times; and would
always call me honey, and pet me and do everything
he could think of for me, and how good he always was;
and at last I struck the time I saved him by telling the
men we had small-pox aboard, and he was so grateful,
and said I was the best friend old Jim ever had in the
world, and the only one he's got now.[27]

In reviewing a book about *Huckleberry Finn*, the NPR
critic Linda Holmes finds less a transformative friendship
between Huck and Jim than the maintenance of the status
quo. She writes:

Huck Finn is full of contradictions: Huck comes to
appreciate Jim's kindness and ultimately proves willing
to "go to hell" to free him—but he treats Jim as exceptional, a worthy person because he's not the way Huck
expects a black man to behave. As he puts it after Jim
extends compassion to Tom Sawyer, "I knowed he
was white inside." On the one hand, it's an extension
of respect. On the other, it's equating integrity with
whiteness. Its basic racism and its wisp of understanding are both real; they're both sitting right there.[28]

---

[27]   Ibid., loc. 3341 of 4604, Kindle.
[28]   Linda Holmes, "In 'Huckleberry Finn,' A History In Echoes,"
December 30, 2014, https://www.npr.org/2014/12/30/3738346
35/in-huckleberry-finn-a-history-in-echoes.

"Equating integrity with whiteness" is the narrator's point of view through the novel. Huck's generosity is to imagine Jim a white man.

Novelist and critic Jane Smiley, a Pulitzer Prize winner, created a stir when she penned a piece about the novel after reading it for the first time since her schooldays.[29] Smiley declares Huckleberry Finn not to be a "great novel;" in fact, she argued, it was inferior to Harriet Beecher Stowe's *Uncle Tom's Cabin,* which should take the former's place in school curricula. She is certainly correct that Twain and Huck were "never even held to account for their choice to go down the river rather than across it."[30] To the north is free Illinois, to the south are the slave states, including Mississippi, where Jim was bought and separated from his family. Both Jim and his family are shipped to Missouri but to different "owners." The fact that during the novel Huck and Jim do become friends, according to Smiley, starkly contrasts with the lack of concern Huck has about taking Jim to freedom: "If Huck *feels* positive toward Jim, and *loves* him, and *thinks* of him as a man, then that's enough. He doesn't actually have to act in accordance with his feelings."[31]

One can imagine Aristotle agreeing with this assessment. Looking back to his *Ethics,* we recall his claim that the social barriers and attitudes created by slavery are insurmountable. Though Twain crafts an evolution in their friendship toward

---

[29]   Jane Smiley, "Say it ain't so, Huck; second thoughts on Mark Twain's 'masterpiece,'" *Harper's Magazine*, 1996, https://www.enotes.com/topics/adventures-of-huckleberry-finn/critical-essays.

[30]   Ibid.

[31]   Ibid.

deepening mutual affection, on his view, it is clear that the white boy and the black slave never completely move beyond their social strata towards what Aristotle calls true friendship.

Classic tales like *The Adventures of Huckleberry Finn* challenge Aristotle's core assumption; namely, that differences of sex, class, education, and virtue cannot be overcome in reaching the highest form of friendship. For example, Aristotle insists that the gap between rich and poor cannot be bridged because true friendship requires more than an equality of spirit—things matter. Generally, I have found his general framework illuminating in understanding the coming and going of relationships, and especially why friendships I considered important withered away. This passage from Aristotle's *Ethics*, like all works in the canon, elicits introspection. These works address the human condition: they surprise us, frustrate our expectations, and make us work to find the meaning. As a result, we can become different persons after we experience them. In some cases, the effect is more than slight.

The Rules of the Game

The question of incompatibilities that can affect friendship is at the heart of Jean Renoir's *The Rules of the Game* (1939), a film considered by most critics to be among the greatest of all time.[32] We saw in Aristotle's theory of friendship how he

---

[32]   *The Rules of the Game*, dir. Jean Renoir (1939; New York: The Criterion Collection, Inc., 2011), Blu-ray.

described the social boundaries that demarcate relationships. In Renoir's film, we will see those boundaries tested.

The story arises from a diverse group of characters who arrive for a weeklong house party at the extravagant country home of Marquis Robert de la Cheyniest and his wife, Christine. The "game" in question is the navigation of social strata, fragile marriages, affairs, and the heavy weight of tradition brought to the story by its setting and its players. Thus, the game is multifaceted, lending a patina of farce to an underlying sad story about two persons from different classes and backgrounds meeting the boundary line of their friendship—Christine, played by Nora Gregory, and Octave, played by the director himself.

Octave is having an affair with Christine's maid, the pert and naughty Lisette, whose husband is the gamekeeper, Schumacher (Gaston Modot). In one of the opening scenes, while still at their Paris home, Christine raises the subject of friendship with Lisette, asking if she has any male friends. "With a man! When pigs have wings!"

Also *en route* to the house is a famous and daring aviator, André Jurieux, who loves Christine. We learn that although Christine has encouraged his amorous attention, her ambivalence is obvious—she does not go to meet him at the airfield as promised. "Telling lies is such a weight to bear," she says to Lisette, regarding André.

Surrounded by hundreds of cheering Parisians, ten years after the Lindbergh flight, Andre is handed a radio microphone by a host who awaits a profound statement from the hero. Instead, he is distraught: "She is not here . . . I did it all for her . . . am very unhappy. I made this flight for a woman.

She is not here." His voice is heard over the radio by Christine as she enters her husband's bedroom. Making public his love for a married woman, even in 1930s Paris, was breaking "the rules." Octave calls his friend Christine, begging her to invite the now-suicidal André to the house party—another breach of the rules (note that not all the rules are unfair—some make great sense). On the way to the estate, Octave tries to console André by reminding him, "She's a society woman, and society women have strict rules." Indeed. What will ensue, the viewer wonders, for those who play by the rules and those who don't, like André?

The scene changes to Robert and Christine arriving at their country estate, La Colinière, the rituals soon to commence. Complications and inequalities abound: Christine is from an upper-class German family, her father a celebrated conductor. Octave, her dear friend, is an impoverished composer dependent upon the charity of the Marquis. They met while Octave studied in Austria with her father, and the relationship has lasted for years, held together by their shared love of music and high culture. Octave values her rich cultural background, but Christine's deportment and German heritage, we learn, have been a social barrier—after all, France and Germany were about to go to war when the film premiered. The Aristotelian sinews of usefulness and enjoyment are present in their friendship, with their inequality an apparent source of tension.

Robert, Christine's husband, is a very wealthy merchant familiar to high society despite his Jewish ancestry in a country where anti-Semitism had long flourished. His Jewishness is discussed among his guests, even his own servants, but never in front of his face. He dotes on expensive wind-up toys—the type where bells are struck by mechanically driven figures—which function to both display his wealth and to distract him from the growing chaos of the weekend, especially the two men—the friend and the lover—who are pressing his wife for attention. Throughout the film, Robert is the one who, above all, follows the rules with an unflappable charm even, as we shall see, in the face of death—a death he could have prevented.

We learn quickly that Robert's shrewish mistress, Genevieve (Mila Parely), whom he would like to jettison, is also to attend, which disappoints Christine. Robert has promised his wife that the affair has ended. Lisette, meanwhile, has started a dalliance with a poacher, Marceau (Julien Carette), who, while being caught in the act of poaching, catches the fancy of Robert, who hires him as a servant. The expansive Robert puts his arm over Marceau's shoulder as if they are to be lifelong friends, but, predictably, this is not to be. "The rules of the game" will have the last word.

In a scene that lays bare the cruelty of the rules, Renoir stages a hunt, as was common at such parties.[33] The guests, adorned in their best tweed shooting outfits, stand in place with servants supplying cartridges and piling up carcasses, as a dozen men beat the floor of the woods to flush every animal at the closest possible range to the shooters. The

---

[33]   *The Shooting Party, 1985,* directed by Alan Bridges, starring James Mason, based upon a novel by Isobel Colgate. As in *The Rules of the Game*, a group of aristocrats staying at a country estate go shooting, but their intense competition to see who can kill the most game leads to a death.

director shows close-ups of the animals being hit, falling, and in the case of a rabbit, curling up to die. Only Christine and Octave withhold their approval of the carnage, yet it is all done in "good form" and by the rules. When the shooting ends, Robert asks mechanically, "Shall we display the kill?"

At one point, Christine is encouraged to look through binoculars upon what looks like her husband Robert kissing and caressing his "former" mistress, Genevieve. She doesn't know that Robert has told Genevieve he is through, he doesn't love her, and she must leave him alone. What Christine sees is the mistress clinging to him and Robert, ever the gentlemen, trying to resist. At a masquerade ball that evening, Christine offers to leave with André immediately. André says he must tell Robert, and she is aghast: "But since we're in love, what difference does it make?" André, to our surprise, replies, "But there are rules." Christine muses to herself that she offered him her love and he worries about "proprieties."

As the masquerade entertains the guests, Schumacher obsesses over Marceau's effort to seduce his eminently seducible wife, Lisette. He takes out his gun and starts hunting him, firing shots inside the house, scaring the guests. In his rage, Schumacher fails to hit anyone, but he is fired by Robert, along with Marceau.

In the meantime, Christine has turned her affection from André to Octave and plans to run away with him. Lisette disapproves, saying that all the romantic escapades up till now have been "just for fun." Together in the greenhouse, Christine and Octave decide to leave on the 3:00 a.m. train. Schumacher and Marceau are watching them from the woods but mistakenly think Christine is Lisette because she is wearing her hooded coat. Octave returns to the house for his coat but lends it to André asking him to bring Christine back from the greenhouse. But the farce of mistaken identities yields to tragedy as Schumacher kills André, thinking he is Octave running away with his wife, Lisette.

Renoir brings the film quickly to an end, with Robert addressing his guests outside the house, standing on the steps over which André's body has just been carried into the house. Robert coldly covers up the accidental murder by calling it a "hunting accident," which quickly subdues and sobers everyone. The "rules of the game" have held fast. He says of André, flippantly, "We are in mourning for this delightful friend, who made us forget he is famous," and asks his guests to come in out of the cold.

Octave, who has already left the chateau with Marceau, said earlier in the film what became its most famous line: "The awful thing about life: Everybody has their reasons." He talks of reasons, not rules. The rules to Octave would be only another set of "reasons" for one's actions. There are also "reasons" for breaking the rules and reasons for covering up a murder.

The premiere of the film on June 28, 1939, at the Colisée Theatre was a disaster, reminiscent of Stravinsky's premiere twenty-six years earlier, also in Paris, of *The Rite of Spring*. Fights broke out; people yelled for the film to stop; catcalls were aimed at the director; seats were broken. A man tried to burn down the theatre by setting his newspaper alight. The scandal and wretched character of the players was too much for some. The film closed after three weeks. Renoir was crushed by the reception, and in interviews later in life his disappointment remained apparent. "The laurels came too late," he said in one.[34]

In this film, Renoir chronicles the decline and decadence of the French aristocracy and upper class, who pretend to obey the rules, at least when they are to their advantage. The stratification of Aristotle's Greece was firmly in place in the fifth century BC, but Parisian society just before the Second World War had become porous, with a blurring of the lines between the old aristocracy and the nouveau riche. In spite of its fluidity and pretense to the contrary, no new friendships are formed or deepened at this mini-society gathered at La Colinière. The final scene, after Robert and his guests return to the house, underscores this failure. Octave and the poacher/shoe polisher Marceau are walking down the driveway and while saying goodbye mention the possibility of seeing each other again. Octave, now a realist, replies, "We probably won't," and walks away. "We probably won't" gives the film a sad but realistic ending. We've seen a widely disparate group of people put in a large manor house for days of ritualized festivity. Intimacies are quickly created and just as quickly cast aside. Romantic desires that seemed ardent flame out when difficulties arise. All that transpired at La Colinière will be soon forgotten, even the death of the innocent and sincere André. "We probably won't" casts a nullity over the entire story where nothing of substance has been formed to last.

---

[34]   Video supplement to the *Criterion Collection* edition of *The Rules of the Game*, dir. Jean Renoir (1936; New York, *The Criterion Collection, Inc.*, 2011) Blu-ray.

This film, I believe, confirms Aristotle's distinction between friendships of use and pleasure and those sealed by sharing of firm beliefs about a life well lived. Only Charlotte and Octave touched upon these deeper issues, but the friendship that might have emerged was sidetracked by his infatuation with her and her dissatisfaction with her own life. Neither had the equanimity to focus their conversation on what they had in common, a deep love of music.

Recommended

Books

William Shakespeare, *Hamlet*, 1623.
Jane Austen, *Pride and Prejudice*, 1813.
Emily Brontë, *Wuthering Heights*,1847.
Louisa May Alcott, *Little Women*, 1868–1869.
Ford Maddox Ford, *A Good Soldier*, 1915.
D. H. Lawrence, *Women in Love*, 1920.
F. Scott Fitzgerald, *The Great Gatsby*, 1925.
Evelyn Waugh, *Brideshead Revisited*, 1945.
Samuel Becket, *Waiting for Godot*, 1953.
Fred Uhlman, *Reunion*, 1971.

Music

W. A. Mozart, *Così fan Tutte*, 1790.
W. A. Mozart, *Die Zauberflöte*, 1792.
Georges Bizet, *The Pearl Fishers*, 1863.
Richard Wagner, *Die Meistersinger von Nürnberg*, 1867.
Giacomo Puccini, *La Bohème*, 1895.

Film

Charlie Chaplin, *City Lights*, 1931.
Tod Browning, *Freaks*, 1932.
Jean Renoir, *La Grande Illusion*, 1937.
Orson Welles, *Citizen Kane*, 1941.
William Wyler, *The Best Years of Our Lives*, 1946.
John Schlesinger, *Midnight Cowboy*, 1969.
Michael Cimino, *The Deer Hunter*, 1979.
Louis Malle, *Atlantic City*, 1980.
Sergio Leone, *Once Upon a Time in America*, 1984.
Alain Resnais, *Mélo*, 1986.
Frank Darabont, *The Shawshank Redemption*, 1994.
Terrence Malick, *The Thin Red Line*, 1999.
Claire Denis, *Beau Travail*, 2000.
Steven Spielberg, *A.I. Artificial Intelligence*, 2001.

CHAPTER 15

Eros

Juliet:
How cam'st thou hither, tell me, and wherefore?
The orchard walls are high and hard to climb,
And the place death, considering who thou art,
If any of my kinsmen find thee here.

Romeo:
With love's light wings did I o'erperch these walls,
For stony limits cannot hold love out,
And what love can do, that dares love attempt:
Therefore thy kinsmen are no stop to me.
(Shakespeare, *Romeo and Juliet*, Act 1, Scene 2)

With these words, "And what love can do, that dares love attempt," Shakespeare describes both the natural goodness of Eros and its capacity for destruction. What begins with the simple beauty of awakened desire between two teenagers ends in a double suicide, "For never was a story of more woe, / Than this of Juliet and her Romeo."[1]

---

[1]   William Shakespeare, *Romeo and Juliet*, V, iii.309-310, *The Riverside Shakespeare*, ed. G. Blackmore Evans (Boston: Houghton Mifflin Company, 1974), 1093.

There are love stories that capture our imaginations for a lifetime, stories of couples whose desire lead them astray and towards disaster: Adam and Eve, Orpheus and Euridice, David and Bathsheba, Paris and Helen, Antony and Cleopatra, Aeneas and Dido, Lancelot and Guinevere, Abelard and Heloise, Tristan and Isolde, Paolo and Francesca. We find them in canonical works such as *The Sorrows of Young Werther*, *Anna Karenina*, *Madame Bovary*, *The Scarlet Letter*, *Wuthering Heights*, *The Age of Innocence*, *The Sun Also Rises*, *Of Human Bondage*, and *Lolita*. This list, as the reader knows, goes on and on. In telling love stories—of Eros, Philia, Storge, or Agape—we portray the human condition. All stories, in one way or another, are love stories.

Animated as it is by passion and drama, Eros provides the richest tableau for the storyteller. Its "light wings" can soar in any direction without respect for limits—"And what love can do, that dares love attempt." In modernity, depictions of Eros have been reduced to romantic love, eroticism, or sexual desire. As we shall see, the idea of Eros was originally, until the Middle Ages,[2] an irresistible urge that needed to transcend the physical to find its final object.

Eros entered the Western literary tradition at its earliest stage—as a god of Greek mythology. The earliest philosophers, however, treated Eros as an idea of the human desire

---

[2]   As discussed in a later chapter, the notion of Romantic love, love for its own sake, emerges in the twelfth century with the rise of the Troubadour poets and the myth of Tristan and Isolde; see Denis de Rougemont, *Love In the Western World*, trans. Montgomery Belgion (New York: Harper Colophon Books, 1972).

for wholeness, a resting place where desire can find its true end.

The Symposium

In his great dialogue on love, *The Symposium*, Plato presents the narrative of Socrates and a small group of friends attending a banquet, where wine will be served and drunk in abundance. Agathon, a renowned tragic poet, hosts the event as Socrates announces that each of the guests must make a speech in praise of Eros. The result is seven points of view as expressed, in order, by Phaedrus, Pausanias, Eurymachus, Aristophanes, Agathon, Socrates, and a very drunk Alcibiades. Each of these prominent men of Athens approaches Eros from differing points of view: legal, medical, mythical, political, comic, poetic, and personal.

As the argument advances, Socrates makes the basic point that a lover feels the lack of the thing he desires: "Now such a person who feels longing, longs for what is not at hand, for what he isn't himself, and for what he lacks."[3] As the wine flows, the friends' animated conversation drifts predictably towards Eros as the desire for physical beauty. Socrates, as he so often does, redirects the conversation. He tells those gathered about how Diotima, an ancient Greek philosopher and prophetess, instructed him about the genealogy of Eros. It was typical of Socrates's use of irony to have his teachings come from the mouth of another character, and in this case,

---

[3]   Plato, *The Symposium of Plato*, trans. Suzy Q Groden (Boston: University of Massachusetts Press, 1070), 77. All subsequent quotations are taken from this book.

from a woman. Diotima lays out the basic outline of what
has become known as "Platonic Love." Recall that Socrates
was no fan of the written word, so we know his teachings
from the writings of his greatest student, Plato.

Plato uses beauty (*kalos*) to describe the object toward
which one ascends. Don't be confused; beauty is how the
good attracts us. Beauty brings the appetite to rest. It simultaneously lifts the mind above everydayness, and we see with
eyes raised to a higher power.

Diotima explains that love for another's beautiful body
is only the beginning of love. Eros awakens a higher desire,
to love the beauty of souls—this stepping upward can be
described as ascending a "ladder of love." This ladder became
the basis of Neo-Platonic metaphysics, seen in the works of
the Neo-Platonists such the pagan Plotinus culminating in
the *Paradiso* of Dante's *Divine Comedy*.

The last step described by Diotima is the vision of Beauty
itself: "[Beauty] exists by itself in itself, eternally, and in one
form only, and all other beautiful things participate in it in
such a way, that, while they come into being and perish, it
does not, nor does it become greater or less, nor is it affected
by anything."[4]

An individual's Eros must submit to *sublimation* so that
the force of Eros constantly propels us towards our final end,
our happiness (*eudaimonia*).[5] To sublimate means to raise

---

4   *Symposium*, 211b, 92-93.
5   *Eudaimonia* is not a feeling or simple psychological satisfaction,
     it is more closely related to blessedness and flourishing, and it
     belongs to those whose Eros is directed by virtue. See *Happiness
     and the Limits of Satisfaction*, 64–65.

something to a higher level,[6] in this case redirecting physical desire to seek towards a non-physical object. Sublimation does not come naturally to everyone. Some recognize that physical love creates a hunger for something more. Some do not. The virtues which order thoughts, emotions, and actions are required to incline an individual towards sublimation.

That Eros stems from natural desire, the ancient philosophers and the theologians of the Patristic and medieval periods agree. This desire comes with the human condition, a built-in desire that you possess whether you know it or not. But the early Christian theologians decisively differed with the Greeks: Platonists and Aristotelians consider that final end to be the Good (*agathon*), which remains abstract and conceptual, an ideal. In the Christian view, that ideal has been replaced by a person, Jesus Christ. When Christian believers look at history or eternity, they encounter a person, the three-person God of Love, not an abstract ideal.

Love Songs

Lovers sing. They sing spontaneously to express a wonderment inexpressible by spoken words (unless, of course, a lover is a proficient poet). Love ballads can be traced back to the English composer John Dowland (1563–1626). The performer Sting must agree—he recorded a set of Dowland songs on his 2006 CD "Songs from the Labyrinth."[7] A Catholic convert, Dowland spent much of his composing

---

6   https://en.oxforddictionaries.com/definition/sublimate.
7   Sting sings some Dowland songs and explains his choice to record them here: https://www.youtube.com/watch?v=8QkqXvLLDRo.

life outside of Elizabethan England, where "papists" were often treated roughly. After eight years serving in the court of King Christian IV of Denmark, he returned to England, finding employment with the more tolerant James I. From 1592 to 1612, Dowland composed ninety-six songs for lute and voice.

These songs remain fresh to the ear more than four centuries later. Among the songs, I suggest starting with "Dear, if you change"[8] and "Come away, come sweet love,"[9] both from Dowland's *1st Booke of Songs* (1597). Direct and melodic, with poetically crafted lyrics, these are the kind of songs some think have never been surpassed—they were gems then as they are now. They encompass all the experiences familiar to all lovers: from desire and disappointment to melancholy and pure joy.

Dowland's songs often sound a note of sadness probably due to vicissitudes in his personal life. He never rose to the prominence he felt he deserved in his lifetime, perhaps because of his chosen faith, yet history has righted any wrongs. Once the songs have hooked you, try listening to the roughly ninety compositions for solo lute played by Paul O'Dette.[10] His advocacy of Dowland combined with the

---

[8]   Dowland's "Dear, if you change" sung by John Elwes and played by Mattihas Spaeter on the lute can be heard here: www.youtube.com/watch?v=7ReVhLys278&list=PLwFq8431xj18AnpTSyfUEMCydI vkpbMP8&index=18&t=0s.

[9]   Dowland's song, "Come away," sung by Emma Kirkby and Joel Frederiksen, accompanied by the Ensemble Phoenix Munich is found here: /www.youtube.com/watch?v=UjWYw-w9rKg&list=RDUjWYw-w9rKg&start_radio=1.

[10]   Paul O'Dette can be heard playing Dowland's "Lachrimae" on the lute: www.youtube.com/watch?v=zSzSNN7ETvM.

recordings by Anthony Rooney's *Academy of Ancient Music* has given this generation virtually all of his music in superb performances.[11] Listening to his love songs makes you realize Eros has not changed in the last five centuries.

Vertigo

The sins of Eros are recounted over and over in song, verse, fiction, and film: the sadness following a one-night stand, the depression of the sexual adventurer, the sudden disappointment in finding out what we thought was love was only infatuation—all these experiences are commonplace. We are "looking for love in all the wrong places," or at least in all the wrong ways.

In *Vertigo*, the viewer witnesses a train wreck of Eros.[12] In this 1958 classic film, Alfred Hitchcock creates an as-yet-unequaled modern parable of disordered passion, in which an idol is made of feminine beauty and a cross of masculine desire.[13] Every element of *Vertigo* is essential—the script, cinematic techniques, use of color filters, animation, and in particular the soundtrack of composer Bernard Herrmann. Herrmann's *Vertigo* score stands at number twelve on the American Film Institute's list of greatest film scores.[14] It is as essential to *Vertigo* as his work in *Psycho* (1960) was to that

---

[11]   Dowland's entire *The Firste Booke of Songes* (1597) is played by The Consort Of Musicke and conducted by Anthony Rooley, is heard here: www.youtube.com/watch?v=_TbIE1JNj2I&t=2s.

[12]   *Vertigo*, dir. Alfred Hitchcock (1958; Universal City, CA: Universal Pictures Home Entertainment, 2014), Blu-ray.

[13]   In 2012, *Vertigo* replaced *The Rules of the Game* as the no. 1 film of all time in the 2012 *Sight and Sound* poll of over 1,000 film critics.

[14]   "AFI's Greatest 25 Film Scores of All Time," www.afi.com/100Years/scores.aspx.

memorable film. Who can forget those screeching strings of the shower scene?

Set in San Francisco, *Vertigo* is about a recently retired LA policeman, Scottie, played by James Stewart, who agrees to help an old friend, Gavin Elster (Tom Nelmore), by following his wife, whom he fears is losing her mind. His wife, Madeleine, played by Kim Novak, believes she is becoming possessed by the spirit of Carlotta Valdes, a woman who died a century before.

Scottie did not want the job initially, but Elster sets a trap to ensure Scottie's interest. That night at Ernie's Restaurant, Scottie is sitting at the bar. The camera pans from Scottie through the restaurant until we see the back of a beautiful blonde woman relaxing with Elster. We hear Hermann's memorable "Madeleine" theme (1.12).[15] The camera cuts back to the bar from where Scottie sees the couple rise from their table. Madeleine gets up in a low-cut black velvet gown with a deep green cloak hanging from her shoulders. As she walks towards him in the bar, we see Scottie trying not to be seen seeing.

Everything about Madeleine, as Hitchcock presents her, is irresistible—even her movements are seductively feline. Hitchcock has her stop and stand ninety degrees to the camera and Scottie's gaze. The camera lingers on her profile and then on Scottie. When the camera returns to Madeleine, the dark red wall covering has a new, fiery luster, which serves to both frame her beauty and warn the viewer. If Scottie is

---

[15]   Bernard Herrmann's "Madeleine" theme begins 24 seconds into this clip from the movie, *Vertigo*, https://www.youtube.com/watch?v=Beac86mN8XM.

stunned by her beauty, his face does not betray, but we bet he is, because Hitchcock has made sure that we are. The viewer is not surprised that the camera cuts to him sitting in his car in front of Madeleine's apartment building, where she lives apart from her now-estranged husband. He has taken the job he couldn't resist.

Scottie is now a captive—not to the beautiful woman, but to Eros. As the unsavory plot unfolds, the viewer learns more about how Scottie was carefully chosen by Madeleine's husband and manipulated into unwittingly participating in his dark scheme. At a crucial point, we again see Scottie overcome by vertigo, enhanced in the film by an animated downward spiral and Hermann's swirling score.

Since I highly recommend this film to the mature viewer, I'll spare you plot spoilers, except perhaps this hint, as it sheds light on Eros deformed. Scottie is at a certain point so distraught that he spends a year in a mental hospital, emerging to try and understand his loss. He finds on the busy streets of San Francisco a beautiful woman who is a dead ringer for Madeleine, but with different hair and style. Scottie obsesses over her, even coercing her into adopting Madeleine's style and dress. He is so consumed by erotic desire and misery that he has no concern for the woman, Judy, as a person.

Deep into the film, Hitchcock carefully orchestrates one scene in which Scottie and Judy, in a lusty panic, confront one another.

> Scottie: Oh Judy, I tell you these past few days have been the happiest days I have known in a year.

Judy: I know, I know because I remind you of her and not
     even that very much.
Scottie: No, it's you too, there's something in you that . . .
     (Scottie cradles her face within his hands but lets her go
     and starts to turn away.)
Judy: You don't even want to touch me.
Scottie: Yes, yes, I know.

In this scene, Hitchcock lights Scottie and Judy differently:
Scottie's face is cool, an icy blue with ominous shadows.
Judy's face is warmly lit, her skin glows with affection and
submissiveness. Saying, "OK, I'll do it. I don't care anymore
about me," she walks into the bathroom. Returning, Scottie
says her hair is not "pinned up" like Madeleine's. He asks
her to go back. She complies. Coming out of the bathroom,
Judy/Madeleine walks through a cloud, wearing a grey suit
Madeleine wore. The music crescendos. Hermann's frankly
erotic music is not subtle. She tries to smile as she walks up
to him. He turns passionate. With a technique that would
be used in many romantic films, the camera swirls around
them as they embrace and kiss for over a minute and Hermann's famous "Scène d'amour" swells (4.57).[16] The background turns dark as the camera turns, and the room fills
with a green light from the hotel sign.[17]

Unrestrained Eros is still very much the dominant force,
and a scene that in some films may have indicated a turn
toward a more real love between persons, one which ascends

---

[16]   Ibid.
[17]   A portion of the scene from *Vertigo* can be seen here: www.
       youtube.com/watch?v=tesqTwX7cpc.

"the ladder," is instead used by Hitchcock as a harbinger of the tragic, ironic conclusion. Disorientation associated with a fear of falling is an apt metaphor, and Hitchcock's visionary approach to the tragedy of depersonalized Eros is anything but a glorification of lust and sex.

As with so many other great works, *Vertigo* was disparaged by most of the major film critics of its time, even as it is now considered among the greats. In the late fifties, were men and women not ready to see their love affairs displayed on screen, or was the story just too dark? It's not easy to watch the romantic and sublime turned inside out, but great art is never about the shortest, most direct route to what is true, good, and beautiful. We are often left to infer what is good from a sober recognition of evil in a tragedy that reaches a dark and logical conclusion.

Leaves of Grass

As I read Walt Whitman's *Leaves of Grass*, I'm continually struck by the sense of Eros, the unabashed hunger for the universe, that resounds from the classic poetic work. In the history of love, Whitman retains the Eros of Platonism and Christianity but without their absolutes. Whitman lives in a world where there is no God, but he expresses a passionate gratitude towards Nature; that is, all that exists.

Leaves of Grass has a complicated publishing history: first published in 1855, it contained twelve poems. Every time Whitman republished an edition, it included new poems and some revisions to older ones, running through six or nine editions, depending on which scholar you ask. The last, the "deathbed" edition, was published in 1892, two months before Whitman's death. It contains over four hundred poems.

Whitman and his poetry were controversial from the start, partly due to his treatment of Eros and sexuality. His frank depictions of the erotic impulse and celebration of the naked body startled the reading public in the mid-nineteenth century. In 1860, walking around Boston with his first supporter Ralph Waldo Emerson, Emerson tried to convince his friend to cut some of the more explicit sexual lines not only in "I Sing the Body Electric" but also in the "Children of Adam" section. Whitman declined his friend's advice.

An example of what upset Emerson can be seen in one of the twelve original poems from the 1855 edition, starting with the opening line, "The bodies of men and women engirth me, and I engirth them." In the 1867 edition, Whitman added a title, "I Sing the Body Electric,"[18] which only underscores the enthusiastic celebration of the human body. Sample these lines from the 1891–1892 edition:

> I believe the likes of you shall stand or fall with my poems,
>   and that they are my poems,
> Man's, woman's, child's, youth's, wife's, husband's, mother's,
>   father's, young man's, young woman's poems,
> Head, neck, hair, ears, drop and tympan of the ears,
> Eyes, eye-fringes, iris of the eye, eyebrows, and the waking or
>   sleeping of the lids,

---

[18]   Huck Gutman, "I Sing the Body Electric, 1855," https://whitmanarchive.org/criticism/current/encyclopedia/entry_9.html.

Mouth, tongue, lips, teeth, roof of the mouth, jaws, and the
     jaw-hinges,
Nose, nostrils of the nose, and the partition,
Cheeks, temples, forehead, chin, throat, back of the neck,
     neck-slue,
Strong shoulders, manly beard, scapula, hind-shoulders, and
     the ample side-round of the chest, . . .
Womanhood, and all that is a woman, and the man that
     comes from woman,
The womb, the teats, nipples, breast-milk, tears, laughter,
     weeping, love-looks, love-perturbations and risings, . . .

Read aloud at Socrates's *Symposium*, *Leaves of Grass* would
have received little, if any, applause. Whitman's Eros cele-
brates the physical, focusing the reader on the details of the
body's shape and sexuality. Where the Greeks would have
started climbing the ladder towards the abstract ideal, Whitman stoops over and looks even closer. In his personal life,
it should be added, Whitman disapproved of pornography
and sexual libertinism.[19]

As Whitman grew older, the *Leaves of Grass* grew and it
also changed. By the 1872 edition, Whitman scholar David
S. Reynolds sees a change of Whitman's voice—his "I"
becomes one expressing "an urgent desire to escape to the
spiritual realm."[20] In "Passage to India," we find Whitman
seemingly trying to escape the earth, the physicality he celebrated. The poet and his soul, the "we" in the poem, are

---

[19]   David S. Reynolds, *Walt Whitman's America: A Cultural Biography*
         (New York: Alfred A. Knopf, 1995), 195.
[20]   Ibid., 500.

about to "launch out on trackless seas" and to sail "on waves of ecstasy" singing "our song of God," a spiritual exploration.

> O we can wait no longer,
> We too take ship O soul,
> Joyous we too launch out on trackless seas,
> Fearless for unknown shores on waves of ecstasy to sail,
> Amid the wafting winds, (thou pressing me to thee, I thee to
>   me, O soul,)
> Caroling free, singing our song of God,
> Chanting our chant of pleasant exploration.

The soul hopes to make contact with the divine: "Bathe me O God in thee." Whitman's poet seeks nothing less than to be immersed—a baptism in the divine. In that hope, they continue their journey.

> O soul thou pleasest me, I thee,
> Sailing these seas or on the hills, or waking in the night,
> Thoughts, silent thoughts, of Time and Space and Death,
>   like waters flowing,
> Bear me indeed as through the regions infinite,
> Whose air I breathe, whose ripples hear, lave me all over,
> Bathe me O God in thee, mounting to thee,
> I and my soul to range in range of thee.

Then the poet addresses God as "O Thou transcendent,/ Nameless," as the source of light and cosmic design and a "moral, spiritual fountain." The poet "shrivels at the thought of God, / At Nature and its wonders," but he expects the soul to bring about a harmonious reconciliation with these forces.

> O Thou transcendent,
> Nameless, the fibre and the breath,
> Light of the light, shedding forth universes, thou centre of
>   them.

Note how Whitman alternates between the personal, "Bathe me," and the impersonal, "O Thou transcendent," an uncapped *transcendent* with a capitalized *Thou*. Are we losing both in a mystical vision? No, because the poet is overcome with fear and falls back to contemplate only "the vastnesses of Space."

> Swiftly I shrivel at the thought of God,
> At Nature and its wonders, Time and Space and Death,
> But that I, turning, call to thee O soul, thou actual Me,
> And lo, thou gently masterest the orbs,
> Thou matest Time, smilest content at Death,
> And fillest, swellest full the vastnesses of Space.[21]

Just what is the reader to make of this? Has Whitman done an about-face? No, the poet and his soul are not escaping the earth but looking for its center. The journey has not transcended the boundaries of nature, within the world Whitman celebrated his entire life. Whitman has proposed a spirituality of naturalism, which a century later was employed and trivialized by the gurus of the New Age.

---

[21]   Walt Whitman, Section 8, "Passage to India," *Walt Whitman: Complete Poetry and Collected Prose* (New York: Literary Classics of the United States, 1982), 537–38. "Passage to India" was first published in the 1872 edition.

A Sea Symphony

What happens when a composer of the same sensibility sets Whitman's words above to music? In *A Sea Symphony*, English composer Ralph Vaughan Williams (1872–1958) multiplies the power of Whitman's words, interpreting them in a way that reveals more meaning than reading them does alone.

This work will not be familiar to most readers, yet it deserves to be part of the regular repertoire of concert orchestras around the world. It is a masterpiece, and in its historical context, it is highly innovative. A *Sea Symphony* was first performed in 1910 with Williams himself conducting. It's a long work, lasting seventy minutes in most recordings, for large orchestra, chorus, and two soloists—a baritone and a soprano. All the texts are taken from *Leaves of Grass*. He was introduced to Whitman in 1892 by a fellow undergraduate, Bertrand Russell, who would go on to be a world-famous philosopher. Williams cared so much about *Leaves of Grass* that he kept a volume in his pocket while he served in the First World War.[22]

A great-nephew of Charles Darwin, Williams was a religious skeptic. His father, an Anglican pastor, died when he was two and a half years old, all but eliminating the possibility of firm religious direction. In her memoir, his second wife, Ursula, describes Williams as "a cheerful agnostic, but he was never a professing Christian."[23] Thus he shared

---

22   Bryon Adams, Program Notes, American Symphony Orchestra, http://americansymphony.org/wp-content/uploads/2018/10/10-17-ASO-Final.pdf.
23   Ursula Vaughan Williams, *R. V. W.: A Biography of Ralph Vaughan*

something with Whitman: both were raised as Christians, distanced themselves from institutional religion, and sought to express a spirituality without dogma, only a yearning for a universal principle, regardless of the name used to describe it. This unreligious, or immanent, spirituality would later become common in the West, as traditional Christian faith retreated.

A Sea Symphony consists of four movements.[24] The fourth, "The Explorers," is thirty minutes long. At first "The Explorers" appear to be climbing the ladder of love described in the *Symposium*. Whitman's and Williams's vision, unlike Plato's, is not dualistic. Their explorers do not want to leave the world; they want to see more deeply into it. There's a pantheism lurking just below the surface of both Whitman's poem and Vaughan William's orchestral setting. Some Whitman scholars refer to this as "inverted mysticism."[25] The first three movements of the symphony are about the earth, the physical, with the fourth, Whitman's poet and his soul have been transported, "now it is the planet itself and its cosmic context which are addressed."[26]

The chorus, orchestra, baritone, and soprano combine in one continuous, unfolding melody with a sense of propelled upward movement shared by all. Nearly midway through the fourth movement, the baritone and soprano launch into

---

Williams (New York: Oxford University Press, 1964), 29.

[24]   I urge the reader to watch this complete video performance of *A Sea Symphony*: https://www.youtube.com/watch?v=Lp4G5vtd SWc&t=1202s. It's impossible to appreciate Vaughan Williams achievement from a verbal description.

[25]   *Walt Whitman's America*, 244.

[26]   Ibid., 144.

a rapturous duet filled with a sense of wonder at what lies at the end of the journey, with the baritone declaiming, "O we can wait no longer, / We too take ship O Soul, / Joyous we too launch out on trackless seas." The soprano enters here singing the same line just as the baritone ends. This canon structure of overlapping is used throughout, like waves falling against the shore, like the motions of lovers.

When the baritone sings "O soul thou pleasest me, I thee," the music begins rising in pitch, building tension slowly, an anticipation of the vision to come. "Waking in the night" intensifies our expectation, but the voices frustrate us, drifting dreamily, as if floating upward, until they reach the line, "Bear me indeed as through regions infinite." Then, with a big intake of breath, they sing in unison, "Whose air I breathe, whose ripples hear, lave me all over," as if the dam is about to burst, and it does, with the soprano entering on "Bathe me O God in thee," joined in a few bars by the baritone, with an ecstatic plea to God to allow them into His presence. After a moment of rest, the baritone enters with great nobility, and it's clear they have been allowed to rise to a higher level, "mounting to thee." Suddenly another burst of emotion is released as the baritone joins with the soprano rising up a ladder of notes to a high pitch, singing "and my soul in range of thee."

What follows is one of those moments in music that leaves the listener speechless, dazzled by a beauty seemingly beyond the power of a human artist to create. On "O Thou transcendent," the two voices rise and merge in one of the most sublime passages in music, until the end of the stanza, "Light of the light, shedding forth universes, thou centre of them." The music is climatic and shattering and succeeds in conveying the unique power of Whitman's poetic voice.

What did Whitman's poet and his soul meet in their vision as rendered by Vaughan Williams? Plato's Beauty or the person of the Revealed God seen "face to face"? They met neither. Whitman has an understanding of being where the physical and spiritual may be distinguished in language but not in reality.[27] I'd say that Whitman, aided by Vaughan Williams, goes as far as unaided Eros can go, but both must fall back because without faith there is no person to welcome them.

What makes Eros this powerful? For one thing, it is integral to our human nature, and cannot be removed. Eros is existence pushing us forward. Deny Eros and you remain in the dark about what and who you are. Eros naturally moves our will towards anything perceived as beautiful and good. Delighting in each spring flower is invigorating and harmless. Delighting in the beauty of faces passing by on the street is also, unless you are Scottie looking to find a replacement for a lost love. In our world, peopled as it is with us, with fallen humanity, many men and women treat Eros as a kind of drug, and the person at whom it's misdirected as a useful object.

Romantic Love

Romantic love was invented in the twelfth century according to Denis de Rougemont in his classic study of *Love In*

---

[27]   Ibid., 244.

the Western World.[28] The Troubadour poets who performed at French courts composed and sang songs of love about unattainable ladies. Their songs were representative of what is called "The Tristan Myth," a love characterized by the desire for someone who cannot be possessed. The intensity of Romantic love grows as the object of desire is denied. Most would agree this is the opposite of how love grows in an ordered relationship. But in Romantic love, the inflamed emotions become valued as an ideal type of love and passion. Here de Rougemont describes the relation between Tristan and Isolde as told by the twelfth-century medieval writer Béroul: "Tristan and Iseult do not love each other. They say they don't and everything goes to prove it. *What they love is love and being in love.*"[29]

The ferocity of the felt love and desire is admired rather than the "humdrum" everyday love of, say, a mature marriage. Such love was not left behind in the twelfth century— it remains both in life and fiction. Writers prefer unhappy love because "Happy love has no history," remarks de Rougemont.[30] He explains, "Romance only comes into existence where love is fatal, frowned upon and doomed by life itself. What stirs lyrical poets to their finest flights is neither the delight of the senses nor the fruitful contentment of the settled couple; not the satisfaction of love, but its *passion*. And passion means suffering."[31]

---

[28]   *Love In the Western World*, 41.
[29]   Ibid., Italics in the original.
[30]   Ibid., 15.
[31]   Ibid.

Here de Rougemont overstates his case, though his analysis of the passion malady remains true. We saw it vividly in *Vertigo*. A comparison can be made with *Leaves of Grass*: Whitman's erotic desire flourishes in the journey itself—reaching the destination doesn't matter. His Eros is like that of the Troubadour poets whose ardor is intensified by being denied the woman whose praises he sings. This shift of attention from the object loved to the subject loving became central during the Renaissance and, especially, the Romantic era. The turn to the subject became a theme present in all modern philosophy, as more and more doubt was cast on the knowledge we have of the outer world. The concept of happiness itself slowly transitioned to becoming a psychological state, the enjoyment of the chase but not the capture.[32]

French existentialist author Albert Camus depicted the less than happy outcome of this journey in his *Myth of Sisyphus* (1942). Using a character from Greek mythology, Camus tells the story of Sisyphus, who spends his life rolling a rock up a hill only to see it roll down again. But Sisyphus never stops rolling it back up the mountain. However, Camus concludes that "all is well," and indeed, that "one must imagine Sisyphus happy."[33] Camus's Sisyphus represents the nihilism that results from chasing the chase, from moving on after every capture because after capture comes the immediate lessening of desire; the air goes out of the balloon.

We can disagree with Camus's harsh portrait of human existence while seeing his point: this is what happens when

---

[32]   *Happiness and the Limits of Satisfaction*, 73.
[33]   Albert Camus, *The Myth of Sisyphus & Other Essays*, trans. Justin O'Brien (New York: Alfred A. Knopf, 1955), 91.

human love seeks only the Self. Camus makes us think about the consequences of what we believe and the ways in which our beliefs affect how we live and love. Human Eros sets us down a specific path of life. At some point, hopefully, each of us will stop, look in the mirror, and ask, "What is it I am looking for?" That moment is the beginning of wisdom.

Recommended

Books

Old Testament, *Song of Songs.*
Plato, *Phaedrus*, 370 BC.
Andreas Capellanus, *The Art of Courtly Love*, 1184.
St. Thomas Aquinas, "Treatise on Love," *Summa Theologica*, 1265–1274.
William Shakespeare, *Sonnets*, 1609.
Johann Wolfgang von Goethe, *The Sorrows of Young Werther*, 1774.
Stendhal, *On Love*, 1822.
Søren Kierkegaard, *Works of Love*, 1847.
Martin Buber, *I and Thou*, 1923.
Anders Nygren, *Agape and Eros*,1930–1936.
Jose Ortega y Gasset, *On Love: Aspects of a Single Theme*, 1940.
M. C. D'Arcy, *The Mind and Heart of Love*, 1945.
Hans Urs von Balthasar, *Love Alone*, 1966.
Robert G. Hazo, *The Idea of Love*, 1967.
Dietrich von Hildebrand, *The Nature of Love*, 1971.

Music

Giovanni Pierluigi da Palestrina, *Canticum Canticorum* (choral setting of the *Song of Songs*), 1584.

W. A. Mozart, *Le Nozze di Figaro*, 1786.

Franz Schubert, *Die Schöne Müllerin*, 1823.

Frédéric Chopin, Piano Concerto No. 1, 1830.

Hector Berlioz, *Symphonie Fantastique*, 1830.

Richard Wagner, *Prelude* and *Liebestod*, from *Tristan and Isolde*, 1859.

Georges Bizet, *Carmen*, 1875.

Giacomo Puccini, *La Boheme*, 1895.

Arnold Schoenberg, *Transfigured Night*, 1899.

Richard Strauss, *Der Rosenkavalier*, 1910.

Leos Janacek, String Quartet No. 2 ("Intimate Letters"), 1928.

Frederick Delius, *Idyll* (with text by Walt Whitman), 1933.

Leonard Bernstein and Stephen Sondheim, *West Side Story*, 1957.

Movies

F. W. Murnau, *Sunrise*, 1927.

Kenji Mizoguchi, *The Story of Last Chrysanthemums*, 1939.

Marcel Carné, *The Children of Paradise*, 1945.

David Lean, *Brief Encounter*, 1945.

William Wyler, *The Best Years of Our Lives*, 1946.

Douglas Sirk, *All That Heaven Allows*, 1955.

Billy Wilder, *The Apartment*, 1960.

Ken Russell, *Women in Love*, 1970.

Krzysztof Kieślowski, *A Short Film About Love*, 1988.

Krzysztof Kieślowski, *The Decalogue*, 1989–1990.
Martin Scorsese, *The Age of Innocence,* 1993.
Wong Kar-wai, *In the Mood for Love*, 2000.

CHAPTER 16

Agape

1 Corinthians 13:1–13

Next, we consider a text that has probably influenced the Western understanding of love more than any other, St. Paul's tribute to love from his *First Letter to the Corinthians*. Written around AD 53, this letter contains the most widely-recognized words about love ever written, such as, "If I speak in the tongues of men or of angels, but do not have love, I am only a resounding gong or a clanging cymbal." Though the words are eloquent, for St. Paul, love is action, not words, even if spoken by the greatest poets or philosophers. In the next verse, he says that without love, regardless of our attainments, we are "nothing." And any actions lacking love, no matter how sacrificial, "gain nothing" (v. 3).

All of St. Paul's references to love are about ἀγάπην, Agape. St. Paul describes this love as the necessary foundation for all moral action—without love, whatever is done has no merit. In fact, the Greek word *Eros* is not used at all in the New Testament, whereas the other loves—Storge and Philia—are found there alongside Agape.

At verse 4, the apostle begins to describe the attributes of true love: "Love is patient and kind; love is not jealous or boastful; it is not arrogant or rude. Love does not insist on its own way; it is not irritable or resentful; it does not rejoice at wrong, but rejoices in the right. Love bears all things, believes all things, hopes all things, endures all things" (13:4–7).

"Love keeps no record of wrongs"—taken literally no one does that, but St. Paul's intent is clear: past wrongs must be put aside, reconciled in some way, for love to continue and thrive. Indeed, this why "Love never ends" (v. 8). Agape as the perfect realization of God's will replaces everything imperfect—including prophecies, tongues, and knowledge (v. 8–10). Through this love, we become fully grown, the man replaces the child: "When I became a man, I gave up childish ways" (v. 11).

In verse 12, we read a passage reminiscent of Plato: the apostle moves our eyes upward: "For now we see in a mirror dimly, but then face to face." The resemblance to Plato's ascent to Beauty is there, but St. Paul immediately qualifies the vision he describes: "then I shall know fully, even *as I am fully known*" (emphasis added). Plato's Good does not look back and does not seek to recognize the lover. In a Christian universe, however, each of us is "fully known" by God whether we seek him or not.

This characterization of Agape by St. Paul reverberates so deeply in the collective memory of Western civilization that it has become a standard reference point for selfless love. Agape is the love that "never fails" (v. 8), but as we have seen, Eros is a love that can go wrong, and in countless ways. St.

Paul's Agape should be regarded as the corrective to unrestrained, unredeemed Eros as well as the defects in Storge and Philia.

Os Justi

It is an intriguing question: What great musical work best evokes the sense of Agape love, the "perfect love" that descends from God to his beloved creation? Some possible choices immediately came to mind: Duruflé, *Ubi Caritas;* Victoria, *O Magnum Mysterium;* Byrd, *Ave Verum Corpus;* Faure, *Requiem;* Haydn, *Creation;* Mozart, *Requiem;* Bach, *Mass in B Minor;* Elgar, *The Dream of Gerontius.* The list could go on—there are centuries of sacred and classical music devoted to God's love and our love for him.

One criterion has guided me in my selection of books, music, and films: each is a work from the canon that has special meaning for me. I'm very fond of all the music listed above, but I know another piece of music that sounds to me like pure Agape: I'm talking about the motet *Os Justi* (1879)[1] by Anton Bruckner (1824–1896).

From the first time I heard *Os Justi* (The Mouth of the Righteous) forty years ago as a graduate student in Atlanta, I've considered it the closest thing I could imagine to what God's love might sound like. The performance by Robert Shaw and his chorus completely stunned me. When I return to it, *Os Justi* never loses its luster. The words of this motet, a

---

[1]   Here is a video of a very fine performance by the Bavarian Radio Chorus conducted by Michael Gläser: www.youtube.com/watch?v=I7MjBNDuNd0.

Gregorian chant performed/prayed in liturgical settings for centuries, do not refer directly to love: the text from Psalm 37 speaks of a "just man:" the wisdom, judgment, and divine love he has "in his heart." But the music, to my ear, expresses in sound the overflowing gift of God's love to his creatures.

Anton Bruckner was an earnest Catholic. Music historian Derek Watson says about Bruckner, "For him, God and the world of transcendent spirit were realities he never questioned."[2] He wrote eleven symphonies, though only nine of them are numbered. His unfinished Ninth Symphony was dedicated to God. Music historian and critic Paul Henry Lang describes Bruckner as a "medieval soul living in the nineteenth century, struggling with the problem of finding an artistic relationship to God."[3]

Bruckner began his musical career as a choirboy at St. Florian's Monastery near his home in Ansfelden, Austria. After some years as a teacher, Bruckner returned to St. Florian, where he became one of the finest organists in Europe with a reputation for stupendous improvisation. From there, Bruckner returned to Linz and started compositional training. Just as he began to compose for orchestra, Bruckner was appointed professor of harmony and counterpoint at the University of Vienna. He never married, though he had the habit of proposing marriage to much younger women. Nothing ever came of it; he was not predatory in the least, but he earned much scathing gossip. Bruckner did not appear to be much of a catch; his homeliness and unkempt

---

2   Derek Watson, *Bruckner* (New York: Schirmer Books, 1996), 49.
3   *Music in Western Civilization*, 918.

appearance did not fit easily into Viennese society. But, to his credit, he did not isolate himself. His biographer Derek Watson reports that Bruckner danced well and attended carnival balls well into his fifties.[4]

Transcendent moments occur throughout Bruckner's work. Sometimes they happen amidst a ninety-minute symphony, others visit your ear quickly, and you are left wondering how such sublimity is possible. One of our era's most celebrated conductors, Colin Davis, said, "Bruckner could create a melody that is like an arc from heaven." About Bruckner's Third Symphony, Davis said to the interviewer, "If I have not conveyed to you why I think the passage starting at the 11:57 mark in this performance resembles just such an arc from heaven, I have been wasting my time."[5]

Everything in the five-minute *Os justi* happens quickly. Written as an eight-part setting for a cappella mixed chorus, the motet uses texts from Psalm 36, verses 30 and 31: "The mouth of the just shall meditate wisdom, and his tongue shall speak judgment. The law of his God is in his heart, and his steps shall not be supplanted. Alleluia." Derek Watson comments, "Despite the severity of these restrictions, this motet is profoundly emotional in its effect."[6]

The piece opens simply with the choir singing together in harmony through the first two bars: "Os justi, meditabitur sapientiam." At the third bar, the same line is repeated with

---

4   Ibid., 46.
5   R. J. Stove, "Anton Bruckner and God," *Catholic World Report*, August 2, 2015, www.catholicworldreport.com/2015/08/02/anton-bruckner-and-god/.
6   *Bruckner*, 93.

the lower male voices entering on the first word *os*. Then the higher women's voices enter on *os* just as the men have sung *sti*. So far the music is lovely but straightforward. But just as the women finish *justi*, the men's voices rise quickly on *meditabitur*, creating an unexpected chord, matched by the ladies as they start the same word. The chord creates tension, with a hint of unresolved discord, but then something magical happens. At *sapientiam*, the choir's steadily descending notes create four bars of astonishing beauty, their falling suggests a wisdom (sapientia) coming from above, not man-made.

In a personal letter to me, music scholar Francis O'Gorman wrote, "What's striking about that first 'sapientiam' is that it is a prominent moment of a discord resolved. The alto part has an expressive figure on <pi> but on <en> is suddenly in a tone clash with the treble/soprano part, a clash that is beautifully resolved in the four-note descending scale to <tiam>. The clarity and simplicity of the treble part expressively contrast with this inner movement."[7] In *Os Justi*, Bruckner has made God's love audible in music.

What all loves have in common is a desire for unity with another, whether a person or God. We've seen this with a mother's love for her child; in friendship between friends; and in Eros, which, starting with the physical, rises along the ladder of love towards perfect Beauty, the Good itself.

Agape can be described in two ways, from above and from below. Viewed from above, God's love descends and transforms as an act of grace. From below, agape is human love so surprising and powerful we cannot explain it without

---

[7]   Prof. Francis O'Gorman email to the author, February 3, 2019.

pointing toward the mystery or the miraculous. In either case, Agape is a love that dwarfs our resources. We wonder where it comes from unless we have faith.

For the believer, Agape does not originate from below but descends from God, "for God so loved the world" (Jn 3:16). Non-believers recognize extraordinary acts of love, which seem miraculous and mysterious to them. But without a transcendent reference point, their recognition cannot fully comprehend the deepest meaning contained in acts of extreme self-sacrifice, heroism, kindness, and personal transformation.

Contrast Agape then with Greek Eros. In the case of Eros, the lover strives for the Beautiful and the Good, but these ideals do not love back. Only a *person* can love in return. The sense of unity attained by spiritual Eros, though satisfying, remains a vision of possibility, of what might be: the Good is never actualized though in the way Christians believe it was with the Incarnation.

Christian Agape is the culmination of what C. S. Lewis termed "Gift-love" because God has no *need* to give it. Those who receive it by faith need it and need to love in return. Human love for God is only fully actualized when a person loves the self for God's sake—this was the theological insight of St. Bernard of Clairvaux and other mystical theologians of the Middle Ages.[8]

---

[8]   Bernard of Clairvuax, *Treatises II: The Steps of Humility and Pride & On Loving God*, trans. Robert Walton OSB (Kalamazoo: Cistercian Publications, 1980, 119–21.

A Memoir of Mary Ann

The Southern writer Flannery O'Connor (1925–1963) wrote an introduction to a non-fiction book about a girl named Mary Ann. Mary Ann Long was born with a disfiguring cancerous tumor on her face.[9] When she was three, the doctor told her parents that Mary Ann had only six months to live. She went to live with a group of seventeen Dominican sisters[10] at the Our Lady of Perpetual Help Cancer Home in Atlanta. Mary Ann received love and care from the sisters until she died at the age of twelve.

Several years later, one of the Dominican sisters wrote to O'Connor about the remarkable life and sanctity of Mary Ann, suggesting she write a novel about her. O'Connor, who lived close by in Milledgeville, Georgia, responded with the suggestion that the sisters send her their memories of Mary Ann which she would edit into a book and write the introduction. The sister's letter had enclosed a picture: "Her small face was straight and bright on one side. The other side was protuberant, the eye was bandaged, the nose and mouth crowded slightly out of place. The child looked out at her observer with an obvious happiness and composure. I

---

[9]   Lorraine V. Murray, "Saying 'Yes' to God: Flannery O'Connor and Mary Ann," *Georgia Bulletin*, March 27, 2011, https://georgiabulletin.org/news/2011/03/saying-yes-to-god-flannery-oconnor-and-mary-ann/.

[10] The Dominican Sisters of Hawthorne were founded in 1900 by Rose Hawthorne, daughter of the famous writer, to minister to incurable cancer patients: https://hawthorne-dominicans.org/about-us.html.

continued to gaze at the picture long after I had thought to be finished with it."[11]

After looking at Mary Ann's picture, the introduction became an eighteen-page reflection on love, suffering, and faith. O'Connor comments on Mary Ann's funeral where the bishop naturally spoke to her family. But "he could not have been thinking of that world, much farther removed yet everywhere, which should not ask why Mary Ann would die, but why she should be born in the first place."[12] O'Connor acknowledges that a child's suffering is often used to discredit God and his goodness. Suffering doesn't fit into a therapeutic culture where people cling to comfort. Where comfort is paramount, the question will arise why someone like Mary Ann "should be born in the first place."

Such a question arises because, "in this popular pity, we mark our gain in sensibility and our loss of vision."[13] The vision of the *source* of life is being lost. Living through World War II, O'Connor had already made the connection how *the idea of death as a solution* issues from the loss of belief: "When tenderness is detached from the source of tenderness, its logical outcome is terror. It ends in forced labor camps in the fumes of the gas chamber."[14] Writing in 1961, Flannery O'Connor foresees a culture that accepts parents disposing of their child, a newly-conceived life. Love does not remove

---

[11]   *A Memoir of Mary Ann By the Dominican Nuns Who Took Care of Her*, introduction by Flannery O'Connor (New York: Farrar, Straus and Cudahy, 1961), 5–6.

[12]   Ibid., 18.

[13]   Ibid., 19.

[14]   Ibid.

suffering by eliminating the sufferer: love, as writes St. Paul, "always protects, always trusts, always hopes, always perseveres" (1 Cor 13:7).

The Straight Story

Can we describe Agape from below without any reference to God? O'Connor would very likely say it is sheer foolishness to try. But here I go: Let's start by paying attention to those narratives where an event occurs that dazzles onlookers and leaves them either speechless or filled with joy. They might call it a mystery or a miracle, even if they don't believe in them. They may thank God, who they believe doesn't exist. A particularly striking example of this can be a sudden change in character or complete moral transformation. For instance, in *The Bicycle Thieves*, why did the man in the crowd on that street in Rome decide to let the father go? Rossellini does not celebrate that decision by focusing on the man among the group but instead focuses on the father and son walking home, reunited and free from danger. There was no such change of character in either *The Rules of the Game*, *Vertigo*, or *Autumn Sonata*, no matter how much we may have hoped for them.

For a character undergoing a transformative change, let's call it a non-religious *metanoia*.[15] I can think of no better example than *The Straight Story* (1999),[16] directed by David Lynch. Lynch is best known for his mind-bending TV series

---

[15]   The Greek word for "conversion."
[16]   *The Straight Story*, dir. David Lynch (1999; Burbank, CA: Walt Disney Pictures, 2000), DVD.

Twin Peaks (1991–1993) and his myth-exploding portrayal of 1950s America, *Blue Velvet* (1986). Lynch has shown, however, he can make a brilliant film in any genre. His first major success, *Elephant Man* (1980), demonstrated that a thirty-four-year-old American from Missoula, Montana could make a classic directing a who's who of British actors, including Anthony Hopkins, John Gielgud, and Wendy Hiller.

The setting of *The Straight Story* is about as far as you can get from *Elephant Man's* nineteenth-century London of starched collars and women's corsets. Alvin Straight (Richard Farnsworth), age seventy-three, lives in Laurens, Iowa and hears his older brother Lyle (Harry Dean Stanton), who lives three hundred miles away, has had a stroke. Alvin decides he must see him, though they've not spoken for ten years after an argument left them estranged. Alvin does not own a driver's license or a car, so he sets out on his riding lawnmower, pulling a cart with the essentials needed for a long trip.

David Lynch called *The Straight Story* his "most experimental film."[17] Reading this, I first wondered if the famously eccentric director was joking, but then I took into account both the simplicity and boldness of the story. In a television interview, Lynch explains he wanted to make the movie because he fell in love with the script. He recognized and felt the big emotions of the story and wanted to bring that

---

17   Christopher Runyon, "The David Lynch Retrospective: 'The Straight Story,'" July 26, 2013, http://moviemezzanine.com/the-david-lynch-retrospective-the-straight-story/.

emotion to the screen, as only film can do.[18] The script, by the way, is based upon a true story.[19]

The Straight Story is the story of a journey where we learn about Alvin. Alvin is not a religious man.[20] He does not join in opportunities to discuss faith with strangers during his voyage. Once a farm hand and former alcoholic and bar brawler, only seven of his fourteen children have survived. Despite a tough life, what impacted him most was when he accidentally shot a fellow soldier as a sniper during WWII. Returning from the war, he became dissolute. Hearing about the rough-and-ready of Alvin's background is important. The face of the actor Richard Farnsworth, and especially his blue eyes, make him look almost saintly.[21]

At some stops along the road, Alvin helps some strangers to resolve serious difficulties—the pregnant teenager run away from home, and the two brothers, both mechanics, who can't stop arguing with each other. When asked why he is making this trip, Alvin answers that he wants to see his brother, adding, "I want to sit with him and look up at the stars, like we used to, so long ago." Walt Whitman would have appreciated that comment, as the camera pans across

[18] American Film Institute interview with David Lynch, August 13 2009, https://www.youtube.com/watch?v=O8qM05l9tIs.

[19] Roger Ebert, "The Straight Story," October 15, 1999, https://www.rogerebert.com/reviews/the-straight-story-1999.

[20] This original 1999 trailer of *The Straight Story* gives the flavor of the film: www.youtube.com/watch?v=e0zb_baTzkk.

[21] This clip from the film shows Alvin telling his daughter, Rosie, that he must go see his brother and shows the power of Farnsworth's face and acting: www.youtube.com/watch?v=aCzAetSFRC8.

a panorama of trees, corn, and wheat fields blown by the wind.

As the lawnmower goes by, the camera often widens out to take in the nature around him: its beauty is reassuring, reflecting the peaceful and reassuring disposition of its eccentric captain.

When Alvin reaches his brother's shack, they say very little to each other. The depth of emotion is communicated by the warmth of the hug between brothers. This is not just, "I'm glad to see you." This is, "I am so glad to see you, my brother, after all these years." More dialogue would have weakened the effect. In the last scene, the brothers sit on the front porch gazing out into the valley and the sky. Is this a miracle? Think about it: a seventy-three-year-old man, having fallen out with his brother ten years ago, drives his grass mower three hundred miles for reconciliation. Yes, it's a miracle.

We never find out exactly why Alvin changed in his attitude towards Luke, but we know something happened. Perhaps it was merely the news of his brother's illness, but the change comes from deep inside him. This kind of inexplicable transformation points only to Agape.

Ordet

Carl Theodor Dreyer's 1955 Danish film *Ordet,* translated "Word," is about Christian love and the possibility of miracles.[22] There's no irony, no tongue-in-cheek, the film is

---

22   *Ordet,* dir. Carl Theodor von Dreyer (1978; London: The British Film Institue, 2015), Blu-ray.

completely representational. Despite its near-biblical tone, Dreyer's film earned praise from critics across the spectrum. Ranked twenty-fourth among the fifty best movies ever made in the 2016 *Sight and Sound* poll,[23] *Ordet*, according to Roger Ebert, "stands utterly and fearlessly alone. . . . Many viewers will turn away from it. Persevere. Go to it. It will not come to you." Glenn Erickson, another major critic, effuses, "For this is nothing less than a miracle story. Maybe it was a cumulative spell, but by the end of *Ordet* I was transported and experienced a little dramatic miracle of my own."

How does Dreyer pull this off when so many films about religion become kitschy when depicting the supernatural? He had done it before in his most famous movie, *The Passion of Joan of Arc* (1928), ranked ninth in the *Sight and Sound* poll. Starting in 1919 Dreyer had become world famous as a silent film director, often portraying religious stories; religious concerns also informed three of his five "talking" movies, *Day of Wrath* (1943), *Ordet* (1955), and *Gertrud* (1964). Strangely, though raised Lutheran, Dreyer was not very religious.

The question arises how such a man can make some of the most realistic and probing films about faith and spirituality. Perhaps having some distance from his subject matter, as did the agnostic Mark Twain when he wrote his marvelous biography of St. Joan, allowed Dreyer the kind of objective portrayal that gives these films such power. Dreyer did not manipulate his material, looking for additional dramatic

---

[23]   "The 50 Greatest Films of All Time," https://www.bfi.org.uk/news/50-greatest-films-all-time.

effect; he just told the story. With *Ordet*, he was determined to remain faithful to the play upon which the film was based, Kaj Munk's *I Begyndelsen var Ordet* (*In the Beginning was the Word*).[24] Munk, a Danish national hero, was martyred by the Nazis for his sermons condemning the occupiers. Dreyer met regularly with Munk's widow to assure her, and himself, his adaptation was faithful to her husband's play.

Dreyer was meticulous in his aesthetic choices for the film. His casting of the main characters is astute, especially Henrik Malberg as Morten, the Borgen family patriarch, whose face comes right out of a Rembrandt masterpiece: looking in his deep-set expressive eyes we believe this is a man of faith. His three sons—Mikkel (Emil Hass Christensen), Johannes (Preben Lerdorff Rye), and Anders (Cay Kristiansen)—are not the same physical type, they are etched individually. The unbelieving oldest son married to the saintly, pregnant Inger (Birgitte Federspiel); Johannes, the second son, who wanders around the village proclaiming himself Jesus Christ after going insane studying theology; and young Anders, who wants to marry Anne Petersen (Gerda Nielsen), the only daughter of the local tailor.

The director considered Johannes the key character, the apparent madman who comes out of his room as in a trance, constantly quoting Scripture as if he was the man who first spoke the words. Dreyer explains, "From the character of the

---

24   Norman Berdichevsky, "Pastor Kaj Munk: Martyr of the Danish Resistance: Why Christians Must Never be Pacifists in the Face of Evil," November 2015, https://www.newenglishreview.org/ Norman_Berdichevsky/Pastor_Kaj_Munk:_Martyr_of_the_ Danish_Resistance/.

man Johannes, the film will find its true style. I must pour into *The Word* an atmosphere in which a miracle is possible. Life—*Life* must be the watchword."[25] In other words, the director wants Johannes to be a holy fool who disturbs all present.

Dreyer's choice of settings is also highly intentional: he shot all the exterior scenes in a barren part of Jutland near the church of Pastor Munk, author of the original play. *Ordet*'s setting is sparse, shot in black and white, without a hint of luxury. The handful of outside shots reveal a stark but beautiful landscape—a constant wind bends the high reeds, and the sand blows across the dunes.

Next, in spite of the simple setting, the cinematographer, Henning Bendtsen, shot scenes of extraordinary beauty— but Dreyer restrained himself and the cinematographer from allowing visual splendor to detract from the story. In the climactic scene, Bendtsen shot what has been called one of the most exceptional scenes in cinema history: "a late-film, almost three-minute pan around the possibly mad character Johannes and his niece, Marren, fearful of her mother's [Inger] death. Though the camera doesn't for a moment stop its slow rotation around the two of them, we never see their backs; they are subtly rotating along with the camera."[26] This was three years before the spiraling shot in Hitchcock's *Vertigo*.

---

[25]   Jan Wahl, *Carl Theodor Dreyer and Ordet: My Summer with the Danish Filmmaker* (Lexington: The University of Kentucky Press, 2012), 26.

[26]   "Henning Bendtsen, 1925–2011," www.criterion.com/current/posts/1751-henning-bendtsen-1925-2011.

Emphasizing the sense of isolation, in an homage to the film's theatrical origins, most of the movie takes place in the main room of the family's ancestral home and a bedroom. There's nothing extraneous to distract from the questions raised about belief and unbelief. All the plotlines intertwine to culminate at the open coffin of Inger, a beautiful young woman, a wife, and mother of two. Standing at the end of the bed is a man holding the hand of a young girl, praying for a miracle.

Once the characters are established, the plot of *Ordet* quickly focuses on one source of conflict, the fight to save the life of Inger and her baby during childbirth. The initial conflict is created by Anne's parents, Peter and Kristin, who oppose the marriage between their daughter and Anders because they believe only evangelicals like themselves are true Christians. Morten, the patriarch whose faith is more cheerful, is outraged to hear his son has been rejected. Morten rushes to the Petersen's home, where the conversation turns ugly when Peter refuses to reconsider. As Morten is leaving, the phone rings, summoning him home due to Inger's pregnancy going bad. Frustrated that Morten will not convert, Peter welcomes the news of Inger's possible death because it will bring Morten to the true faith. Morten smacks him on the head, leaves with Anders, and we see the carriage rushing through the night.

At this point in the film, the viewer has seen a father badgering his eldest son about his lack of belief; a young man driven to insanity by the study of theology; two families estranged over different versions of their Christianity; and the most sympathetic character, Inger, fighting for her life. Dreyer's films raise questions for both skeptics and the religious.

When father and son get home, we hear her cries of pain, we see Mikkel's near-hysteria, and Morten starts questioning God, while Johannes frantically begs his family to pray for a miracle. The doctor, a skeptic, arrives to help Inger and performs an abortion to save Inger's life. After a brief rally, Inger dies, which Johannes had predicted after having a vision of the Grim Reaper, to the scorn of his father. The household grieves while Johannes keeps telling Morten to have faith enough to ask for a miracle. Morten waves him off.

Morten stands at the open coffin. The Petersens arrive to apologize to Morten; they embrace. Anne and Anders can be married, Peter adds. Johannes decides to pray for the miracle himself. Everyone goes into the room, scoffing at Johannes, but no one tries to stop him from praying for Inger to come back to life. His first try fails. He comes to realize that he has not entirely relied on God, and he undergoes a transformation. His insanity leaves him. One daughter takes his hand and prays with him. In this image there's an allusion to Jesus's teaching, "Whenever two are gathered in my name, I am with them;" and "Unless you become as little children, you will not enter the Kingdom of God." Inger comes back to life.

Dreyer wanted to challenge the rejection of faith by modern intellectuals like the doctor: "To me, the best believers are the child and the deranged person, since their minds are not rational and limited by proof-positive facts like ours. They have a wider universe, where such things are possible."

Ordet confronted the viewer with a literal miracle—there's no waffling on its significance, no backdoor explanation. Dreyer portrays the literal meaning of the miracle story while using his art to tell that story to an audience—that, to me, denotes greatness.

Paradiso

Centuries of often contentious theological debate have been devoted to explaining how Agape ("the perfect love") connects with the human loves. It is one of the debates that divided the Church between Catholic and Protestant. The question is this: Is human nature capable of cooperating in any way with God's grace? That question leads to enumerating the effects of the Fall. Did human nature become so corrupted after being thrown out of Eden that grace never really penetrates human character? Grace, rather, is a means of reconciling God and man through Christ's sacrifice. Man is, therefore, justified before God, but his ways remain the same—there is no infusion of grace into human habits where the will allows grace to perfect its actions.

This last sentence was the argument of the original Protestant reformers—Martin Luther, Ulrich Zwingli, and John Calvin. Henry VIII is not a reformer in this sense. The Church of England which he created by a declaration in 1534 replaced the Roman pontiff but not the substance of traditional Catholic moral teaching. The early Protestants generally agreed that Agape is a grace given entirely by the benevolence of God and given to a creature whose nature is far too corrupted to claim any merit.

In 1520, Luther wrote a public letter, *Address to the Nobility of the German Nation*, that announced the need for Germany to free itself from the Roman power.[27] In his next treatise of the same year, *The Babylonian Captivity of the Church*, Luther proclaims that it is by faith alone we are justified before God.[28] This was far more than a doctrine; Luther and his followers were severing themselves from the Catholic Church and the authority of the pope.

Catholic theologians had long held that Storge, Philia, and Eros play a role by being infused with Agape and raised to a higher power. One of the bedrock principles of St. Thomas Aquinas was that "grace does not destroy nature but perfects it."[29] Luther, as a well-educated Augustinian monk, would have known this teaching, as would Zwingli and Calvin, and would have been perfectly aware he was rejecting what was considered dogma. When Luther went to Augsburg to be scrutinized by a papal legate, the legate was none other than the leading Thomistic scholar of his generation, the Dominican scholar Thomas Cajetan.[30] They talked for three days, just the two of them, but failed to reach any agreement— Luther tried to leave Augsburg quickly that evening but

---

27   Mark Greengrass, *Christendom Destroyed: Europe 1517-1648* (New York: Viking Penguin, 2014), 332.

28   Richard Marius, *Martin Luther: The Christian Between God and Death* (Boston: The Belknap Press of Harvard University, 1999), 253. For a primary source see Martin Luther, *The Bondage of the Will*, V. xiv, trans. J. I. Packer and O. R. Johnston (Grand Rapids, MI: Baker Academic, 2012), 235–38.

29   *Summa Theologica* 1.1:8.

30   Heinz Schilling, *Martin Luther: Rebel In an Age of Upheaval*, trans. Rona Johnston (Oxford: Oxford University Press, 2017), 150–51.

found the city gates already locked. Finally, a friend found a key and let him out.[31]

The divide over religious questions that led to such turmoil in Europe in the fifteenth century had been festering a long time. For example, the argument about nature and grace was very much in the air when Dante Alighieri (1265–1321) wrote his *Divine Comedy*. Dante was born in Florence nine years after the death of Aquinas, which left him standing between the ending of one world and the beginning of another. The Middle Ages would continue in other parts of Europe for another century, but in Florence, a new era was being born, with a renewed interest in antiquity, the pre-Christian West. Elites sought more freedom for the individual from Church authority, as well as new paradigms for the arts, from poetry and music to sculpture, painting, and architecture.

The writer most identified with what become known as the Italian Renaissance was the poet Petrarch. He was born in 1301, when Dante was already thirty-six and had published his first major work, *La Vita Nuova*. That Dante championed writing in the vernacular rather than Latin marks him as a man who did not seek to imitate his predecessors. He was exiled from his Florence in 1302 for merely identifying with a political faction no longer in power. He would never return.

His masterpiece, therefore, was conceived and completed as an exile. Dante started working on the epic poem in 1306, finishing a year before his death in 1320. Like St.

---

[31]   Ibid, 151.

Thomas Aquinas's *Summa Theologica*, Dante's work was a *summa* of sorts: In the three parts of his *Comedia—Inferno*, *Purgatorio*, and *Paradiso*—he combined one man's spiritual journey in the afterlife with a commentary on all Western history known during his lifetime. Famous philosophers, writers, theologians, scriptural figures, and political leaders are placed not just in hell, purgatory, or paradise, but onto a specific ring or level. Each level corresponds to a degree of mortal sin, the purgation for different venial sins, or the intensity of love for God.

The levels in hell, for example, correspond to the "seven deadly sins" of lust, gluttony, avarice, sloth, wrath, envy, and pride; ranked by degrees of destructive rebellion by the poet. Purgatory reflects the same order except they are in the process of being purged by various punishments. In hell, there is only punishment; the damned have not sought redemption or wished for it.

Dante's pilgrim descends into hell, a pit where Satan is stuck in ice, flapping his wings helplessly for eternity. In purgatory, Dante ascends a rock staircase through its circle until the pilgrim reaches the earthly paradise and the first ring of paradise. Until he reaches paradise, his guide is the wisest of pagans, the poet Virgil. But the poet of the *Aeneid*, not being a Christian, cannot enter paradise. Here is where the pilgrim meets his Beatrice, the name of the Florentine woman whose beauty in real life struck so deeply into Dante's heart.

The rings of paradise grow wider, unlike those of hell, as the pilgrim is lead higher, like petals on a rose. The closer he gets to the outermost circle, the *Primum Mobile*, the closer he comes to the vision of God.

In canto 3, the pilgrim meets nuns who "were neglectful in our vows," and he asks if "you desire a place of greater height / to see more, know more, and be held more dear?" (3:55–66).[32] One sister replies,

> Brother, the virtue of our charity
> Brings quiet to our wills, so we desire
> but what we have, and thirst for nothing else. (3:70–72)

Dante begins to understand God's grace, for each one's place in paradise corresponds to their love for him. The Agape love bestowed in paradise brings to everyone a spiritual fulfillment, though each remains aware of their relative distance to the outermost ring.

> Then it was clear to me that everywhere
> in Heaven is Paradise, though the high Good
> does not rain down His grace on all souls there
> Equally. But as it happens that one food
> satisfies, and you give thanks, while you yearn
> for yet another and you beg for it. (3:88–91)

The sins of earthly life, even when redeemed and purged, limit the ability to receive the fullness of God's love, Agape. This is not to say the nuns feel any lack; they don't—they are filled with the divine vision to the extent their lives made it possible. The nun's explanation no doubt irritated Martin Luther, who considered a person's earthly life obliterated by God's forgiveness. Everyone in heaven, for Luther, should be

---

[32]   Dante, *Paradise: A New Translation by Anthony Esolen* (New York: Modern Library, 2004). All quotations from the *Paradiso* are from this volume.

seated the same distance from God—their relative human merit makes no difference.

After the poet gains a new understanding, "you yearn / for yet another and you beg for it." In canto 7, the conversation between Beatrice and Dante turns to Christ's act of atonement, specifically "why God chose / that man should be redeemed in just this way" (7:56–57). Because of the Fall and the exile of Adam and Eve from Eden, humankind suffered a loss of "nobility" (7:79). Humankind's condition takes on a criminal status from the perspective of divine justice. Beatrice explains there are only two ways nobility can be regained: "Either the Lord alone for courtesy / pardon the sin, or for his foolishness / mankind make satisfaction on his own" (7:91–93). If God pardoned the sins of humanity, he would be ignoring the demands of divine justice. Thus, God, in the act of divine love, paid the debt which humankind cannot pay. Despite their extraordinary sanctity, the saints cannot redeem themselves, or earn their way into heaven.

Dante's view of satisfaction—atonement—derives from what is called the "satisfaction theory"[33] of St. Anselm of Canterbury (1033–1109). Jesus Christ's death is understood to satisfy the justice of God. Satisfaction here means restitution, the mending of what was broken and the paying back of debt. In this theory, Anselm emphasizes the justice of God and claims that sin is an injustice that must be balanced. St. Anselm proposed his interpretation in response to the "Ransom theory," which held that the death and resurrection of

---

[33] Anselm of Canterbury, *The Major Works: Including Monologion, Proslogion, and Why God Became Man*, ed. Brian Davies and G. R. Evans (Oxford: Oxford University Press, 2008), 260–356.

Christ was payment to Satan rather than satisfaction of God's justice. The assumption in this theory is that the Fall and the subsequent sins placed humankind under Satan's reign. As hostages, humankind must be ransomed back. Anselm, on the other hand, argued the debt belongs to God, not Satan. Anselm saw the Ransom theory as logically flawed, because what does God owe Satan? Therefore, in contrast with the Ransom theory, Anselm taught that it is humanity who owes a debt to God, not God to Satan.

Beatrice explains that God's payment through his Son's death to obtain pardon made his grace an act of love that can never be surpassed.

> Unto earth's final night from earth's first day
>   no deed so grand or lofty has been done
>   by justice or by pardon, nor shall be,
> For when God gave Himself, enabling man
>   to rise again, His gift was all the more
>   mighty than had He pardoned him, alone. (7:112–17)

"His gift was all the more," this is the gift-love beyond compare.

In the final canto, the pilgrim reaches his goal, the vision of God. Until now, the pilgrim had been ascending, but he suddenly finds himself *being moved*, his will and desire turned by another power, Agape.

> As a geometer struggles all he can
>   to measure out the circle by the square,
>   but all his cogitation cannot gain
> The principle he lacks: so I did stare

at this strange sight, to make the image fit
the aureole, and see it enter there:
But mine were not the feathers for that flight,
   Save that the truth I longed for came to me,
   smiting my mind like lightning flashing bright.
Here ceased the powers of my high fantasy.
   Already were all my will and my desires
   turned—as a wheel in equal balance—by
The Love that moves the sun and other stars. (33:133–45)

The translation, "But mine were not the feathers for that flight," recalls the Platonic ladder of love which the human will ascends, drawn upward by the beauty above. There is more here than the pull of Beauty; this is an act of being taken over by the love of God.

This ecstatic vision as an encounter with and envelopment in divine love anchors the worldview of Christians. Other monotheistic faiths have similar views of eternity. But to generalize about the worldview of the non-believer is dangerous, if only for the fact that some have embraced a spirituality that contains remnants of various religions including those that are animist, polytheistic, and pagan. These eclectic spiritualities offer their own forms of consolation, empowerment, and self-actualization. Whether we agree with them or not, these beliefs are expressions of ultimate concern. Such beliefs may dismay orthodox Christians, but it's a mistake to forget the natural desire for God at their root. None of us has the vantage point from which to judge with finality where God's love is at work and where it is not.

Those who have no religious beliefs at all do recognize, at the very least, that some factors are more beneficial to human lives than others. When children grow up to be self-destructive adults, the first question asked is about their upbringing. What kind of parents, family, education, nutrition, healthcare, and community did they belong to? Such external factors so determinative of a child's future can be seen as analogous to Christian grace, meaning that factor which shapes and directs a life toward well-being. In fact, it's common for grown men and women to express their gratitude for having these advantages—these external factors are viewed as gifts.

Thus, the push-and-pull between the power of nature and nurture repeats the question of nature and grace at another level. Instead of asking what part of a good life we attribute to God's grace, the non-believer asks what kind of factors in upbringing incline a person towards living well. A good upbringing becomes a kind of natural grace that brings order to nature.

For a Christian, however, God's grace is the main factor considered and encompasses all the nurturing factors mentioned above. Christians are grateful too but not for merely being lucky but for a God whose very Being is Love.

Every child is born with a natural desire for all that is good, for God himself. But each child is born into uncertain circumstances. It's impossible to know in advance whether a child's natural desire will be respected and nurtured. The future of any child depends first of all on Storge, the love of a family. Then comes the experiences of Philia which are central to the formation of character in young adults, often determining how a person handles the promptings of Eros. Whether Agape will play a role in these loves, fulfilling all three loves in Itself, is life's most decisive mystery.

Recommended

Books

Bernard of Clairvaux, *On Loving God*, 1128.
St. Thomas Aquinas, "Treatise on Love," *Summa Theologica*, 1265–1274.
William Shakespeare, *A Winter's Tale*, 1623.
Victor Hugo, *Les Misérables*, 1862.
C. S. Lewis, *The Allegory of Love: A Study in Medieval Tradition*, 1936.
Georges Bernanos, *The Diary of a Country Priest*, 1936.
Harper Lee, *To Kill a Mockingbird*, 1960.
Shūsaku Endō, *Silence*, 1966.
Dietrich von Hildebrand, *The Nature of Love*, 1971.
Benedict XVI, *Deus Caritas Est*, 2006.

Music

Tomás Luis de Victoria, *O magnum mysterium*, 1572.
William Byrd, *Ave verum corpus*, 1605.
Johann Sebastian Bach, *St. Matthew Passion*, 1727.
George Frideric Handel, *Messiah*, 1741.
Wolfgang Amadeus Mozart, *Requiem*, 1791.
Joseph Haydn, *Creation*, 1798.
Gabriel Fauré, *Requiem*, 1890.
Edward Elgar, *The Dream of Gerontius*, 1900.
Ralph Vaughan Williams, *Five Mystical Songs*, 1911.

Maurice Duruflé, *Requiem*, 1948.
Stephen Edwards, *Requiem for My Mother*, 2017.

Films

Marcel Carné, *Children of Paradise*, 1945.
Frank Capra, *It's a Wonderful Life*, 1947.
Yasujirö Ozu, *Ikiru*, 1953.
Robert Bresson, *Au Hasard Balthazar*, 1966.
Krzysztof Kieślowski, *Three Colors: White*, 1994.
Paul Thomas Anderson, *Magnolia*, 1999.
Xavier Beauvois, *Of Gods and Men*, 2010.
Terrence Malick, *The Tree of Life*, 2011.

CHAPTER 17

The Human

William Shakespeare and Miguel de Cervantes both died in 1616. Their period of actual writing was nearly the same, 1588–1615. In the West, Shakespeare is regarded as the greatest playwright who ever lived. Harold Bloom goes farther, calling Shakespeare "the Inventor of the Human."[1] Shakespeare's plays offer "extraordinary instances not only of how meaning gets started, rather than repeated, but also of how new modes of consciousness come into being."[2] Here, Bloom means "the human" as we, in the modern world, understand the term "humanity." Bloom is saying that in his plays, Shakespeare created the framework for narrating the human drama, a framework that was dramatically different from that which preceded the sixteenth century, before the changes brought about by Renaissance and Reformation.

Cervantes, we are told, invented not only the novel but all of Western fiction with *Don Quixote*. As famed literary

---

[1] Harold Bloom, *Shakespeare: The Invention of the Human* (New York: Riverhead Books, 1998), xviii.

[2] Ibid.

critic Lionel Trilling says of Cervantes, "It can be said that all prose fiction is a variation on the theme of *Don Quixote.*"[3]

It is intriguing that these two giants appeared in the same time. It leads one to wonder whether there was something about the Western world in the late sixteenth and early seventeenth centuries that provoked such startling intellectual invention. Well, there was: the tumult of the Reformation. In the sixteenth century, Europe broke in two, one adopting a form of Christianity in protest of the Catholic Church ("Protestant"), the other retaining its ancient Catholic faith. The first half of the century saw Martin Luther excommunicated in 1521 followed the next year by King Henry VIII of England. Luther soon commanded a following in most of Northern Europe and Scandinavia. Henry's new Church of England also became the religion of Scotland along with portions of the American colonies. Ireland stubbornly maintained its ties with Rome, promising further division in the United Kingdom.

The Reformers, including not only Luther but John Calvin and Ulrich Zwingli, set off a period of religious war and persecutions that lasted until the middle of the next century, and beyond. When Mary I, daughter of Henry VIII, married Philip of Spain and tried to reimpose Catholicism in England, the persecution of Protestants began, and Sir Thomas Wyatt lead an unsuccessful revolt. In 1558, Elizabeth I returned England to Protestantism, leading to decades of intrigue with Spain culminating with the defeat

---

[3]   Lionel Trilling, *The Liberal Imagination: Essays on Literature and Society,* ed. Pascal Covici (New York: Viking, 1950), 203.

of the Spanish Armada in 1588. Spain had already been at war with the Netherlands since 1546, the year before Cervantes was born. The Eighty Years War between Spain and the Netherlands didn't end until 1648.

Those who ask why some of Shakespeare's plays such as *Titus Andronicus* (1589),[4] *Cymbeline*,[5] and *King Lear* (1608)[6] are so bloody need only look closer into his time and place. Among his fellow playwrights, Christopher Marlowe was murdered, Thomas Kyd tortured, and Ben Jonson branded. Shakespeare kept a low profile. As we will see, violence and cruelty figure prominently in *Don Quixote*; its author, a soldier, had experienced it all firsthand.

What had been the sole moral authority of the Western world since the eleventh century[7] now had a rival: religious leaders who proclaimed that the truth of Scripture was accessible to anyone who could read. (Note the role played by technology; before Gutenberg's printing press, Bibles were hand-copied by scholars for very few owners.) Now, God's Word needed no mediator, whether a priest or the pope; its truth was evident to all. People were naturally confused: they had been told there was only one Truth, and now another

---

[4]   On stage, several body parts are chopped off, along with rape, cannibalism, and a person buried in sand up their neck and left to die.

[5]   Prefiguring *The Godfather*, young Imogen wakes in bed thinking she is beside her lover only to find Cloten, her half-brother, beheaded.

[6]   In Act 3, scene 7, Gloucester's eyes are gouged out on stage by Cornwall and Regan. Cordelia is hung offstage, Goneril poisons Regan, and Goneril kills herself.

[7]   In 1054, the Catholic Church split into the Roman Catholic Church in the West and the Orthodox Church in the East.

version of Truth was being proclaimed and spreading rapidly. The resulting skepticism soon found an eloquent advocate in Montaigne whose *Essays* appeared in 1580, on the eve of Shakespeare's rise to glory. As historian Michael Buckley points out, the *Essays* "permeated the intellect of Europe" with a skepticism so profound it led to Descartes's attempt in the *Meditations* to find a foundation for epistemological certainty.[8]

With skepticism came secularization: once-earnest believers realized if a king (Henry VIII) and an Augustinian monk (Luther) could ignore papal authority, then why not themselves? Some factions within the Church tried to restore its dominance by force—war, persecution, and the Inquisition—though, truth be told, each of these had as much to do with related political fracture as it did with doctrine.

Popes Leo X (1513–1521) and Clement VII (1523–1534) did not want Scripture translated into the vernacular. Thus, when John Tyndale published his first English translation of the Bible in 1525, he became a marked man. In 1535, Tyndale was tried and executed in a court of the Holy Roman emperor at the request of Henry VIII. To get a sense of how quickly things were changing, one need only consider that within four years his translations were being published by Henry VIII, now self-declared head of the Church in England. Martin Luther's translations into German began to appear at the same time, but by then he had the protection of German princes, who preferred to be out from under the

---

[8]   Michael J. Buckley, S.J., *At the Origins of Modern Atheism* (New Haven: Yale University Press, 1987), 69.

thumb of the pope and the Holy Roman emperor. (It should be noted that prior to Luther's translation, there had been eighteen complete translations into German of the Catholic Scriptures.)[9]

Add to this religious confusion the discovery in 1543 by Copernicus that the earth revolved around other bodies in the sky.[10] The earth was no longer the center of the universe. For Protestants, the pope was no longer head of the Church. The earth became smaller in the cosmic scheme of things. The pope had also shrunk in stature. When the Church found Galileo guilty of heresy, a line was crossed for many among the elite: the Church no longer held a monopoly over scholarship and learning. By 1611, English translations of the Bible, including the *King James Bible*, and Homer's *Iliad*, by George Chapman,[11] freed these foundational books to be read by others than those trained in Greek and Latin.

Born in 1564, William Shakespeare was raised in an England of intrigue, war, and deception. Six years earlier, Elizabeth I became queen of England, vowing to restore the Protestantism of her father, Henry VIII. With this return came a persecution of Catholics that outdid the previous one in bloodiness and scope.

---

[9] See http://pblosser.blogspot.com/2004/09/luthers-bible-translation.html.

[10] Nicolaus Copernicus, *On the Revolution of Heavenly Bodies*, 1543.

[11] This translation was called "Chapman's Homer" which inspired an 1816 poem by John Keats, "On First Looking into Chapman's Homer." The poem can be read here: https://www.poetryfoundation.org/poems/44481/on-first-looking-into-chapmans-homer.

Young William grew up in Stratford, receiving an education in Latin literature that exposed him to poetry and drama. He probably left school at fourteen, which was then common, but we know nothing about him until he married Anne Hathaway four years later at age eighteen. The next we hear of Shakespeare was in 1592 when he appeared in London. He acted, wrote, and produced for theatre until 1611 before retiring to Stratford where he died five years later at age fifty-two.

His thirty-eight plays, written over twenty-four years, reflect the tumult of the Elizabethan-Jacobean age but are not bound by them. As we discussed previously, modern academic iconoclasm has not spared Shakespeare, whose works have been dismissed as mere products of the age, written by a Dead White Man, with little if any relevance to our own time. To those scholars who view Shakespeare as merely a *product* of his age, Shakespeare scholar A. D. Nuttall replies that his plays are performed, successfully, in various historical settings, all very different from those described by the playwright. Nuttall calls Shakespeare a "natural time-traveler."[12] His historical period, I would add, was a time of thinking globally; travel and exploration had become common in Elizabethan England: other, newer, worlds were being discovered and elements of their culture brought home by explorers.

Shakespeare's *The Winter's Tale* takes place in Sicily and Bohemia, locales not too exotic but far enough away to

---

[12]   A. D. Nuttall, *Shakespeare the Thinker* (New Haven: Yale University Press, 2007), 22.

stretch the imagination. One of his last plays, *The Winter's Tale* was first performed at London's Globe Theater in May 1611.[13] It takes little effort to connect with its plot and characters. Shakespeare's story belongs to every age and audience, depicting as it does the gall of jealousy, its blindness, and its rage. *The Winter's Tale* is not about the jealousy of an ordinary man but of a king: the order of a kingdom can be destroyed by a king whose thoughts have turned to nihilism and the need for revenge.

As the play opens, Polixenes, the king of Bohemia, has been visiting for nine months at the court of his boyhood friend, Leontes, king of Sicily. Polixenes tells Leontes that he must return home immediately.[14] Leontes encourages him to stay longer, perhaps a week. Polixenes firmly refuses: "There is no tongue that moves, none, none i' th' world, / So soon as yours, could win me" (1.2:19–20). Leontes turns to his pregnant queen and asks if she is too "tongue tied" to speak. She replies, "You, sir, / Charge him too coldly" and recommends Leontes take a gentler approach. But not waiting for her husband, she takes over, cajoling Polixenes for "the borrow of a week." He refuses, twice, with an emphatic "Verily!" Then Hermione cleverly poses him an alternative.

> You shall not go: a lady's 'Verily' 's
> As potent as a lord's. Will you go yet?
> Force me to keep you as a prisoner,

[13]   The full text of *A Winter's Tale* can be read online here: http://shakespeare.mit.edu/winters_tale/full.html.
[14]   An audio recording with Sir John Gielgud as King Leontes of *The Winter's Tale* can be heard here: https://www.youtube.com/watch?v=6h3Uv8SILj4.

Not like a guest; so you shall pay your fees
When you depart, and save your thanks. How say
    you?
My prisoner? Or my guest? by your dread 'Verily,'
One of them you shall be. (1.2.50–57)

Polixenes agrees to stay another week, to my reading, because he's charmed by Hermione's verbal jousting and by the king's encouragement. As we will see, the king discerns different motives for his change of mind. Leontes, who has been attending to other matters, turns and asks Hermione, "Is he won yet?" When Hermione affirms that he is, Leontes is startled, his mood changes quickly. An aroused jealousy catches fire, and he does not attempt to dowse it. His anger mounts, "*At my request* he would not. / Hermione, my dearest, thou never spokest / To better purpose" (italics added). Hermione innocently asks, "Never?" which opens the door for Leontes to compare her wooing of Polixenes to their betrothal: "Never, but once," he adds:

Why, that was when
Three crabbed months had sour'd themselves to death,
Ere I could make thee open thy white hand
And clap thyself my love: then didst thou utter
'I am yours for ever.' (1.2.101–4)

Leontes describes his three months of courtship as "crabbed" and "sour'd," comparing his courtship to how quickly Hermione changed the mind of Polixenes. Hermione, not realizing her husband's mind is unhinging, confirms the equivalence:

I have spoke to the purpose twice:

The one for ever earn'd a royal husband;
The other for some while a friend. (1.2.105–8)

There is only so much a reader of a play can make of its meaning from the text alone—these are words meant to be performed. For example, what Leontes does on stage at this moment is crucial to following the progression of his madness. Leontes, as played by the actor Anthony Sher, does not pull away from Hermione until this moment.[15] Sher's face becomes a mask, his mouth open but saying nothing, his anger building. After a long silence, he lets go of Hermione's hand, turns his back, and walks towards the audience. He looks back to see Hermione and Polixenes dancing. The playwright does not prescribe this, but by having them dance, the director Robin Lough adds a visual reference point for Leontes's unhinged imagination and his rage. Now all the friendly playfulness between his wife and Polixenes corroborate his rash judgment. Leontes says in an aside:

Too hot, too hot!
To mingle friendship far is mingling bloods.
I have *tremor cordis* on me: my heart dances;
But not for joy; not joy. This entertainment
May a free face put on, derive a liberty
From heartiness, from bounty, fertile bosom,
And well become the agent; 't may, I grant;
But to be paddling palms and pinching fingers,
As now they are, and making practis'd smiles,

---

15   *The Winter's Tale*, dir. Robin Lough (New Hope, PA: Kultur Video, 1999), DVD.

As to a looking-glass; and then to sigh, as 'twere
The mort o' the deer; O, that is entertainment
My bosom likes not, nor my brows! Mamillius,
Art thou my boy? (1.2.108–17)

The young prince Mamillius is nearby but has taken no notice of the change in his father when he hears him asking, "Art thou my boy?" After all, Polixenes has been with them for nine months. Mamillius doesn't know that his father now doubts that he is his son. For the next twenty-six lines, Leontes continues in the same angry vein with his son still nearby. "Art thou my calf?" He asks, and his son answers, "Yes, if you will, my lord."[16]

Throughout Act I, Leontes's madness escalates while his wife, Polixenes, his young son, and his court, bewildered, are afraid of what he will do next. Have we been given any clues to a deeper cause of his breaking mind? Earlier, Polixenes had spoken to Hermione about his boyhood friendship with Leontes:

We were, fair queen,
Two lads that thought there was no more behind
But such a day to-morrow as to-day,
And to be boy eternal. (1.2.62–64)

Hermione interrupts his idyllic description with a pointed question, "Was not my lord / The verier wag o' the two?"

---

[16]   Leontes calling his son a "calf" prompted me to think about the story of Abraham being commanded by God to kill his son Issac (Gn 22:1–19). If Shakespeare intended the allusion, it would have been a grotesque contrast between a father who acts in obedience to God and a father tempted to break divine law and kill his son.

Polixenes dodges it by suggesting that both of them began their friendships as innocents, "What we changed / was innocence for innocence. But he admits that less innocent pursuits followed:

> Had we pursu'd that life,
> And our weak spirits ne'er been higher rear'd
> With stronger blood, we should have answer'd heaven
> Boldly 'not guilty;' the imposition clear'd
> Hereditary ours. (1.2.71–74)

Hermione quickly asks, "By this we gather / You have tripp'd since."

Polixenes dodges again by reminding her that during those years both she and his wife had been girls. Hermione persists, wanting to know whether either of them had "sinn'd" or "slipp'd with any but us." Polixenes is saved from answering when Leontes returns to ask the fatal question, "Is he won yet?" From this brief conversation, we learn that Leontes and Polixenes were the closest of friends, and as they grew older, their "stronger blood" took hold. In other words, they faced adult temptations, but he provides no details.

Given the close bond between these two kings, it's apparent that Leontes is doubly hurt. His best friend now seems more intimate with Hermione than with himself. A friend who spends nine months in your home, with whom you share the idyllic memories of boyhood, along with those of post-pubescent pursuits, is more than a friend, but nearly a brother. "Brother" is what Polixenes calls Leontes as they enter the room, to which Leontes replies "brother" a few lines later. Though Leontes's dive into madness is ground-less, the bonds he feels broken lie deeply in his heart.

After Hermione, Polixenes, and his son leave the room, Leontes seethes,

> Should all despair
> That have revolted wives, the tenth of mankind
> Would hang themselves. Physic for't there's none;
> It is a bawdy planet, that will strike
> Where 'tis predominant; and 'tis powerful, think it,
> From east, west, north and south: be it concluded,
> No barricado for a belly; Know't;
> It will let in and out the enemy,
> With bag and baggage: many thousand on's
> Have the disease, and feel't not. (1.2.198–207)

For Leontes, the world has turned "bawdy," one-tenth of all wives cheat on their husbands, and against this "disease" there is no remedy. Leontes condemns his wife, his friend, womanhood, and the world itself. This is the first step Leontes takes into pure nihilism and unbridled murderous revenge. He will order the death of his wife and their two children. Antigonus, his subject, is given the grim job of taking the king's infant to the beach to leave her there to die. Mamillius dies offstage after his mother is imprisoned. With the news of his son's death, Leontes begins to come back to his senses: "I have too much believed mine own suspicion" (3.2.151).

Harold Bloom spoke of seeing "how new modes of consciousness come into being," and in the figure of Leontes, we meet one of them. The jealous lover is found in literature before Shakespeare, but not one whose interiority is revealed so fully and whose intelligence, spurred by impulse, turns against everything good in his life. *The Winter's Tale* prefigures similar tales in Dostoevsky's *The Eternal Husband*, Thomas Hardy's *Tess of the d'Urbervilles*, Tolstoy's *The Kreutzer Sonata*, Graham Greene's *The End of the Affair*, and Saul Bellow's *Herzog*.

Don Quixote

Cervantes was born in Spain seventeen years before Shakespeare in 1547. He spent much of his life as a professional warrior and sailor.

Before joining the army, he spent a year in Rome (1569–1570), the same year the excommunication of Elizabeth I was being prepared. He was recognized for his bravery at the Battle of Lepanto (1572), taking two harquebus[17] balls in the chest and one in the left hand, leaving it useless.[18] He was captured by Ottoman Turks in 1575 (the "Barbary Pirates") and held prisoner in Algeria for five years. After four escape attempts, Cervantes was ransomed after an arduous effort by his family, and with the aid of two Trinitarians, he returned to Spain in 1580.

He spent the remainder of his life in Spain writing and making a living doing various jobs, including as commissioner of supplies for the Spanish Armada in Seville.[19] He

---

[17] A harquebus is an early form of a long rifle.
[18] William Byron, *Cervantes: A Biography* (Garden City, NY: Doubleday & Company, Inc., 1978), 132.
[19] Ibid., 323.

served briefly as a spy in Portugal.[20] He married Catalina de Salazar y Palacios in 1584, but they had no children. In the same year, before he was married, Cervantes had an affair with actress Ana Franca de Rojas, with whom he had a daughter, Isabel de Saavedra. He arranged for Ana Franca to marry a friend, and when she was widowed in 1599, Cervantes recognized the child and took both of them into his home: Ana Franca became a servant. Cervantes was excommunicated briefly in 1587 for being a tax collector, and he was imprisoned two times, both in 1592 and 1597, found guilty for money missing from the king's accounts. Cervantes, it's safe to say, was something of a rascal.

I could imagine a man like Cervantes, after all his mistakes and disappointments in life, becoming bitter and turning inward. Instead, during his second prison sentence in Seville, he conceived of a story set in a space between the world of medieval chivalry and his inglorious present. With what I would call a gleeful, even a mischievous spirit, he poured all his experience into the creation of characters never before seen in Western literature.

Before publishing his masterpiece, *Don Quixote*, Cervantes had written some twenty plays, all lost, and a pastoral novel, *La Galatea,* in 1585. Nothing survives of his writing that anticipates the creation of a new form of literature. *Don Quixote* was published in two parts: part one in 1605 (the year that Shakespeare wrote *King Lear*) and part two in 1615.[21] The work traveled abroad promptly, with the first

---

[20]   Ibid., 255–56.
[21]   Part I is divided into three parts: The First Sally (chapters 1-5); the Destruction of Don Quixote's library (chapters 6-7), and

part translated into English by 1616 and the second part in 1620.[22] Translations into other languages quickly followed, making *Don Quixote* known throughout the Western world by 1650.[23] It's now the most published work of literature in history.[24]

When picking up a book like *Don Quixote*, a lengthy, highly-revered work of literature, I look for an angle that helps me settle into it more quickly. From my first reading, I remembered *Don Quixote* as a series of mad romps in and out of villages and inns, scuffles with windmills and sheep, the loyalty of a peasant servant, all the misadventures of an elderly man who had lived too long in books about the past age of chivalry. But a recent book by William Egginton, *The Man Who Invented Fiction: How Cervantes Ushered in the Modern World*, cured me of that caricature. Egginton made me see that I had not appreciated the role of Sancho Panza: "The introduction of this stout, simple neighbor changes everything."[25]

---

the Second Sally which has six subsections. This Sally starts with chapter 11 and goes to the end, chapter 52. Part 2, published ten years later, contains "The Third Sally."

[22]   In the year Shakespeare died in 1616, the first English translation of *Don Quixote* appeared in English by Thomas Shelton. The second part of *Don Quixote* appeared in 1615 with Shelton's English translation published in in 1620.

[23]   This article about the history of *Don Quixote* in translation is fascinating: Ilan Stavans, "One Master, Many Cervantes," *Humanities* (September/October 2008) vol. 29, n. 5, https://webarchive.library.unt.edu/eot2008/20080916011930/http://neh.gov/news/humanities/2008-09/OneMaster.html.

[24]   William Egginton, *The Man Who Invented Fiction: How Cervantes Ushered in the Modern World* (New York: Bloomsbury, 2016), xxvii.

[25]   Ibid., xviii.

As the story begins, the old man in a knight's armor is treated derisively by almost everyone he meets, but Sancho Panza reacts quite differently. When his new master challenges the windmills to a fight, calling them "giants," Sancho calmly explains to him that these are not giants. Don Quixote ignores the warning. Sancho watches as his master calls out the giants and, lance in hand, spurs his horse, Rocinante, towards the windmill. Both horse and rider are picked up by the sails of the windmill and dropped to the ground. You might imagine Sancho Panza calling him a nut and heading for home. No, Sancho chooses to accept him and believe his vision. "'It's in God's hands,' said Sancho, 'I believe everything your grace says, but sit a little straighter, it looks like you're tilting, it must be from the battering you took when you fell.'"[26]

For the remainder of their journey, Sancho Panza warns Don Quixote about the trouble he is stirring up but defends the knight regardless of the consequences. This costs them some severe beatings that come close to killing them.

It is in part Sancho Panza's empathy for Don Quixote that persuades us to keep turning the pages in the book. He makes what could have been a Monty Python story into one that investigates what it means to be human, to serve an ideal, to fail in that service. Egginton writes, "That ability to experience different and at times contradictory realities without rejecting one or the other is one of the main reasons we are so drawn to fiction, in all its forms."[27] In the creation

---

[26]   Miguel de Cervantes, *Don Quixote*, trans. Edith Grossman, intro. Harold Bloom (New York: Ecco, 2003), 60.

[27]   *The Man Who Invented Fiction*, xix.

of the relationship between Don Quixote and Sancho Panza, Cervantes created an imaginative space where we, the readers, can try on different identities, perspectives, and moralities in total safety. Egginton refers to this as wearing a mask[28] to tell the truth, "truths of who we are, which we can discover solely by imagining ourselves otherwise."[29]

Another reason we keep reading is Sancho Panza himself. We first meet him when Don Quixote rides to a nearby farm looking for a squire. Sancho is a poor farmer with a wife and children, but he is persuaded by Don Quixote to serve as his squire. "Among other things, Don Quixote said he should prepare to go with him gladly, because it might happen that one day he would have an adventure that would gain him, in a blink of an eye, an insula [island], and he would make him governor. With these promises and others like them, Sancho Panza, for that was the farmer's name, left his wife and children and agreed to be his neighbor's squire."[30]

Once on the road, Sancho begins to remind his master of his promise to make him a governor. Don Quixote, being a chivalric knight, promises him more: a kingdom if one falls into their hands. Sancho asks if his wife would become queen, but his intention is not what we think: "'Well, who could doubt it?' responded Don Quixote. 'I doubt it,' replied Sancho Panza, 'because in my opinion, even if God rained kingdoms down on earth, none of them would sit well on the head of Mari Gutiérrez. You should know, *Señor*, that she

---

28   Ibid., 164.
29   Ibid.
30   *Don Quixote*, 55-56.

isn't worth two maravedis [silver coins] as a queen; she'd do better as a countess, and even then she'd need God's help.'"[31]

Sancho Panza reveals himself to be far more interesting than a mere loyal servant; he is something of a rascal, like the author. Their subsequent conversations reveal their deepening friendship, one that would have perplexed Aristotle. Sancho Panza proves himself articulate, espousing his realism so eloquently that several times he earns praise from his master who calls him "philosophical."

As readers, our experience is like that of Sancho Panza: We begin asking ourselves about his master; who is this fool? And, why am I reading about him? Isn't he just an old man whose head has been so occupied with chivalric tales he now believes himself to be living in one? The narrator of *Don Quixote* has already appraised him as such:

> The truth is that when his mind was completely gone, he had the strangest thought any lunatic in the world ever had, which was that it seemed reasonable and necessary to him, both for the sake of his honor and as service to the nation, to become a knight errant and travel the world with his armor and his horse to seek adventures and to engage in everything he had read about that knights errant engaged in, righting all manner of wrongs and, by seizing the opportunity and placing himself in danger and ending those wrongs, winning eternal renown and everlasting fame.[32]

---

[31]   Ibid., 57.
[32]   Ibid., 21.

Young men naturally dream of glory, but it is rare for a man of "about fifty" to go on such a quest. For a man of that age, it's an act of sheer foolishness or great courage. The literary achievement of Cervantes is enabling the reader to believe both, holding them in contradiction until the final chapter. The same is true for some characters in the novel.

In Part 2, chapter 59, Don Quixote and Sancho stop at an inn for dinner and the night. The knight hears a conversation between two men in the next room discussing whether or not to read Part 2 of *Don Quixote*. Don Quixote knows the book is a fake and calls them out. (There had been a fake version of Part 2 published before Cervantes wrote his own.) With help from Sancho, Quixote convinces them the book was written by someone else. Thus, the reader is faced with the fictional Don Quixote talking to strangers who had read Part I and are about to read a fake Part 2. But there's another layer of complication: At the beginning of Part I, the reader is told that it was not written by the author but given to him by a Moor (a Muslim). Yes, circles within circles.

The two strangers, Don Juan and Don Jerónimo, view the knight errant through a kind of bifocal glasses that create a single image: "The two gentlemen were exceedingly happy to hear Don Quixote relate the strange events of his history, and they were as amazed by the nonsensical things he said as by the elegant manner in which he said them. Here they considered him intelligent, and there seemed to slip into foolishness, and they could not determine where precisely to place him between intelligence and madness."[33]

---

[33]   Ibid., 847.

This dimensionality of character and setting is what makes *Don Quixote* so unique and the aspect of the novel that changed the nature of fiction for all who followed. In accepting the psychological and moral complexity of the knight, we recognize it in ourselves. Our own fictions, the ones that help us to cope with unhappiness, are staring back at us as we read. The multiple perspectives at play make us aware of the contradictions, both ironic and humorous, that are part of our lives. For example, how we commonly use storytelling to paper over our stumbles and falls. For Cervantes, there's no shame in that; instead, it is necessary, and should be the source of laughter, not regret.

I doubt if I'm the only reader who wished, like Sancho Panza, that Don Quixote had remained a knight errant until the end. Before he dies, Don Quixote renounces all his chivalric idealism and takes back his real name, Alonso Quixano.[34] Reading the final pages, I felt the magic disappear, but that's as the author intended it. Into his bedroom come the physician to take his pulse, the priest to hear his confession, and a scribe to whom the dying man could dictate his will. Sancho Panza begs him not "to let himself die, just like that, without anybody killing him or any other hands ending his life except those of melancholy."[35]

But Cervantes will not let this be a sad scene. Don Quixote dictates the terms of his will; the beneficiaries of which include his niece, his housekeeper, and his loyal squire. Afterward, he swoons and collapses in his bed, not yet dead: "The house was in an uproar, but even so the niece ate, the

---

34   Ibid., 936.
35   Ibid., 937.

housekeeper drank, and Sancho Panza was content, for the fact of inheriting something wipes away or tempers in the heir the memory of the grief that is reasonably felt for the deceased."[36]

Perhaps Cervantes thought the ending should tie back to the beginning, before the transformation of Alonso Quixano. We followed Don Quixote and Sancho Panza into a world of giants, wizards, castles, and damsels-in-distress; when we come out the other side, knight errantry is disavowed and the loyal squire's pleadings are followed by grief assuaged by money.

But life, I observe, is just like that. How precious, then, is this flight into a world where one man was willing to die for love, honor, loyalty, and to keep a promise. Life can be like that too. In *Don Quixote*, the world of our aspirations is brought together with the world of lies, broken promises, violence, and failure. Together the two worlds make one reality, the one in which we live.

***

How do works like these keep you from losing your mind? After all, Don Quixote lost his mind reading books. How do we know that we have not repeated his mistake? I think the answer is this: what we have read, heard, and seen has immersed us more deeply in the human condition. Like learning a language, we learn best when immersed in it, when we are forced to learn it to live day to day. Our minds are found, so to speak, when we connect with the real, when

---

[36] Ibid.

we think beyond the media script and reject the catechism of postmodernism. In the last century, countless millions lost their minds to various forms of utopianism, in search of a land that would never be. Under the influence of delusional academics, many treated human nature as if it could be reconstructed. Unfortunately, many continue the attempt today in increasingly perverse ways. Don't submit to them.

The effects of this assault on human nature—in large part perpetrated by obscuring what is good, true, and beautiful—have been manifold and extreme. In the works presented, and others in the canon, however, we find that the individual person *can* change, with jarring rapidity, his or her fundamental orientation either towards heaven or hell. Human beings have freedom, but they can lose their freedom when their rationality breaks down—think of Leontes and Scottie.

In a typical day of a typical busy life, we often miss moments that affect us with the mourning of poet Dana Gioia, the ecstatic joy of Finzi's *Dies Natalis,* the frenzied eroticism of *Vertigo*, the heroic love of Telemachus, or a witness to human depravity like that described by Joseph Conrad. These works, and other classics of film, music, and literature, heighten the reality of what they depict, pressing their impressions into our memory. There comes a time in all our lives when we need to remember these things—both angels and demons appear suddenly.

Fiction, like music and film, may succeed in teaching us where standard explanations fail. In *The Winter's Tale*, we are put inside the mind of an insanely jealous man and hear, with horror, his thoughts as he turns against all those who love him. A description of jealousy by a psychologist won't horrify you or leave you with the felt experience of its destructiveness. For most of us, artistic representations are remembered longer than definitions. This is why Jesus spoke in parables and why churches make use of painting, sculpture, and stained-glass windows.

The next time you meet someone who defends Communism, you can remember the story of Rubashov from *Darkness at Noon*. If someone tells you that "people never change," you will recall Alvin in *The Straight Story* or Hightower in *3 Godfathers*. If a friend complains about all those awful people in the world, you can reflect on the fact that we are all fallen, as Baudelaire depicts in *The Flowers of Evil*. To those who have forgotten the sacrifice of our soldiers, introduce them to the poetry of Wilfred Owen.

In a world that has done all it can to erase or obscure the civilizational memory of the West, *remembering* becomes a moral obligation, and a key to recovering our sanity. Sometimes such memories are more abstract and emotional than descriptive. There are encounters with the classics that are easily remembered because it is not a matter of getting the exact words right: Beethoven's "Ode to Joy" from the Ninth Symphony, the moment when Inger comes back to life, or Telemachus standing up to the suitors in his father's court.

What we remember comes to us through our entire body, not just the intellect. Take another example: St. Thomas Aquinas defines love as "willing good for the other."[37] What

---

[37]   *Summa Theoligica*, I-II.24.4, http://www.newadvent.org/summa/ 2026.htm#article4.

will you remember more easily, his definition or the words of St. Paul in 1 Corinthians?

Which has the better chance of changing your life?

Cervantes tells us a truth about human life: we are capable of serving and suffering for noble causes, but we often fail because we lack what is needed to face a world riddled with unforeseen minefields. Cervantes acknowledges this with a sigh but also with a laugh. The laughter of Sancho Panza is the sound of hope—we get up and try again.

Recall what Aristotle said, "All men by nature desire to know."[38] And, what Aquinas argued, we desire to know more than finite things; we desire to know God.[39] We lose our minds when that desire is derailed, when we are seduced by simple-minded, lopsided, or inverted worldviews. False narratives play out in two ways. Either the suffering they cause leads to an awakening, as we saw in the character of Leontes, or they remain stubbornly in place, and the suffering they cause is turned outward, demanding recognition, approval, and, as we saw in *Darkness At Noon*, conformity. *Miser amor companorum. Misery loves company.*

My goal in this book has been to reengage you, the reader, with the classics and, hopefully, incite a new passion for the greatness which lies so close to hand. We only have to "pick one up" and start reading, listening, or watching. I've tried to facilitate your reengagement by clearing away the untruths that dominate public conversation and reminding you to

---

[38]   *Metaphysics* 1.1.980a, 689.
[39]   *Summa contra gentiles* III.I.48, 162–67.

prepare a setting where your mind can work with minimal distraction. I've warned you against the cultural gurus and the postmodern despots who want to tell you what to think and how to feel. I have armed you with arguments about a human nature that is shared by all. I've defended truth, goodness, and beauty as transcendental aspects of being, and we have witnessed these present in the films, music, and books discussed. And we have seen how the great works speak to each other and to us about the human and its place in the universe.

We need to continue looking for connections within our expanded canon. I hope those who have the expertise to include other disciplines, such as science and psychology, and forms of art, like painting, sculpture, and dance, will lead the way. It's been a privilege for me to write this book because it has deepened my own love and gratitude for the men and women who have left behind what we call classics and what we call great. I will have succeeded if readers take up the journey from here on their own, perhaps inspired by whatever wisdom and delight they may have encountered in this book.

Bibliography

Adams, Byron. Program Notes. October 17, 2018. American Symphony Orchestra. http://americansymphony. org/wp-content/uploads/2018/10/10-17-ASO-Final.pdf.

Adler, Mortimer J. *Art, the Arts, and the Great Ideas.* New York: Scribner, 1994.

Adler, Mortimer J. and Robert Hutchins. *Great Books of the Western World.* 54 vols. Chicago: Encyclopædia Britannica, Inc., 1952.

Adler, Mortimer J. *Haves without Have-Nots.* New York: Random House, 1996.

———. *Philosopher At Large: An Intellectual Biography.* New York: Macmillan Publishing Co., Inc., 1977.

———. *Six Great Ideas.* New York: Touchstone, 1997.

"All Nobel Prizes in Literature." https://www.nobelprize. org/prizes/lists/all-nobel-prizes-in-literature/.

"All-Time Box-Office Top 100 Films." https://www.filmsite.org/boxoffice.html.

Aquinas, Thomas. *Summa Contra Gentiles* III. Translated Vernon J. Bourke. London: The University of Notre Dame Press, 1975.

———. *Summa Theologica.* Translated by the Fathers of the English Dominican Province. 3 vols. New York: Benziger Brothers, Inc., 1947.

A Memoir of Mary Ann By the Dominican Nuns Who Took Care of Her. Introduction by Flannery O'Connor. New York: Farrar, Straus and Cudahy, 1961.

American Film Institute interview with David Lynch. August 13 2009. https://www.youtube.com/watch?v=O8qM05l9tIs.

American Movie Critics: An Anthology From the Silents Until Now. Edited by Phillip Lopate. New York: Literary Classics of the United States, 2006.

Anselm of Canterbury. *The Major Works: Including Monologion, Proslogion, and Why God Became Man.* Edited by Brian Davies and G. R. Evans. Oxford: Oxford University Press, 2008.

Apkon, Stephen. *The Art of the Image: Redefining Literacy In a World of Screens.* Foreword by Martin Scorsese. New York: Farrar, Straus, and Giroux, 2013.

Applebaum, Anne. *Iron Curtain: The Crushing of Eastern Europe:1944-56.* New York: Doubleday, 2012.

Aristotle. *The Basic Works of Aristotle.* Edited by Richard McKeon. Introduction by C. D. C. Reeve. New York: Modern Library Classic, 2001.

———. *Nicomachean Ethics.* Translated by Martin Ostwald. Indianapolis: Bobbs-Merrill Educational Publishing, 1962.

———. *Metaphysics.* Translated by Hippocrates G. Apostle. Grinnell, Iowa: The Peripatetic Press, 1979.

———. *Aristotle's Poetics: A Translation and Commentary for Students of Literature.* Translated by Leon Golden. Upper Saddle River, NJ: Prentice-Hall Inc., 1968.

Ayer, A. J. *Language, Truth and Logic.* London: Victor Gol-lancz Ltd, 1936.

Baginni, Julian. *A Short History of Truth: Consolations for a Post-Truth World.* London: Quercus, 2017.

Baker, Nicholson. *Human Smoke: The Beginnings of World War II, the End of Civilization.* London: Simon & Schuster, 2008.

Banks, James A. "The Canon Debate, Knowledge Construction, and Multicultural Education." *Educational Researcher,* v. 22, n. 5 (Jun.-Jul., 1993).

Barnhart, Francis. "The Siegfried Idyll: Jewel of the Wagner Romance." https://web.archive.org/web/20071211050 734/http://francisbarnhart.com/projects/siegfried-idyll/.

Barzun, Jacques. *Berlioz and the Romantic Century.* 2 vols. New York: Columbia University Press, 1969.

Benda, Julian. *The Treason of the Intellectuals.* Introduction by Roger Kimball. New York: Routledge, 2006.

Benjamin, Walter. "The Work of Art in the Age of Mechanical Reproduction." (1936). Translated by Harry Zohn. https://www.marxists.org/reference/subject/philosophy/works/ge/benjamin.htm.

Berdichevsky, Norman. "Pastor Kaj Munk: Martyr of the Danish Resistance: Why Christians Must Never be Pacifists in the Face of Evil." (November 2015). https://www.newenglishreview.org/Norman_Berdichevsky/Pastor_Kaj_Munk:_Martyr_of_the_Danish_Resistance/.

Beilin, Elaine V. *Redeeming Eve: Women Writers of the English Renaissance.* Princeton: Princeton University Press, 1987.

Bergman, Ingmar, dir. *Autumn Sonata,* 1978; New York: The Criterion Collection, Inc., 2013. Blu-ray Disc, 1080p HD.

"Berlioz's *Symphonie Fantastique.*" https://www.pbs.org/ keepingscore/berlioz-symphonie-fantastique.html.

Bernard of Clairvaux. *Treatises II: The Steps of Humility and Pride & On Loving God.* Translated by Robert Walton OSB. Kalamazoo: Cistercian Publications, 1980.

Bernstein, Leonard. *The Unanswered Question: Six Talks at Harvard.* Boston: Harvard University Press, 1976.

Birkinshaw, Julian. "The Post-Truth World - Why Have We Had Enough Of Experts?" *Forbes,* May 22, 2017. https://www.forbes.com/sites/lbsbusinessstrategyreview/2017/05/22/the-post-truth-world-why-have-we-had-enough-of-experts/#7e19a0d154e6.

Bloom, Allan. *The Closing of the American Mind: How Higher Education Has Failed Democracy and Impoverished the Souls of Today's Students.* Foreword by Saul Bellow. New York: Simon and Schuster, 1987.

Bloom, Harold. *Shakespeare: The Invention of the Human.* New York: Riverhead Books, 1998.

———. *The Western Canon: The Books and School of the Ages.* New York: Riverhead Books, 1994.

Borstlap, John. *The Classical Revolution: Thoughts On New Music In the 21st Century.* New York: Dover Publications, 2017.

Buckley, Michael J. *At the Origins of Modern Atheism.* New Haven: Yale University Press, 1987.

Campbell, Roy. *Poems of Baudelaire.* New York: Pantheon Books, 1952.

Camus, Albert. *The Myth of Sisyphus and Other Essays.* Translated by Justin O'Brien. New York: Alfred A. Knopf, 1955.

Carey, Kevin. *The End of College: Creating the Future of Learning and the University of Everywhere.* New York: Riverhead Books, 2015.

Carnochan, W. B. "Where Did Great Books Come From Anyway?" *Stanford Humanities Review*, vol. 6 (1995). https://web.stanford.edu/group/SHR/6-1/html/carnochan.html.

Cervantes, Miguel de. *Don Quixote.* Translated by Edith Grossman. Introduction by Harold Bloom. New York: Ecco, 2003.

Christie, Ian. "The 50 Greatest Films of All Time," July 30, 2018. https://www.bfi.org.uk/news/50-greatest-films-all-time.

Christodoulou, Daisy. *Seven Myths About Education.* The Curriculum Center. London: Routledge, 2013.

Claret, Lluis, "Pablo Casals: Artist and Humanitarian." https://www.cellobello.org/legacy-cellists/pablo-casals-artist-and-teacher/.

Conrad, Joseph. *The Heart of Darkness and Selected Short Stories.* New York: Barnes & Noble Books, 2008.

Cooper, Elinor. "Women in (New) Music: Timeline of Women Composers," October 11, 2016. http://www.classical-music.com/article/10-female-composers-you-should-know.

Cowden, Catarina. "The Long-Term Movie Attendance Graph Is Really, Really Depressing." https://www.cinemablend.com/new/

Long-Term-Movie-Attendance-Graph-Really-Really-De-
pressing-68981.html.
Culshaw, Peter. "Andrei Tarkovsky – 'a mystic and a
fighter,'" *Telegraph*. December 1, 2007. https://www.
telegraph.co.uk/culture/film/starsandstories/3669621/
Andrei-Tarkovsky-a-mystic-and-a-fighter.html.
Dante. *Paradise: A New Translation*. Translated by Anthony
Esolen. New York: Modern Library, 2004.
Darmont, Pierre. *Damning the Innocent: A History of the
Persecution of the Impotent in Pre-Revolutionary France*.
Translated by Paul Keegan. New York: Viking Penguin,
Inc., 1986.
Dautreppe, Corentin. "The mind distracted: technology's
battle for our attention," March 6, 2019. https://news.
yahoo.com/mind-distracted-technologys-battle-
attention-034909034.html?soc_src=community&soc_
trk=ma.
Denyer, Simon. "The walls are closing in: China
finds new ways to tighten Internet controls."
Washington Post, September 27, 2017. https://
www.washingtonpost.com/world/asia_pacific/
the-walls-are-closing-in-chinafinds-new-ways-to-
tighten-internet-controls/2017/09/26/2e0d3562-9ee6-
11e7-b2a7-bc70b6f98089_story.html?utm_term=.
aac2d0229d1d.
Derrida, Jacques. *Of Grammatology*. Translated by Gayatri
Chakravorty Spivak. Baltimore: Johns Hopkins Press,
1976.

Derrida, Jacques. *The Other Heading*. Translated by Pascale-Anne Brault and Michel B. Haas. Bloomington: Indiana University Press, 1992.

"Domestic Movie Theatrical Market Summary 1995 to 2019." https://www.the-numbers.com/market/.

Dreyer, Carl Theodor, dir. *Ordet*. 1955. *The Carl Theodor Dreyer Collection*. London: The British Film Institute, 2015. Blu-ray Disc, 1080p HD.

Dubal, David. *The Essential Canon of Classical Music*. New York: North Point Press, 2003.

Ebert, Roger. "*Bicycle Thieves*," March 19, 1999. https://www.rogerebert.com/reviews/great-movie-the-bicycle-thief--bicycle-thieves-1949.

———. "*The Lives of Others*," September 20, 2007. https://www.rogerebert.com/reviews/the-lives-of-others-2007-17.

———. "Mishima: A Life in Four Chapters," December 5, 2007. https://www.rogerebert.com/reviews/great-movie-mishima-a-life-in-four-chapters-1985.

———. "The Straight Story," October 15, 1999. https://www.rogerebert.com/reviews/the-straight-story-1999.

Enginsson, William. *The Man Who Invented Fiction: How Cervantes Ushered in the Modern World*. New York: Bloomsburg, 2016.

Eksteins, Modris. *Rites of Spring: The Great War and the Birth of the Modern Age*. Boston: Marriner Books, 2000.

Eliot, T. S. "Ash Wednesday." *The Poems of T. S. Eliot: The Annotated Text, Collected and Uncollected Poems*. vol. 1. Edited by Christopher Ricks and Jim McCue. Baltimore: Johns Hopkins Press, 2015.

————. "Baudelaire." *Selected Essays*. New York: Harcourt, Brace, & World, 1964.

"European Dreams; Rediscovering Joseph Roth." *The New Yorker*, January 19, 2004. https://www.newyorker.com/magazine/2004/01/19/europeandreams.

European Music Archaeology Project. http://www.emaproject.eu.

Figes, Orlando. A *Revolutionary Russia:1891-1991: A History*. New York: Metropolitan Books, 2014.

Finkielkraut, Alain. *In the Name of Humanity: Reflections on the Twentieth Century*. Translated by Judith Friedlander. New York: Columbia University Press, 2000.

Fogelin, Robert J. *Understanding Arguments: An Introduction to Informal Logic*. New York: Harcourt Brace Jovanovich, 1982.

Ford, John, dir. *3 Godfathers*, 1978; Burbank, CA: Warner Brothers, 2007. DVD Disc, 480p SD.

Gambetta, Diego. "Primo Levi's Last Moments." *The Boston Review*, July 1, 1999. https://bostonreview.net/diego-gambetta-primo-levi-last-moments.

Gardiner, John Eliot. *Bach: Music In the Castle of Heaven*. New York: Vintage Books, 2015.

Gilmour, David. *The Film Club: A Memoir*. New York: Twelve, 2008.

Gioia, Dana. "Clarify Me, Please, God of the Galaxies: In Praise of the Poetry of Elizabeth Jennings." *First Things*. May 2018.'

————. "Introduction." *Best American Poetry 2018*. Dana Gioia, guest editor. The Best American Poetry series. New York: Scribner, 2018.

————. *99 Poems*. Reprint Edition. Port Townsend, WA: Graywolf Press, 2017.

"Glossary of Philosophical Terms." http://global.oup. com/us/companion.websites/9780199812998/studentresources/pdf/perry_glossary.pdf.

Gornick, Vivian. "Good Feminist." *Boston Review*, December 8, 2014. https://bostonreview.net/books-ideas/ vivian-gornick-good-feminist-solnit-rhode-cobble-gordon-henry.

Gössman, Elisabeth. "The Image of the Human Being According to Scholastic Theology and the Reaction of Contemporary Women." *Ultimate Reality & Meaning*, 11, 1988.

Gray, John. "Deluded liberals can't keep clinging to a dead idea." *Unherd*, October 3, 2018. https://unherd.com/ 2018/10/deluded-liberals-cant-keep-clinging-dead-idea/.

Gray, John. *The Silence of Animals: On Progress and Other Modern Myths*. New York: Farrar, Straus & Giroux, 2013.

Gray, John. *Straw Dogs: Thoughts on Humans and Other Animals*. New York: Farrar, Straus & Giroux, 2007.

Greengrass, Mark. *Christendom Destroyed: Europe 1517-1648*. New York: Viking Penguin, 2014.

"Harold Bloom Creates a Massive List of Works in The 'Western Canon': Read Many of the Books Free Online." http://www.openculture.com/2014/01/harold-bloom-creates-a-massive-list-of-works-in-the-western-canon. html.

"Henning Bendtsen, 1925–2011." https://www.criterion. com/current/posts/1751-henning-bendtsen-1925-2011.

Heer, Friedrich. *The Intellectual History of Europe.* Translated by Jonathan Steinberg. Cleveland and New York: The World Publishing Company, 1966.

Hirsch, E. D. "Cultural Literacy." *American Scholar* (Spring 1983). https://3o83ip44005z3mk17t31679f-wpengine. netdna-ssl.com/wp-content/uploads/2018/03/From_ Cultural_Literacy_1983.pdf.

———. *Cultural Literacy: What Every American Needs to Know.* New York: Vintage Books, 1988.

Hirsch, E. D., Joseph F. Kett, and James Trefell. *The Dictionary of Cultural Literacy: What Every American Needs to Know.* Boston: Houghton Mifflin Harcourt. Revised, Updated edition, 2002.

Hitchcock, Alfred, dir. *Vertigo.* 1958; Los Angeles: Universal Pictures Home Entertainment, 2014. Blu-ray Disc, 1080p HD.

Hoffman, Nicholas von. "Was McCarthy Right About the Left?" *Washington Post,* April 14, 1996. https://www. washingtonpost.com/archive/opinions/1996/04/14/ was-mccarthy-right-about-the-left/a0dc6726-e2fd-4a31-bcdd-5f352acbf5de/?utm_term=.a1321b99a626.

Hohn, Donovan. "Everybody Hates Henry." *The New Republic,* October 21, 2015. https://newrepublic.com/ article/123162/everybody-hates-henry-david-thoreau.

Holmes, Linda. "In 'Huckleberry Finn,' A History In Echoes," December 30, 2014. https://www.npr.org/ 2014/12/30/373834635/in-huckleberry-finn-a-history-in-echoes.

Homer. *The Iliad*. Translated by Robert Fagles. Introduction and Notes by Bernard Knox. New York: Penguin Books, 1990.

―――. *The Odyssey*. Translated by Robert Fagles. Introduction and Notes by Bernard Knox. New York: Penguin Books, 1996.

"How long does it take to form a habit?" August 2, 2009. https://www.ucl.ac.uk/news/news-articles/0908/09080401

Howard, Luke B. "Laying the Foundation: The Reception of Górecki's Third Symphony, 1977-1992." *Polish Music Journal*, vol. 6, n. 2. https://polishmusic.usc.edu/research/publications/polish-music-journal/vol6no2/gorecki-third-symphony/.

Howard, Jacqueline. "Americans devote more than 10 hours a day to screen time, and growing," July 29, 2016. https://www.cnn.com/2016/06/30/health/americans-screen-time-nielsen/index.html.

Hudson, Deal W. *An American Conversion: One Man's Discovery of Beauty and Truth in Times of Crisis*. New York: The Crossroad Publishing Company, 2003.

―――. "How the Beatles, My Great Aunt, and Debussy Changed My Life." http://www.thechristianreview.com/how-the-beatles-my-great-aunt-and-debussy-changed-my-life/.

―――. *Happiness and the Limits of Satisfaction*. Lanham, MD: Rowman & Littlefield Publishers, 1995.

―――. *Onward Christian Soldiers: The Growing Political Power of Catholics and Evangelicals in the United States*. New York: Threshold Editions, 2010.

————. "Adler from An Angel's Eye." *The Aspen Institute Quarterly*, Winter, 1995. vol. 7, n.1.

————. "Contemporary Views of Happiness." *The Great Ideas Today*. Chicago: Encyclopedia Britannica, Inc. 1992.

————. "Human Nature, Gender, and Ethnicity (Part One)." *The Great Ideas Today*. Chicago: Encyclopedia Britannica, Inc. 1994.

————. "Human Nature, Gender, and Ethnicity (Part Two)." *The Great Ideas Today*. Chicago: Encyclopedia Britannica, Inc. 1995.

————. "Three Reactions to Romanticism: Baudelaire, Nietzsche, and Kierkegaard." The Graduate Institute of Liberal Arts, Emory University, 1978.

Huscher, Phillip. "Richard Wagner - Siegfried Idyll." https://cso.org/uploadedFiles/1_Tickets_and_Events/Program_Notes/ProgramNotes_Wagner_SiegfriedIdyll.pdf.

Iyengar, Sunil. "Taking Note: Poetry Reading Is Up— Federal Survey Results," June 7, 2018. https://www.arts.gov/art-works/2018/taking-note-poetry-reading-federal-survey-results.

Jennings, Elizabeth. *Collected Poems*. Edited by Emma Mason. Manchester: Carcanet Press, 2012.

John Paul II. *Fides et Ratio*. September 14, 1998. https://w2.vatican.va/content/john-paul-ii/en/encyclicals/documents/hf_jp-ii_enc_14091998_fides-et-ratio.html.

Johnson, Alex. "The Book List: Meet Sir John Lubbock, Godfather of the must-read listicle." *Independent*, April 24, 2018. https://www.independent.co.uk/

arts-entertainment/books/features/sir-john-lubbock-the-book-list-literature-reading-godfather-mustread-listi-cle-a8320811.html.

Johnson, Paul. *Modern Times: The World from the 20s to the 90s.* London: Weidenfeld & Nicolson, 1983.

Kael, Pauline. "Trash, Art, and the Movies." *American Movie Critics: An Anthology From the Silents Until Now.* New York: The Library of America, 2006.

Kalder, Daniel. *Dictator Literature: A History of Despots Through Their Writings.* London: Oneworld Publications, 2018.

Kennedy, Matthew. "Making History: D. W. Griffith on DVD." https://brightlightsfilm.com/making-history-d-w-griffith-on-dvd/#.XHG10C3Mx0I.

Kenyon, Nicholas. "Jump Up and Shout," *Observer.* April 9, 1989.

Kierkegaard, Søren. *The Point of View for My Work as An Author: A Report to History, and Related Writings.* Translated by Walter Lowrie. Edited by Benjamin Nelson. New York: Harper Torchbooks, 1962.

———. *The Sickness Unto Death: A Christian Psychological Exposition for Upbuilding and Awakening.* Translated by Howard V. Hong and Edna H. Hong. Princeton: Princeton University Press, 1980.

Kimball, Bruce. *Orators & Philosophers: A History of the Idea of Liberal Education.* Expanded Edition. New York: College Board Publications, 1995.

Kirk, G. S. and J. E. Raven. *The Presocratic Philosophers: A Critical History With a Selection of Texts.* Cambridge: Cambridge University Press, 1957.

Kirsch, Adam. "The Five-Foot Shelf Reconsidered." November-December, 2001. http://harvardmagazine. com/2001/11/the-five-foot-shelf-reco.html.

Knox, Bernard. *The Oldest Dead White European Males: And Other Reflections on the Classics.* New York: W. W. Norton, 1993.

Koestler, Arthur. *Darkness at Noon.* Translated by Daphne Hardy. New York: Macmillan Publishing Company, 1941.

Kramer, Fritzi. "Silent Movie Myth: 'The Birth of a Nation' was the first feature and the first film shown at the White House," September 7, 2015. http://moviessilently. com/2015/09/07/silent-movie-myth-the-birth-of-a-na-tion-was-the-first-feature-and-the-first-film-shown-at-the-white-house/.

Lang, Paul Henry. *Music In Western Civilization.* New York: W.W. Norton & Company, 1941.

Lanzmann, Claude. *Shoah: An Oral History of the Holo-caust, The Complete Text of the Film.* Preface by Simone de Beauvoir. New York: Pantheon Books, 1985.

———, Claude, dir. *Shoah. 1985; New York: The Criterion Collection, Inc.,* 2013. DVD Disc, 480p SD.

Leiva-Merikakis, Erasmo. *Love's Sacred Order: The Four Loves Revisited.* San Francisco: Ignatius Press, 2000.

Leonhard, Jörn. *Pandora's Box: A History of the First World War.* Translated by Patrick Camiller. Cambridge, Massa-chusetts: The Belknap Press of Harvard University, 2018.

Levertov, Denise. "Primary Wonder." *Selected Poems.* Edited by Paul A. Lacey. New York: New Directions, 2002.

Levy, Andrew. *Huck Finn's America: Mark Twain and the Era That Shaped His Masterpiece*. New York: Simon and Schuster, 2014.

Levy, Bernard-Henri. *Left in Dark Times: A Stand Against the New Barbarism*. Translated by Benjamin Moser. New York: Random House, 2008.

Lewis, C. S. *The Four Loves*. London: Geoffrey Bles, 1960.

"Lewis on Love." *The Official Website of C. S. Lewis*. http://www.cslewis.com/lewis-on-love/.

Liu, Eric. "What Every American Should Know: Defining common cultural literacy for an increasingly diverse nation." *The Atlantic*, July 3, 2015. https://www.theatlantic.com/politics/archive/2015/07/what-every-american-should-know/397334/.

Lough, Robin. dir. *The Winter's Tale*, 1999; New Hope, PA: Kultur Video, 1999, DVD Disc, 480p SD.

Lukianoff, Greg and Jonathan Haidt. *The Coddling of the American Mind: How Good Intentions and Bad Ideas Are Setting Up a Generation for Failure*. New York: Penguin Press, 2018.

Luther, Martin. *The Bondage of the Will*. Translated by J. I. Packer and O. R. Johnston. Grand Rapids, MI: Baker Academic, 2012.

Lynch, David, dir. *The Straight Story*. 1999; Burbank, CA: Walt Disney Pictures, 2000. DVD Disc, 480p SD.

Macmillan, Margaret. *Paris 1919: Six Months That Changed the World*. New York: Random House, 2002.

Mann, Thomas. *The Magic Mountain*. Translated by H. T. Lowe-Porter. Afterword by the author. London: Secker and Warburg, 1927.

————. *The Magic Mountain.* Translated by John E. Woods. New York: Alfred A. Knopf, 1995.

Mariani, Paul. *The Whole Harmonium: The Life of Wallace Stevens.* New York: Simon & Schuster, 2016.

Marius, Richard. *Martin Luther: The Christian Between God and Death.* Boston: The Belknap Press of Harvard University, 1999.

Martinique, Elena. "10 Brilliant Female Artists of the Renaissance," January 9, 2018. https://www.widewalls.ch/famous-female-renaissance-artists/levina-teerlinc/.

McBride, Joseph. *Searching for John Ford.* New York: St. Martin's Griffin Edition, 2003.

McManners, John. *The French Revolution & The Church.* New York: Harper Torchbooks, 1969.

Melchior, Jillian Kay. "Fake News Comes to Academia." *Wall Street Journal,* October 5, 2018.

McPhee, Peter. *Liberty or Death: The French Revolution.* New York: Yale University Press, 2016.

McSpadden, Kevin. "You Now Have a Shorter Attention Span Than a Goldfish." *TIME,* May 14, 2013. http://time.com/3858309/attention-spans-goldfish/.

McVeagh, Diane. *Gerald Finzi: His Life and Music.* Woodbridge, Suffolk: Boydell Press, 2007.

Mellers, Wilfrid. *Celestial Music? Some Masterpieces of European Religious Music.* Woodbridge: The Boydell Press, 2002.

Mitchell, Stephen. *the rise of the image and the fall of the word.* London: Oxford University Press, 1998.

Mojoo, Farhad. "You Won't Finish This Article. Why people online don't read to the end." *Slate,* June 6, 2013.

https://slate.com/technology/2013/06/how-people-read-online-why-you-wont-finish-this-article.html.

Moore, John. "The 10 most important American plays." *Denver Post*, February 11, 2010. https://www.denver post.com/2010/02/11/ the-10-most-important-american-plays/.

Murray, Lorraine V. "Saying 'Yes' to God: Flannery O'Connor and Mary Ann." *Georgia Bulletin*, March 27, 2011. https://georgiabulletin.org/news/2011/03/ saying-yes-to-god-flannery-oconnor-and-mary-ann/.

Musser, Charles. *The Emergence of Cinema: The American Screen to 1907.* Berkeley: University of California Press, 1994.

Nehme, Farran Smith. "Mothers, Daughters, and Mon-sters." *Ingmar Bergman's Cinema. The Criterion Collection,* 2018.

Nietzsche, Friedrich. *The Gay Science: with a prelude of rhymes and an Appendix of Songs.* Translated by Walter Kaufmann. New York: Vintage Books, 1974.

———. *Human, All Too Human: A Book for Free Spirits.* Translated by Marion Faber and Stephen Lehmann. Lin-coln, NE: University of Nebraska Press, 1984.

Nuremberg Trial Proceedings Vol. I. Minutes of the Open-ing Session October 18, 1945. http://avalon.law.yale. edu/imt/imtmin.asp.

Nuttall, A. D. *Shakespeare the Thinker.* New Haven: Yale University Press, 2007.

O'Connor, Flannery. "Introduction." *A Memoir of Mary Ann: By the Dominican Nuns Who Took Care of Her.* New York: Farrar, Straus, and Cudahy, 1961.

"100 Hilarious College Courses that Really Exist." https://
www.onlineuniversities.com/blog/2009/10/100-hilari-
ous-college-courses-that-really-exist/\.

Ophüls, Marcel, dir. *The Sorrow and the Pity.* 1969; Hertfordshire, UK: Arrow Academy. 2017. Blu-ray Dis-
c,1080p HD.

The Oxford Book of Twentieth Century English Verse. Chosen by Philip Larkin. London: Oxford University Press,
1973.

Paglia, Camille. *Provocations: Collected Essays on Art, Feminism, Politics, Sex, and Education.* New York: Pantheon,
2018.

Pascal, Blaise. *Pensées.* Translated by A. J. Krailsheimer.
London: Penguin Books, 1966.

Perrin, Andrew. "Book Reading 2016," September 1,
2016. http://www.pewinternet.org/2016/09/01/
book-reading-2016/.

Peters, F. E. *Greek Philosophical Terms: A Historical Lexicon.*
New York: New York University Press, 1967.

Pieper, Josef. *Leisure: The Basis of Culture.* Introduction by
T. S. Eliot. Translated by Alexander Dru. London: Faber
and Faber LTS, 1952.

Philip, Robert. *The Classical Music Lover's Companion to
Orchestral Music.* New Haven: Yale University Press,
2018.

Plato. *Euthyphro, Crito, Apology, & Symposium.* Translated
by Benjamin Jowett and Moses Hadas. South Bend:
Regnery/Gateway Inc., 1953.

———. *Republic.* Translated by G. M. A. Grube. Indianapolis: Hackett Publishing Company, 1974.

———. *The Symposium of Plato.* Translated by Suzy Q. Groden. Boston: University of Massachusetts Press, 1970.

Plotinus. *The Enneads.* Translated by Stephen MacKenna. Fourth Edition. New York: Pantheon Books, 1969.

Pluckrose, Helen. "No, Postmodernism is not Dead (and Other Misconceptions." *Areo,* Feb 7, 2018. https://areomagazine.com/2018/02/07/no-postmodernism-is-not-dead-and-other-misconceptions/.

Powys, John Cowper. *One Hundred Best Books: With Commentary and an Essay on Books and Reading.* New York: G. Arnold Shaw, 1916.

Prudhomme, Sully. *The Vain Tenderness.* Dead Dodo Vintage, 2012. https://www.amazon.com/Vain-Tenderness-Annotated-Sully-Prudhomme-ebook/dp/B0083V6B8I/ref=sr_1_3?keywords=Sully+Prudomme&qid=1551387306&s=gateway&sr=8-3-spell.

Purdy, Jedediah. "In Defense of Thoreau: He may have been a jerk, but he still matters." *The Atlantic,* October 20, 2015. https://www.theatlantic.com/science/archive/2015/10/in-defense-of-thoreau/411457/.

Ray, TJ. "The brain's dwindiling attention span." *The Oxford Eagle,* September 23, 2018. https://www.oxfordeagle.com/2018/09/23/the-brains-dwindiling-attention-span/.

Reider, Jon. Letter to the Editor. *Chronicle of Higher Education,* November 21, 2016. https://www.chronicle.com/blogs/letters/jesse-jackson-didnt-lead-chant-against-western-culture/.

Reilly, Robert R. and Jens F. Laurson. *Surprised by Beauty: A Listener's Guide to the Recovery of Modern Music.* San Francisco: Ignatius Press, 2016.

Renoir, Jean, dir. *The Rules of the Game.* 1939; New York: The Criterion Collection, Inc., 2011. Blu-ray Disc, 1080p HD.

Rhode, Eric. *A History of the Cinema: From Its Origins to 1970.* Boston: Da Capo Press, 1976.

Rilke, Rainer Maria. *Requiem and Other Poems.* Translated by J. B. Leishman. London: Hogarth Press, 1949.

Robb, Graham. *Victor Hugo: A Biography.* New York: W. W. Norton & Company, 1998.

Robin, William. "How a Somber Symphony Sold More Than a Million Records." *The New York Times*, June 9, 2017.

Rochefoucauld, François de La. *Maxims: La Rochefoucauld.* Translated by Stuart D. Warner and Stephane Douard. South Bend: St. Augustine's Press, 2001.

Rorty, Richard. *Consequences of Pragmatism.* Minneapolis: University of Minnesota Press, 1981.

Rosenbaum, Jonathan. "The Bicycle Thief." *Chicago Reader*, March 1, 1999. https://www.jonathanrosenbaum. net/2017/06/the-bicycle-thief-2/.

———. *Essential Cinema: On the Necessity of Film Canons.* Baltimore: The Johns Hopkins University Press, 2004.

Roth, Joseph. *Radetzky March.* Translated by Michael Hoffmann. London: Granta Books, 2003.

———. *What I Saw: Reports from Berlin: 1920-1933.* Translated by Michael Hoffmann. New York: W. W. Norton & Company, 2003.

Runyon, Christopher. "The David Lynch Retrospective: 'The Straight Story,'" July 26, 2013. http://movie mezzanine.com/the-david-lynch-retrospective-the-straight-story/.

Sachs, Harvey. *The Ninth: Beethoven and the World in 1824.* New York: Random House Trade Paperback Edition, 2010.

Sacks, Oliver. *Musicophilia: Tales of Music and the Brain.* New York: Vintage, 2008.

Sager, Jeanne. "The Power of Inclusive Sex Education." *The Atlantic,* July 17, 2017, https://www.theatlantic.com/education/archive/2017/07/the-power-of-inclusive-sex-ed/533772/.

Santayana, George. *The Life of Reason: The Phases of Human Progress.* 1905. http://www.gutenberg.org/catalog/world/readfile?fk_files=169068&pageno=115.

Sarris, Andrew. *The American Cinema: Directors and Directions 1929–1968.* New York: Dutton, 1968.

Schickel, Richard. *D. W. Griffith: An American Life.* New York: Limelight Editions, 1984.

Schiller, Friedrich. *Essays.* Edited by Walter Hinderer and Daniel O. Dahlstrom. New York: Continuum, 1998.

Schilling, Heinz. *Martin Luther: Rebel In an Age of Upheaval.* Translated by Rona Johnston. Oxford: Oxford University Press, 2017.

Schmidt, Michael. *The Novel: A Biography.* Boston: The Belknap Press at Harvard, 2014.

———. *The Lives of Poets.* New York: Alfred A. Knopf, 1999.

Schonberg, Harold. *The Lives of the Great Composers*. New York: W. W. Norton & Company, 1997.

Schrader, Paul. "Canon Fodder: Paul Schrader's Canon Criteria." *Film Comment*, September/October 2006.

Schulz, Kathryn. "Pond Scum: Henry David Thoreau's moral myopia." *The New Yorker*, October 19, 2015. https://www.newyorker.com/magazine/2015/10/19/pond-scum.

Senz, Paul. "Catholic Composers: Hildegard von Bingen." *Catholic World Report*, September 17, 2018. https://www.catholicworldreport.com/2018/09/17/catholic-composers-hildegard-von-bingen/.

Shakespeare, William. *The Complete Works of Shakespeare*. Edited by Hardin Craig. Atlanta: Scott, Foresman and Company, 1961.

———. *The Riverside Shakespeare*. Edited by G. Blakemore Evans. Boston: Houghton Mifflin Company, 1974.

Shattuck, Roger. *Proust's Way: A Field Guide to 'In Search of Lost Time*. New York: W. W. Norton & Company, 2000.

Sica, Vittorio de. dir. *Bicycle Thieves,* 1948; New York: The Criterion Collection, Inc. 2016, Blu-ray Disc, 1080p HD.

———. dir. *Umberto D*. 1952; New York: The Criterion Collection, Inc., 2012, Blu-ray Disc, 1080p HD.

Smiley, Jane. "Say it ain't so, Huck; second thoughts on Mark Twain's 'masterpiece.'" *Harper's Magazine*, January, 1996. https://www.enotes.com/topics/adventures-of-huckleberry-finn/critical-essays.

Snyder, Timothy D. *Bloodlands: Europe Between Hitler and Stalin*. New York: Basic Books, 2010.

Speer, Albert. *Inside the Third Reich.* Translated by Richard and Clara Winston. New York and Toronto: Macmillan, 1970.

Stavans, Ilan. "One Master, Many Cervantes." *Humanities* (September/October 2008), vol. 29, n. 5. https://webarchive.library.unt.edu/eot2008/20080916011930/http://neh.gov/news/humanities/2008-09/OneMaster.html.

Steiner, George. *George Steiner: A Reader.* New York: Oxford University Press, 1984.

———. *Real Presences.* Chicago: The University of Chicago Press, 1989.

Stephen, Bijan. "You Won't Believe How Little Americans Read." *TIME,* June 22, 2014. http://time.com/2909743/americans-reading/.

Stevens, Wallace. *The Collected Poems of Wallace Stevens.* Edited by John N. Serio and Chris Beyers. New York: Vintage Books, 2015.

Stern, Sol. "E.D. Hirsch's Curriculum for Democracy." *City Journal,* Autumn, 2009. https://www.city-journal.org/html/e-d-hirsch's-curriculum-democracy-13234.html.

Stove, R. J. "Anton Bruckner and God." *Catholic World Report*, August 2, 2015. www.catholicworldreport.com/2015/08/02/anton-bruckner-and-god/.

Tallerico, Brian. *"Roma."* November 21, 2018. https://www.rogerebert.com/reviews/roma-2018.

"Theatrical Market Statistics 2016." https://www.mpaa.org/wp-content/uploads/2017/03/MPAA-Theatrical-Market-Statistics-2016_Final-1.pdf.

Thomson, David. *"Have You Seen . . .?" A Personal Introduction to 1,000 Films.* New York: Alfred A. Knopf, 2008.

Thoreau, Henry David. *Walden; Or, Life in the Woods.* Dover Thrift Editions. Dover Publications, 2012. Kindle.

Thorne, Ashley. "The drive to put Western civ back in the college curriculum." *New York Post*, March 29, 2016. https://nypost.com/2016/03/29/the-drive-to-put-western-civ-back-in-the-college-curriculum/.

Tillich, Paul. *Dynamics of Faith.* New York: Harper Colophon Books, 1957.

Tommasini, Anthony. *The Indispensable Composers: A Personal Guide.* New York: Penguin Press, 2018.

———. "Richard Wagner, Musical Mensch." *New York Times*, April 10, 2005.

Traherne, Thomas. *Centuries Thomas Traherne 1637-1674.* The Faith Press, 1960. https://archive.org/details/centuries_of_meditations_1412_librivox.

Trilling, Lionel. *The Liberal Imagination: Essays on Literature and Society.* Edited by Pascal Covici. New York: Viking, 1950.

Turan, Kenneth. *Not To Be Missed: Fifty-Four Favorites From a Lifetime of Film.* New York: Public Affairs, 2014.

Twain, Mark. *The Adventures of Huckleberry Finn.* Amazon Classics Edition, 2017. Kindle.

Ullrich, Volker. *Hitler: Ascent 1889-1939.* Translated by Jefferson Chase. New York: Alfred A. Knopf, 2016.

"Unit sales of printed books in the United States from 2004 to 2018 (in millions)." https://www.statista.com/statistics/422595/print-book-sales-usa/.

Wahl, Jan. *Carl Theodor Dreyer and* Ordet: *My Summer with the Danish Filmmaker.* Lexington: The University of Kentucky Press, 2012.

Washington, Bushrod. "NYC Just Released a List of Officially Recognized Genders," May 24, 2016. https://thefederalistpapers.org/us/nyc-just-released-a-list-of-officially-recognized-genders.

Watson, Derek. *Bruckner.* New York: Schirmer Books, 1996.

Weiss, Michael. "The McCarthyism canard." *The New Criterion*, September 7, 2010. https://www.newcriterion.com/blogs/dispatch/the-mccarthyism-canard.

White, Matthew. *The Great Big Book of Horrible Things: The Definitive Chronicle of Histories' 100 Worst Atrocities.* New York: W. W. Norton & Company, 2012.

Zane, J. Peder. *The Top Ten: Writers Pick Their Favorite Books.* Boston: W. W. Norton & Company, 2007.

Zuckerkandl, Victor. *The Sense of Music.* Princeton: Princeton University Press. 1959.